James Von Schilling

The Magic Window
American Television, 1939-1953

"James Von Schilling's *The Magic Window: American Television 1939-1953* reminds us of the fascinating beginning of our video culture. It is a rich companion to familiar reference works, such as Brooks and Marsh's guide to television programming, because it provides a context and more depth about the early programs and their times. Instructors who strive for contemporary relevance in their history lessons will appreciate Von Schilling's chapter-ending links between early video and radar technology and today's sophisticated electronics and military applications.

Those who approach television studies from an economics or organizational perspective will welcome the neat summary of industry changes in place by 1953 that would affect the next thirty years of television. From Desi Arnaz's ownership of the *I Love Lucy* episodes, to the decline of 'the Chicago School of Television' and end of the DuMont Network, to the multimillion-dollar advertising deals, *The Magic Window* traces the evolution of these developments and defines a useful benchmark for delineating two historical television periods, the birth of the medium and the boom that followed.

This book will also be a useful supplemental text for courses in contemporary history. Von Schilling stretches out the early days of television in 1940s America and explores how the nascent industry gradually outgrew its East Coast origins and insinuated itself throughout the country and into American lives."

Tom Mascaro, PhD
Assistant Professor,
Bowling Green State University,
Ohio

More pre-publication
REVIEWS, COMMENTARIES, EVALUATIONS . . .

"**W**ell researched and written, this story of the magic window, the squared glass television screen that brings the images and sounds of the outside world into our homes and daily lives, will delight those who recall the formative years (1939-1953) and intrigue those who missed them. Merging the fields of history, technology, sociology, and entertainment, the book starts with the first flickering images of the 1939 World's Fair, shows how television became 'A Torch of Hope' during World War II, 'Turned the Corner' with the 'Image Orthicon' TV camera developed for the military, and found its permanent place in American culture.

Covering a multitude of people, events, and performances that were either on television or affected what was televised, this book will delight and inform a nation that has entered, in the new millennium, the Television Age.

This book lets you move from boom to Berle, comics to communists, coast to coast. You end up liking Ike and loving Lucy. You will like this book."

Marshall E. Fishwick, PhD
Professor of Humanities
and Popular Culture,
Virginia Tech; Author,
Popular Culture in a New Age

"**V**on Schilling's *The Magic Window* is a fascinating historical highway of the early days of American television with a strong intellectual center line. For those interested in the early instant stages of television, Von Schilling has the correct data; for those interested in what some call the highpoint of television—before it became rotten with commercials—he gives us *I Love Lucy, Dragnet, The Today Show,* and many others. His study is highlighted by the details with which it is recounted and the quality of its style. This is not a book to be consulted for facts but one to be read—cuddled, as it were—for the pleasure of revisiting old entertainment friends and hours. It is indeed a magic window to magic moments of our happier days."

Dr. Ray B. Browne
Secretary/Treasurer,
Popular Culture Association,
Bowling Green, OH

"**J**ames Von Schilling's book *The Magic Window* provides a fascinating glimpse into that forgotten time when television was in its infancy, 1939-1953. The author provides remarkable insight into the era when television was still in its experimental stage, when technology was primitive and programming was unsophisticated. In other words, television was not yet king. This historical analysis reveals how television developed during these years, within the political and economic contexts of the times. In the process the author shoes how, from these humble beginnings, the most dominant medium on earth emerged. In short, this is the story of the beginning of television. Thoroughly researched and well documented, this book is a handy reference tool for teachers and students of broadcast history."

Paul F. Gullifor, PhD
Associate Professor
of Communication,
Bradley, University,
Peoria, IL

More pre-publication
REVIEWS, COMMENTARIES, EVALUATIONS . . .

"James Von Schilling's book, *The Magic Window,* is a bittersweet read for true television aficionados, for it makes us feel that we were born fifty years too late. He captures the excitement of video's pioneer era and reminds us that an infinite number of factors—the personalities of figures such as RCA's David Sarnoff and the FCC's Larry Fly, the interruption of World War II, the parallel development of different technological standards—changed television forever. Von Schilling's almost romantic fourteen-year narrative stands in contrast to the relatively quick and bloodless development of the Internet.

The variety of programs in the early years seems to dwarf the cable TV offering of today. *The Magic Window* is especially compelling in its description of local television programming, such as at Schenectady's legendary WRGB, and Von Schilling does a fine job describing the development of such landmark series as *Kukla, Fran, and Ollie* and *Your Show of Shows.* His examples of how television, even in its infancy, influenced politics are also eye-opening. (As early as 1940, telegenics helped handsome Wendell Willkie wrest the Republican presidential nomination away from the stuffy Robert Taft.) *The Magic Window* is much more than a nostalgia trip; it is a reminder that the television industry would do well to emulate the excitement of its early days."

Robert David Sullivan
Television Critic,
The Boston Phoenix

The Haworth Press®
New York • London • Oxford

The Magic Window
American Television,
1939-1953

THE HAWORTH PRESS
Popular Culture
B. Lee Cooper, PhD
Senior Editor

New, Recent, and Forthcoming Titles of Related Interest

Rock Music in American Popular Culture: Rock 'n' Roll Resources by B. Lee Cooper and Wayne S. Haney

Rock Music in American Popular Culture II: More Rock 'n' Roll Resources by B. Lee Cooper and Wayne S. Haney

Rock Music in American Popular Culture III: More Rock 'n' Roll Resources by B. Lee Cooper and Wayne S. Haney

Popular American Recording Pioneers: 1895-1925 by Tim Gracyk, with Frank Hoffmann

The Big Band Reader: Songs Favored by Swing Era Orchestras and Other Popular Ensembles by William E. Studwell and Mark Baldin

Circus Songs: An Annotated Anthology by William E. Studwell, Charles P. Conrad, and Bruce R. Schueneman

Great Awakenings: Popular Religion and Popular Culture by Marshall W. Fishwick

Popular Culture: Cavespace to Cyberspace by Marshall W. Fishwick

The Classic Rock and Roll Reader: Rock Music from Its Beginnings to the Mid-1970s by William E. Studwell and David F. Lonergan

Images of Elvis Presley in American Culture, 1977-1997: The Mystery Terrain by George Plasketes

The Americana Song Reader by William E. Studwell

The National and Religious Song Reader: Patriotic, Traditional, and Sacred Songs from Around the World by William E. Studwell

The Christmas Carol Reader by William E. Studwell

Popular Culture in a New Age by Marshall W. Fishwick

The Magic Window: American Television, 1939-1953 by James Von Schilling

The Magic Window
American Television, 1939-1953

James Von Schilling

The Haworth Press®
New York • London • Oxford

The Haworth Press, Inc., 10 Alice Street, Binghamton, NY 13904-1580.

Cover design by Lora Wiggins.

Front cover photographs from the David Sarnoff Library, Princeton, NJ, and KYW-TV, Philadelphia, PA.

Library of Congress Cataloging-in-Publication Data

Von Schilling, James A. (James Arthur)
 The magic window : American television, 1939-1953 / by James Von Schilling.
  p. cm.
 Includes bibliographical references and index.
 ISBN 0-7890-1505-6 (alk. paper)—ISBN 0-7890-1506-4 (pbk.)
 1. Television broadcasting—United States—History. I. Title

PN1992.3.U5 V66 2002
384.55'0973—dc21

                    2002068764

CONTENTS

ABOUT THE AUTHOR

James A. Von Schilling, PhD, is a native of Hackensack, New Jersey. He received a BA in English from Princeton University, an MA in education from New York University, and a PhD in American Culture from Bowling Green State University. He has taught English in public schools and at Bowling Green State University, Rider University, and Northampton Community College, where he is a professor of English. He also teaches and writes on diverse topics in American studies, mass media, and popular culture.

Dr. Von Schilling's writings have been published in *The Handbook of American Popular Culture, The Popular Culture Reader, The Journal of Popular Film and Television, American Journalism,* and *The Legal Studies Forum.* He is the American Culture Association's area chair for journalism and media culture, and resides with his wife, Margaret, and his two sons, Scott and Gary, in Somerville, New Jersey.

Preface

Television (TV) may have produced a number of overnight sensations, but it wasn't one itself. A span of more than a decade separated its debut in American society in 1939 from its popular acceptance in the early 1950s. That stretch of time is only an instant in the history of human technology; nevertheless, it's surprising that Americans hesitated so long before making TV a basic part of their lives.

This book tells the story of the period when television struggled to find its place in American culture. It begins with an event that seems too distant for TV to have played any part—the opening of the 1939 World's Fair, and it concludes at a point where some may think TV began, with the success of *I Love Lucy.* In between is a multitude of people, events, and performances that were either on TV or affected what was being televised. For every story that is told in these pages, there is another one that might have been included: the book is not intended to be an encyclopedic reference work. Instead, let it serve its readers as an introduction to television's early history and an encouragement to continue exploring its programs and performers.

The book's title, *The Magic Window,* comes from the first advertisement in the first ad campaign that sold television to the American public, back in the fall of 1939. The "window," of course, is the TV screen—the famous squared glass that captures and holds our vision in millions of American homes. The "magic" is the way TV brings the images and sounds of the outside world into our homes and our daily lives—as it has done for over sixty years.

Chapter 1

The Beginning of Everything

TELEVISION'S DEBUT

John Pavlic was amazed on April 30, 1939, when he saw television for the first time. "I can't believe it. I must be dreaming," the Navy sailor from Youngstown, Ohio, told a reporter for the *New York Herald Tribune.*[1] Pavlic was among hundreds of Americans who watched television for the first time that day, when the New York World's Fair opened in Flushing Meadows, Queens. Dozens of American companies showed off their latest products in pavilions at the Fair, taking advantage of the press and spectacle that surrounded the Fair's opening. The Radio Corporation of America (RCA) was one of these companies, unveiling a display of its first TV sets for sale to the American public.

For Pavlic and nearly all Americans in the spring of 1939, seeing pictures in motion on a small screen was a novelty and a source of wonderment. Pavlic's shipmate, James Vogt of Omaha, "just stared" at the screen of the TV set on display, wrote the *Herald Tribune* reporter.[2] Beatrice Minn, also seeing TV for the first time that day, exclaimed, "I never thought it would be like this. Why, it's beyond conception, and here it is."[3]

Television was at the New York World's Fair because of experiments in the electrical laboratories of the 1920s and 1930s. TV was a natural outgrowth of radio, itself a result of remarkably successful work by inventors, scientists, and engineers over the previous fifty years. The key to both radio and TV was the same: learning to use the electromagnetic spectrum, a basic feature of the universe, to send invisible electrical signals through the air.

Television was also there at the World's Fair in 1939 because America's radio companies, and RCA in particular, were hoping to create a new TV industry. Americans had bought hundreds of millions of new radio sets in the 1920s and 1930s; they might buy millions of TV sets in the upcoming 1940s, or so hoped RCA and other set manufacturers. In fact, RCA's president, David Sarnoff, believed that TV would eventually be in as many American homes as radio was in 1939.

Radio broadcasting had first caught the American public's attention in 1920, when the first radio stations began operating on a regular basis. An industry in radio production and broadcasting soon blossomed and prospered, and radio became the most popular national medium of the 1930s. Every day and every night, most Americans listened to an assortment of entertainment and news programs on their home radio sets. The public loved having music, talk, and other sounds sent over the airwaves and reproduced by the tubes, wires, and speakers of its living-room radio sets; why wouldn't the transmission of moving images be wildly popular as well?

THE JENKINS TELEVISION SYSTEM

By the mid-1920s, inventors in the United States and Europe had demonstrated that images could indeed be transmitted through the air. In June 1925, for example, American inventor Charles Jenkins transmitted a ten-minute movie a distance of five miles to a gathering of government officials in Washington, DC. Later that year, Jenkins predicted that it would "not be very long now before one may see on a small white screen in one's home notable current events, like inaugural ceremonies, ball games, [and] pageants."[4] In 1927, Charles Jenkins took a historic step toward that future when he received America's first license for an experimental TV station, W3XK, transmitting from Wheaton, Maryland.

In the summer of 1928, Jenkins began transmitting a few hours of short television programs six nights a week. The quality was poor, with a resolution of just forty-eight lines per image—less than one-tenth as sharply defined as TV's current picture. The picture was small, only two inches square, and was just a black silhouette in motion, projected silently on a wall. The performers on these short programs were employees of Jenkins and children from the neighborhood, and they danced, jumped, and skipped rope. It was little more than shadow play, but it was motion and image, and it was live. It was television.

Over the next few years, the Jenkins Television Corporation produced a TV set for the home, called the Radiovisor, that sold for around $100. Jenkins also sold do-it-yourself TV kits for under $10, below cost, in an effort to make this new medium popular. With the kit and the purchase of a small motor, radio hobbyists could transform a home radio into a Jenkins television set and watch the live silhouette broadcasts. "It was the beginning of everything," according to Irma Kroman, who worked in Jenkins' television studio and often appeared in these early broadcasts.[5]

These broadcasts were indeed the beginning of regularly scheduled TV programming in the United States. But Jenkins could hardly have picked a worse time to sell America on a new technology. Only a year after his nightly broadcasts began, the U.S. economy plunged into the Great Depression, and the early 1930s saw Americans holding on desperately to whatever income and savings they might have. Radio was free to the public, and most families already had a living-room radio set; the medium remained popular. But sales of phonograph records dropped, as did movie box-office receipts, and only a few thousand people bought the TV sets and kits that Jenkins was promoting.

Jenkins was also thwarted by the U.S. government. The agency that governed the nation's airwaves, the Federal Radio Commission (FRC), had granted Jenkins only an experimental TV license, which kept him from seeking commercial sponsors. Jenkins wasn't even allowed to advertise his own TV sets on the air. Nor did the FRC ever endorse the Jenkins television system. Its commissioners believed instead that a better process for broadcasting images was needed, and they were right.

Jenkins was in fact selling an inferior product to the American public. His Radiovisor sets and do-it-yourself home TV kits used a piece of technology that had serious limitations: the Nipkow disk. Invented by Paul Nipkow of Germany in 1884, the Nipkow disk featured a set of small holes, evenly spaced apart, that spiraled in toward the disk's center. With the disk spinning rapidly, light that was reflected off an object on one side of the disk would travel through each hole and recreate, on the other side, an image of the object.

The Jenkins studio camera used a Nipkow disk that spun fifteen times a second, creating fifteen complete images. Each spot of light was captured by a light-sensitive photoelectrical cell and transformed into an electrical signal that was broadcast on radio waves to Radiovisor sets within range of the transmitting antenna. Electrical circuitry in these sets converted the signal back into light, which flashed through the holes in another Nipkow disk inside the Radiovisor that was synchronized to spin along with the disk at the studio. The light pattern that resulted was projected onto a screen, creating fifteen images per second, and the human eye could see the object back in the studio—but not that well. The picture's size and definition were limited by the number of holes that could be punched into the disk and the size of the disk inside the Radiovisor sets. The best picture Jenkins was able to transmit was six inches square, with a definition of sixty lines per image. Another serious drawback to the Jenkins system was the intensity of the light needed to capture images in the studio: it was nearly too hot and bright for the performers and crew to work.

In 1932, the Jenkins Television Corporation collapsed, and its assets became part of the De Forest Radio Company, which was also experimenting with TV transmission. Within a year the De Forest Radio Company folded, too, and soon the assets of both the De Forest and Jenkins businesses were controlled by America's leading radio company, RCA.

As for Charles Jenkins, he lived only two years longer than his television company. He lost his fortune and his spirit when the Jenkins TV system failed to gain a foothold in American society in the early 1930s. As it turned out, he was correct in predicting that Americans would someday view on a small screen in their homes the events of the outside world, but he was wrong in believing it would happen soon and utilize his technology.

RCA TELEVISION

RCA paid a half million dollars to purchase the De Forest and Jenkins assets, thereby eliminating two competitors in the broadcast industry. That strategy was typical of RCA's leader, David Sarnoff, a giant figure in American mass media. Sarnoff had come to America from Russia as a child; he sold newspapers on the streets of New York, then delivered cable messages. He taught himself Morse code, became an office boy with the Marconi Wireless Telegraph Company, and quickly rose through its ranks. In 1922, when Marconi was bought out by a company from the new medium of radio, Sarnoff stayed and became its general manager and vice president. He was only twenty-one. The new company was the Radio Corporation of America, and by 1930 Sarnoff had become its president.

By the late 1930s, Sarnoff's public speeches had taken on the aura of official proclamations. They would begin with an RCA assistant hand-delivering the prepared text in a black notebook to Sarnoff as he stood at the podium, and they would end with copies of the speech dispatched to the national media and inserted in the *Congressional Record*. On April 20, 1939, the air of magnitude was appropriate, and a portion of Sarnoff's speech that day is quoted as often as any words he ever spoke. The setting was the New York World's Fair just ten days before its official opening. Sarnoff stood at a podium in the gardens behind the RCA Pavilion Building, which was shaped in the form of a giant radio tube, and faced a few hundred people in attendance and an RCA television camera.

"It is with a feeling of humbleness," he said, "that I come to this moment of announcing the birth in this country of a new art so important in its implications that it is bound to affect all society. It is an art which shines like a torch of hope in a troubled world. It is a creative force which we must learn to utilize for the benefit of all mankind."[6] Sarnoff also announced that RCA would begin selling TV sets and offer a regular schedule of TV programs once the Fair opened. In fact, his speech itself was being transmitted throughout the New York City area, and a close-up photograph of Sarnoff, taken off a TV set in Manhattan, appeared in *The New York Times* the next morning.

After Sarnoff's speech and the brief ceremony ended, the live TV program switched across the East River to a makeshift boxing ring in the RCA television studio in Manhattan. There, the new medium that Sarnoff had just described as "an art which shines like a torch of hope in a troubled world" transmitted a three-round boxing match between Golden Gloves champion Jack Pembridge and Police Athletic League boxer Pat Dunne.

The TV sets that David Sarnoff promised would be for sale when the Fair opened were a vast improvement over the Radiovisors that Charles Jenkins had tried to sell to the public. RCA had bought the assets of Jenkins' company in the early 1930s, but Sarnoff doubted that the spinning disks of mechanical TV would ever produce images good enough for public acceptance. Instead, he had Vladimir Zworykin and other RCA engineers, working in Camden, New Jersey, and New York City, develop an all-electronic system that replaced the spinning disk with a scanning beam of electrons. Images up to twelve inches square, clear and detailed, now appeared on the new electronic sets being developed not only by RCA but by General Electric, Philco, and others in the radio industry.

By 1938, RCA had an experimental TV studio in Manhattan's RCA Building, a transmitter atop the Empire State Building, and a mobile van that traveled the streets of the city to test out the technology. Within a fifty mile range of the transmitter were a hundred RCA television sets that picked up the experimental broadcasts. The whole TV project had cost RCA $10 million so far, and not a penny had been made from it. RCA's shareholders were voicing their concerns. The pieces were in place, however, for David Sarnoff to begin promoting television as a new medium and selling RCA's new TV sets.

First, Sarnoff and RCA had to settle with inventor Philo Farnsworth, who held the patent rights for key parts of the electronic TV system. At the age of thirteen, while plowing a field on his family's farm in Idaho, Farnsworth figured out how to capture an image electronically. The precocious boy imagined that beams of electrons could be deflected by magnets into reproducing an image one line at a time, just as a field is plowed row by row. Six years later, in 1927, the young inventor received his first patent for electronic TV technology; in the mid-1930s, he began facing RCA engineers and lawyers in court. The litigation lasted for years, as Sarnoff refused to acknowledge that Farnsworth had invented some of the key aspects of TV's technology. At stake wasn't just RCA's reputation as a pioneer in the industry. Whoever owned the patents would be paid royalties from any other company using the technology; indeed, RCA owned most of the important patents in radio, and Sarnoff felt strongly that RCA "didn't pay royalties; it collected them."[7]

RCA was the last company making TV sets to agree to negotiate a settlement with Farnsworth. Even after the negotiations began, in early 1938, RCA took almost two years to reach a deal with Farnsworth and begin paying royalties. In the meantime, RCA produced TV sets, picture tubes, and cameras, as Sarnoff tried to make his company as dominant in the new TV industry as it was in radio.

When the World's Fair opened officially on April 30, 1939, over a dozen new RCA television sets were exhibited in the "Hall of Televisions" in the RCA Pavilion Building. They were RCA's model TRK-12, in polished wood cabinets and with a price tag of $600. The TRK-12 featured a twelve-inch picture that was reflected out to its viewers by a mirror that popped up from the top of the luxurious art-deco cabinet. In the lobby of the Pavilion stood a fantastic TV set, the Phantom Teleceiver, with a transparent cabinet that allowed fair-goers to view the tubes and circuitry that brought live images magically onto the screen.

Not only was RCA showcasing its new TV sets at the Fair, the company was also starting the nation's first schedule of TV programs by televising the Fair's opening-day ceremonies. Shortly after noon, RCA's telecast began with a live picture of the World's Fair center-pieces, two futuristic structures called the Trylon and Perisphere, under a bright springtime sun that darted between clouds. Seated in front of an RCA television set in the RCA Building in midtown Manhattan, eight miles from the Fair, a viewer told a reporter, "I could tell when the sun went behind a cloud."[8] Other viewers watched the telecast on a dozen sets in the RCA Building and on another hundred or more TV sets scattered about the New York area.[9]

This first TV audience next saw a parade marching through the Fair's center court, the images captured by a TV camera mounted on a high platform. As if it were a window opening magically onto another scene, the TV screen let its audience see for the first time life unfolding at a distance. During the World's Fair parade, for example, TV viewers saw New York's Mayor Fiorello LaGuardia walk up to the platform and look directly into the lens of the camera. LaGuardia was the first in a long line of American politicians to be pulled to the video camera and later critiqued by the press for his appearance. Apparently, LaGuardia looked good on TV. The next day's *New York Times* called him "the most telegenic man" in the city, describing "the violent emphasis in the toss of his head and the dramatic facial expressions" that the *Times* reporter had watched on TV in Manhattan.[10]

President Franklin D. Roosevelt also appeared on live TV that afternoon; he was the first President to do so. He rode in a limousine to the Fair after the parade and later gave the speech that officially opened the Fair to the public. Roosevelt appeared only once more on TV during the next six years that he was President. Television was not a good medium for FDR, even though he watched TV himself on a set he owned at his home in Hyde Park, New York. The TV lens and screen could reveal too much of Roosevelt to the public. Unedited live pictures of him at the Fair, for example, may have showed that his lower body was paralyzed, the result of his bout with polio in the 1920s. He could neither get in or out of the limousine nor walk to or from his seat and the podium without assistance. In photographs and newsreels, Roosevelt never seemed disabled; instead, he projected the carefully framed image of an active and jaunty man. On radio, the President was in his element, using his marvelous patrician voice to reassure and inspire Americans during the Great Depression of the 1930s. On television, Roosevelt's movements could be seen clearly, exposing his physical difficulties. If TV became as popular as radio in the 1940s, President Roosevelt would be challenged as never before to keep his disability from the public's eye.

TELEVISION'S FIRST SEASON

RCA's display of TV sets was a popular attraction at the New York World's Fair throughout the spring and summer of 1939. Over 20 million Americans visited the Fair that year, and they gave the new medium an audience of thousands of daily visitors. These fair-goers needed little to watch in the way of programming. Sights of the Fair and live pictures of one another were enough for a few minutes of viewing as they passed by the TV sets on display.

Occasionally, the TV cameras at the Fair transmitted some notable images. On June 11, in particular, those people who were watching the TV sets in the RCA Pavilion in the midafternoon saw images that the rest of the fair-goers that day missed: close-up views of the King and Queen of England. King George VI and Queen Elizabeth were visiting the World's Fair that day as part of a tour of the United States and Canada, and they were televised as they entered and departed from an exclusive luncheon held on the fairgrounds. Crowds of fair-goers lined the short route taken by the British royalty, kept at a distance by police barricades. But the king and queen walked within twenty-five feet of the RCA television camera at one point, and it transmitted close-up images of them in conversation.

The thousands of Americans who visited RCA's exhibit at the Fair weren't TV's only audience in 1939. On the morning after the Fair opened, Macy's and Bloomingdale's department stores in Manhattan put RCA sets on sale for the first time. Macy's reported over 1,000 shoppers an hour viewing a demonstration of TV—"a surprising interest" from the public, store officials said.[11] Thousands more saw the TV sets in Macy's and Bloomingdale's over the next few months. Although only a few hundred TV sets were sold, the new owners and their families comprised another TV audience that expected to see programs on a regular basis—and not just images from the World's Fair.

To satisfy this small audience—and build a mass audience beyond it—RCA began televising programs from its own experimental TV station, W2XBS, located in the RCA Building in Manhattan. The station averaged ten hours of programming a week, mostly in the late afternoon and early evening to satisfy the crowds at the Fair and the customers in the department stores. On May 2, W2XBS televised its first variety show, with a bill of performers that included Broadway composer Richard Rodgers, radio journalist Lowell Thomas, and the orchestra of Fred Waring. Two nights later, a second variety show aired. No visual record of either program was ever made, but a review in that month's *Billboard* was harsh. "A purchaser of a $400 television set is not going to feel any great love for television," wrote the reviewer, who rated the shows as on "about a par with not very good amateur stuff."[12]

Of course, these shows were produced and performed under difficult conditions. Squeezed into a room not much bigger than a badminton court were all the crew and performers, the stage settings and backdrops, the banks of lighting and boom microphones, and three TV cameras and their operators. This was Studio H on the sixty-second floor of the RCA Building, operated by RCA's radio network, the National Broadcasting Company (NBC). In particular, the TV cameras of 1939 needed very bright lighting; Studio H's lights were so bright that dresses wilted, makeup melted, crew members wore tropical hats, and everyone took salt tablets and sweated.

As the RCA's staff learned and practiced their technical skills, the quality of their work rose; new equipment helped, too. Later in 1939, a review of one of their programs, a 1922 play titled *Dulcy*, marveled at the TV-viewing experience and had little to say about technical glitches: "Until such a performance is viewed in the home, it is difficult to realize how the acting seems to be done right in the living room itself; television makes it all so life-like. . . ."[13]

In this first season of television, RCA also tried broadcasting outdoor sports, including baseball, tennis, horse racing, track and field, and a boxing match from Yankee Stadium. The company's mobile TV unit operated out of a $150,000 "Televan" that housed a camera and all the equipment needed to transmit images back to the RCA building.

Television's first baseball game featured the college teams from Columbia and Princeton, playing on May 10 at Baker Field in Upper Manhattan. The telecast of the game was marred by technical problems: transmitting outdoor sports was a challenge for both the TV equipment and its operators. The bright sun that afternoon made the players look as dark as silhouettes up through the fourth inning. Then the picture improved and, as Orrin Dunlap wrote in *The New York Times* the next day, "The diamond became clear and the skyline of apartment buildings sharply defined in the background," with "New York Central trains running toylike in the background."[14]

Dunlap and other TV viewers saw baseball's first televised home run that day, hit by Ken Pill of Columbia. Here was more of TV's magic in evidence: on its screen could be seen the home run, the stolen base, and other moments of drama and surprise. Viewers could actually see the event happen, instead of reading or listening to the report of someone else who was there. But "where are the peanuts, the pop, the score cards, hot dogs and the mustard pot?" asked Orrin Dunlap in the *Times*. After sitting "for two hours in a darkened room on a beautiful sunny day in May to watch a baseball game on a miniature screen," he decided that "baseball on a sofa" was "no substitute for being in the bleachers." [15]

TEST-MARKETING IN NEWBURGH

Perhaps David Sarnoff had spoken too optimistically about TV's future. There were serious doubts in 1939 that the American public would accept this new medium into their homes. Popular magazines published articles suggesting that Americans would reject TV because the images on the screens were too small. After all, people were used to seeing other people either life-sized in reality or oversized on the movie screen. RCA's sets had screens that were just nine inches square, while other TV sets used mirrors to project a bigger picture that was still much smaller than real life. And the quality of the TV picture itself in 1939 was often poor, usually due to technical problems with the cameras or transmitting equipment.

Also, the economic climate remained a problem for television in 1939. The Great Depression was now a decade old and still lingering. Roughly 10 million Americans were unemployed (17 percent of the population), a number that was higher than both 1930-1931 and 1936-1937, and many of those who had jobs were careful how they spent each paycheck. In such times, a TV set costing around $500 was a luxury item that many Americans could easily forego. A similar fate had befallen the 1939 World's Fair itself. Only half of the 50 million Americans who were expected to attend the Fair in 1939 did so, in part because the experience cost more than many families could afford.

Maybe, too, the quality of TV shows available in 1939 was not enough to entice buyers. Plays such as *Dulcy,* cast with unknowns, were unlikely to stir much interest in the American public. In general, TV in 1939 had little drawing power, especially when most families could hear the country's funniest comedians and most popular Big Bands and singers performing nightly on their household radio sets. For exciting visual entertainment, the public need only go downtown to a movie theater for the latest double feature. The year 1939, in fact, was perhaps Hollywood's greatest, with the release of *Gone With the Wind, The Wizard of Oz, Wuthering Heights, Goodbye, Mr. Chips, Stagecoach,* and other classic films.

By summer's end and with the World's Fair planning to close for the fall and winter, David Sarnoff and RCA were faced with an unpleasant situation. Sales of TV sets were minimal, yet station W2XBS had to continue televising programs to serve its small audience and lure potential customers. The regular schedule of programs was costing RCA $10,000 to $15,000 a week; unlike radio, TV had no sponsors in 1939 to pay for the expense of airing shows. Simply put, television needed a bigger audience to survive and grow: more TV sets had to be sold.

A turning point came in the fall of 1939, when RCA decided to launch a "hard sell" campaign for TV in New York City. The company turned first to Newburgh, New York, sixty miles north of Manhattan but within range of W2XBS's signal, to test their marketing strategies. In October 1939, RCA stocked Newburgh's appliance and department stores with new sets, lowered the price by a third, and ran weekly advertisements in the local newspaper.

Television is a "magic window through which you look on right from the ease of your armchair!" proclaimed the first advertisement for TV sets in Newburgh's *Evening News.*[16] Luring potential customers were pictures of TV screens that showed boxers and football players in action. Included, too, were statements from new set owners, claiming, for example, "I can honestly say that television is the biggest kick I've had in years."[17] The town's 30,000 residents were invited to experience the magic themselves at demonstrations in their local stores.

The publicity, lower prices, and store demonstrations worked. In a few weeks, 200 television sets had been sold, equaling 25 percent of all the sets sold throughout New York in the previous six months. Another 400 sets were sold in Newburgh in the months after RCA's short campaign ended. RCA had shown that TV sets could be sold to the American public at a lower, more affordable price. If 600 sets could be sold in Newburgh in a few months, then perhaps 6,000 or even 60,000 could be sold the same way soon in New York City. America's first big television audience was within sight.

THE FCC'S FIRST REPORT ON TV

The steps RCA took to promote and sell TV sets brought forth a reaction from another force in American society: the federal government. Television signals are transmitted through a public property: the airwaves are part of the electromagnetic spectrum that exists freely and invisibly in nature yet is regulated as a public utility in the United States.

In November 1939, the U.S. agency that governs the spectrum, the Federal Communications Commission (FCC), issued an important report on television. The TV industry, said the FCC, was facing an economic problem. Television stations were costly to build and TV programs expensive to create, and not enough sets had been sold to begin paying the industry back its investment. "It may be that the time is fast approaching," the FCC suggested, "when pioneers must receive a return not only on their huge investment but also . . . for operating expenses."[18] That "return" on their investment of at least $10 million was exactly what RCA was hoping to get through their marketing of new sets in New York City.

The FCC asserted that it had no interest in supporting TV in America with government funds. In England, for example, the government-run British Broadcasting Corporation (BBC) controlled the industry and was already paying to produce TV programs. In the United States, on the other hand, the FCC expected television to follow the path that radio had taken in American society and become a commercial medium, finding sponsors to carry the costs of production.

Nonetheless the FCC warned in its November 1939 report that it was unlikely to approve commercial TV broadcasts for the time being, at least not on a scale large enough for RCA to recoup its investment. Were TV to go commercial too soon, claimed the FCC, Americans would suffer "financial exploitation" at the hands of TV set manufacturers.[19] The public would be lured into buying sets by the appeal of new TV programs paid for by commercial sponsors, despite the fact that the TV sets on sale in 1939 and 1940 might soon become obsolete.

Was the FCC correct in its decision to slow down the TV industry, as its predecessor, the FRC, had been right in holding back the Jenkins television system a decade earlier? To some extent, the issue was rooted in the technology behind the transmission of TV signals. By late 1939, sixteen companies were making or planning to make television sets, but not all the new sets would be able to receive the TV signals from RCA's W2XBS. Philco, the country's leading radio manufacturer, was building a TV set with a higher definition picture: over 600 horizontal lines comprised the image on Philco's set, versus 421 lines on RCA's.

The choice of 421 lines by RCA was based on standards agreed upon in 1936 by a trade board, the Radio Manufacturer's Association, to which most of the industry belonged. Now, however, Philco was promising a television picture 35 percent clearer than the image on the RCA sets. A clearer picture would make for a better product to sell to the American public, which could indeed make the sets of 1939 as obsolete as Jenkins' spinning-disk Radiovisors.

Another issue beleagured the FCC above and beyond the technical decision of the number of lines per image. RCA's push to sell TV in 1939 had given the company such a head start on its competition that a monopoly within the new industry seemed possible and maybe even likely. In other times, during other administrations, a single company might have been allowed to dominate an emerging field, as RCA hoped to do with television—but not in 1939 and 1940 with Franklin Roosevelt in the White House. Roosevelt's New Deal administration was stocked with liberals and progressives who fought with enthusiasm against monopolies and big businesses.

The FCC's chairman, new to the post in 1939, was a young veteran of the New Deal's skirmishes against monopolies and corporate interests. James L. (Larry) Fly was a Naval Academy and Harvard Law School graduate who had begun his career as an antitrust lawyer for the Department of Justice during the Hoover Administration. When Roosevelt and his New Deal cabinet took over Washington from the Republicans in 1933, Larry Fly took a position in a new agency, the Tennessee Valley Authority (TVA), and became its chief counsel in 1937. With the TVA, Larry Fly protected two other types of public property: the flowing waters of the Tennessee River and the electricity that resulted when the TVA built a power dam on the river. In particular, Fly defended the TVA from lawsuits filed by privately owned utility companies—local monopolies—who questioned the very existence of the TVA and its plans to sell electrical power at low rates to rural homes and farms.

When Larry Fly became chairman of the FCC in September 1939, he faced a situation similar to the one he had just left at the TVA. There, he'd dealt with the public properties of flowing water and electricity; here, he managed the public airwaves of radio and TV. Fly was still confronting big business: in this case, RCA and the rest of the broadcast industry. Within a few months, the FCC under Larry Fly had issued its first report on television and adopted a new policy that was described as an "amber light" or a caution for the industry.

With a "green light," the FCC could have quickly granted commercial licenses and opened the door to sponsors and advertising on TV, while a "red light" policy would have keep sponsors out of TV altogether. Instead, the FCC chose to grant commercial licenses to only a few TV stations, and only if the money from sponsors would be used to offset production costs or to improve TV's technology, not for corporate profit. With the amber light, RCA could proceed only with caution in marketing TV sets beyond Newburgh.

Before the amber light was switched on, however, the FCC scheduled a set of hearings in Washington for January 1940. "There are no sharp issues involved," said Larry Fly beforehand, "and we have no desire to retard development or keep the industry guessing."[20] Maybe Fly never realized the economic and social issues that lurked behind the technical matters; maybe, based on his years with the TVA, he did. In any case, the hearings marked another turning point in the history of American television. The federal government was now involved. The issues that emerged before the FCC would thwart, divide, and nearly ruin the TV industry throughout the 1940s and beyond.

THE AMBER LIGHT

For two weeks in January 1940, TV industry executives testified before the FCC and the American public. They discussed the technical standards for transmitting TV signals, argued over FCC's amber light ruling, and debated RCA's push to sell television to the American public. Despite all the talk, when the FCC issued its new rules for TV on February 29, 1940, little had changed from the policy announced in November. Starting September 1, 1940, a few licensed TV stations could begin airing sponsored programs, but the FCC insisted that any "emphasis on the commercial aspects of the operation at the expense of program research is to be avoided."[21] The light was still amber.

Nor was the FCC willing to establish an official number of lines per picture or other technical standards. Instead, the agency called upon the set manufacturers to agree among themselves on all standards. In the meantime, the FCC said, TV sets should be designed for flexibility, with the ability to adjust to whatever lines per image became final. The FCC all but named RCA in declaring that "nothing should be done which will encourage a large public investment in receivers which . . . may become obsolete in a relatively short time."[22]

The FCC was favoring public interests over corporate profits, as might be expected of a New Deal agency headed by a veteran of the TVA. Yet Larry Fly and the other FCC commissioners had bent slightly toward the TV industry by letting stations seek commercial sponsors, although not for another six months. That was enough, however, for *The New York Times* to call the FCC ruling a "A Go-Ahead Signal" in its headline the next day.[23] Apparently, David Sarnoff too saw the ruling as a "go-ahead signal" for commercial television. Within two weeks RCA had invited 400 retailers to Radio City to launch its new campaign to sell TV sets in New York City, behaving as though the FCC's light had changed to green.

Based on their test-marketing in Newburgh, RCA expected to increase the number of TV sets sold in New York City from 2,500 to 25,000. Just as they did in Newburgh, the company cut the selling price of its sets by a third. Advertisements were prepared for New York City newspapers and magazines, along with commercials for radio and even a short film about TV to sway the public.

On March 20, 1940, the first of the newspaper ads ran in New York. "Action . . . Drama . . . Historic Events," read the big RCA ad in *The New York Times,* with photographs of boxers and baseball players in action, of theater performers, and of the king and queen of England at the World's Fair; all of these images had been televised in the previous year.[24] Pictured in another ad was an RCA television set in which the image appeared in a mirror on the top of the cabinet. This set, the model TRK-12, was now priced at $395, although "Only 10% Down Buys It!" one New York dealer, Davega City Radio, cited in their ad.[25]

Another advertisement for TV sets on sale at Bloomingdale's read like a telegram: "New Prices Put Thrilling Programs Within Your Reach."[26] The RCA ad, covering a full page in the *Times,* was labeled "A Statement by The Radio Corporation of America on Television for the Home," and signed, "David Sarnoff, President." The letter began, "It is now possible for the RCA to announce the extension of its plans,"[27] which was to build America's first network of TV stations. Linked together, these stations would jointly air programs from RCA's own National Broadcasting Company, including telecasts of upcoming 1940 presidential campaigns and conventions.

RCA was courting trouble with its sales campaign, which tested the FCC's order that "nothing should be done to encourage a large public investment" in TV sets.[28] The FCC responded quickly. Three days after the ads began, on Saturday, March 23, 1940, the FCC dealt a serious blow to RCA's plan to sell thousands of TV sets: the agency withdrew its permission to allow commercial stations as of September 1. The amber light had suddenly changed to an angry red.

In its statement that Saturday, the FCC warned the public against "premature purchase in a rapidly advancing field," then complained specifically about RCA's sales campaign. The agency promised to re-open its hearings from the previous January to decide if RCA was "unduly retarding research, experimentation, and development of television transmission."[29] Only then would the FCC decide when to allow the start of commercial stations.

"I am amazed," David Sarnoff told the press the following morning.[30] He met with his executives the next day and issued no statement. But RCA's marketing campaign in New York City ended abruptly, and sales of TV sets, which had been brisk the previous week when the ads were running, now dropped back down. A group of appliance dealers had by now spoken out against the FCC, and once again Chairman Larry Fly was confronting corporate executives with government policies that were designed to work for the good of the public.

The issue of TV's future was soon taken up in the nation's political arena, in the midst of a big election year, with the Presidency and most of Congress in contention. A leading critic of the White House and its New Deal policies, Senator Ernest Lundeen, jumped to RCA's side in its fight with the FCC. In early April, Lundeen warned the public on network radio that "a new industry is being throttled by a government bureau exercising power never granted by Congress." He called on the Senate's Interstate Commerce Committee, which had some authority over the FCC, to investigate whether the agency had "exceeded its authority."[31]

Larry Fly also spoke on the radio a few nights later, asking the TV industry to "go slow" in selling sets to the public. Without naming RCA, he described a TV company that was engaging in "extravagant promotion of sales to people of modest incomes" and then accused it of trying to dominate the industry and the public. "Don't take this stripling," Fly warned the TV set manufacturers about their intentions for the new medium, "and sell it down the river for a few pieces of silver."[32]

HEARINGS IN WASHINGTON

On Monday, April 8, 1940, the FCC reconvened its hearings on TV. The first day's crowd of 175 people heard another TV set manufacturer, Allen Du Mont of Du Mont Laboratories, claim that he had found a solution to one of TV's technical problems. Du Mont was ready to produce a "flexible" TV set that could handle a range of horizontal lines per image. He guaranteed that his TV sets would not become obsolete—at least not for two years.

Larry Fly was anything but flexible when he spoke in support of the red light at the next day's FCC hearings. He warned that New York City would soon be "saturated with 30,000 receivers of one manufacturer, sold on the installment plan and promoted by a sales campaign and pep talks."[33] A day later, Fly made the same point on Capitol Hill, where the Senate Interstate Commerce Committee was deciding whether to investigate the FCC's rulings on TV. A monopoly, he said, could result from the sale "of a large number of RCA receivers" that picked up signals "only from RCA telecasting units."[34]

Testifying after Larry Fly was David Sarnoff, who claimed that television, if given a green light, would become a billion-dollar industry providing jobs for over a half million Americans. These were appealing numbers for an audience of politicians in the midst of an election year, and apparently they were noticed by President Roosevelt, too. Roosevelt soon summoned Larry Fly to the White House for a meeting. Afterward, Fly took questions from the press, and his resolve seemed to have softened. When would the FCC allow stations to become commercial? "As soon as the industry is ready to go ahead," Fly said. "In a few months, I am hopeful that we will have a flock of receivers capable of receiving all types of transmissions." Did he mean that when such TV sets were available the restrictions would be lifted? His answer: "Why not?"[35]

Later that same day, the Senate Interstate Commerce Committee called off their hearings on the FCC after holding only one day of testimony. The FCC and the Senate Republicans entered what resembled a cease-fire, perhaps brokered by the White House. As *The New York Times* explained, "with a Presidential campaign in the offing," 1940 was "no year . . . to delay a science that holds promise of becoming a billion-dollar industry, giving employment to 600,000 people."[36] As ardent New Dealers, the President and his agency chiefs were committed to fight monopolies. However, even "New Dealers," reported the *Times,* "are said to recognize that this is no year to stir up a new cry of monopoly, bureaucratic control or government power over anything that holds as much promise of reaching out to the masses."[37]

The next day, April 12, President Roosevelt spoke at some length about television during a press conference. He first offered support to Larry Fly and the FCC: it was the New Deal's policy of preventing monopolies, the President explained, that had led to the halt on allowing commercial stations. The FCC was concerned, he said, that one company not control transmissions, nor keep the public from picking up all available telecasts on all sets on the market. Roosevelt also said that he expected a solution within the coming months. He revealed, too, that he'd acquired a television set for his home at Hyde Park. He hoped to watch both local town meetings and prizefights, he said, although there was "little essential difference" between them.[38]

With that small quip, the President moved to a new topic and the public debate over TV's near future ended, for the time being. The FCC quickly ended its own hearings and announced it was reconsidering its last rulings on TV. What had Roosevelt and Larry Fly said at their White House meeting the previous day? Did they discuss, as New Dealers, how to develop TV and its industry in the best interests of the American public? Did they talk of monopolies and commercialism, of green and red and amber lights? Did the President simply tell Fly that the FCC was giving his political opponents an issue—one that wasn't worth the fight in an election year?

Perhaps they discussed a much bigger issue that loomed on the horizon. American TV was basically one year old in April 1940, but had changed little since being introduced at the 1939 World's Fair. What *had* changed dramatically in those twelve months was the world outside TV. Europe was at war in April 1940, and America was responding with the first steps of building a wartime economy. Franklin Roosevelt, David Sarnoff, and Larry Fly could surely see the ominous signs that the future for TV would be affected by events beyond anyone's control.

Chapter 2

A Torch of Hope

THE FUTURE APPEARS IN NEWBURGH

In the spring of 1940, the New York World's Fair opened for a second season. The Fair's theme was "Building the World of Tomorrow," and this particular world of the future was a consumer's paradise. The TV sets and other new products on display gave a tantalizing view to fair-goers of what a post-Depression America might offer. The most popular exhibit at the Fair was General Motors' Futurama, a miniature display of the United States as it might appear in 1960. Fair-goers waited hours in line for a fifteen-minute ride through Futurama, to overlook its half million tiny buildings, roads, and cars.

As it turned out, the America of 1960 did resemble the Futurama version, with its sleek buildings and strands of curved highways. Another prominent feature of the real American landscape in 1960, however, was missing from the Futurama exhibit, although it did make its first appearance in 1940—not at the Fair, but in Newburgh, New York. A writer for the *Saturday Evening Post,* Alva Johnston, visited Newburgh in 1940, and the first thing Johnston noticed was that "the sky line of Newburgh has been changed by television. Tourists stop their cars to gaze at what appear to be newfangled lightning rods."[1]

These new television antennas were installed on the roofs of the roughly 600 homes in Newburgh with TV sets in 1940. Johnston spent time in several of these homes and was struck by how popular TV had quickly become in the neighborhoods. The home of Frank R. Dutcher, for example, had "a small television set which packs them in regularly. The capacity of his cottage is thirty people, which includes standees in the kitchen, from which the television screen is visible."[2]

FCC Chairman Larry Fly watched TV in the Dutcher home, reported Johnston, while on a fact-finding visit to Newburgh in 1940.

"The first thing that Chairman Fly said," according to Mrs. Dutcher, was "'This is going to kill the movies.'" The big attraction that night was a televised wrestling match. At the home of Mr. and Mrs. J. E. McGrath, wrote Johnston, "on wrestling nights groups gather on the sidewalk and watch the show through the parlor window." Fly visited the McGrath's home, too, and commented, "This is better than a ringside seat."[3]

The TV subculture that had developed in just a few months in Newburgh was living proof of the new medium's potential to attract the American public and to alter its lifestyle. How soon would the rest of the country follow in Newburgh's footsteps? As soon as Larry Fly and the FCC gave the industry a green light, tens of thousands of TV sets would be marketed and sold: that was the prediction of RCA's advertising director Thomas Joyce in April 1940. Thirty stations in eighteen cities had already applied for licenses, Joyce noted, with a potential audience of 10 million American families.

THE WAR IN EUROPE

Newburgh, television, RCA, and the FCC were hardly front-page news in April 1940. Instead, Americans were caught up in the shocking and riveting drama in Europe that was unfolding on the radio, in newspapers, and on movie newsreels. Back in September 1939, Hitler's German army invaded and swiftly conquered Poland; in response, Britain and France declared war against the Nazis. Then, after a relatively peaceful winter (the *sitzkrieg* or "phony war"), the real war suddenly broke out in April.

The blitzkrieg of the German Army across Europe began with Germany quickly conquering Denmark and Norway. America's radio airwaves were filled with reports and analysis from the capitals of Europe, as German troops next stormed through Belgium and the Netherlands. By the end of May, England was evacuating its 300,000 troops from the European mainland, along the shores of Dunkirk, France, retreating to defend their homeland from Nazi invaders.

Live pictures on TV from Europe would have given Americans "ringside seats" on the war in Europe, but it was not to be. The technology to transmit images from Europe to the United States had yet to be developed. Instead, the small TV audience of 1940 watched radio journalist Lowell Thomas reading the news on RCA's station

W2XBS for fifteen minutes several nights a week. At times, Thomas narrated newsreel films of the war and related world and national events. Often the images on TV were delayed by days from the time of the actual events—and in Europe in 1940, historic events happened only days apart.

In the midst of the British evacuation from the shores of Dunkirk, Germany invaded France; on June 10, Italy joined the war, siding with Germany and declaring war on France. Just two weeks later, the Battle of France was over. France surrendered to Germany and Paris was occupied, with Britain standing alone on its isles and preparing to defend against a German invasion.

In secret, British and American scientists and engineers were perfecting a new technology closely related to TV to use as a weapon of war against Germany: radar. Both TV and radar used the electromagnetic spectrum to send signals through the air; both used a beam of electrons striking the wide end of a cathode-ray tube to change the signals into pictures. So similar were the two technologies, in fact, that some of the earliest radar units were made from TV tubes.

These two siblings had developed along parallel lines since the early 1930s. Similar to television, radar's first real use came in 1939, aboard the Navy battleship USS *New York*. Using a single radar unit built by the U.S. Naval Research Laboratory, the *New York* detected buoys, birds, mortar shells, and distant aircraft and mountains—whether in daylight or at night, under clear skies or in fog. In early 1940, when RCA launched and then aborted its TV sales campaign in New York City, the same company also began building twenty radar units for the Navy.

In May 1940, as the German army rolled through Western Europe, President Roosevelt called for a tenfold increase in airplane production. By this time, British engineers working together with their American counterparts were developing radar for airplanes. Roosevelt's order meant that some 50,000 new planes would have installed radar units to track enemy aircraft and to spot targets on land. Contracts to build these radar units were sent out to RCA and other electronics firms; they would soon be using the same factories, personnel, material, and machines that might otherwise have gone to building TV sets and equipment.

Thus each radar unit meant, in practical terms, one less TV set to sell to the American public. Whatever the signal from the FCC—

green or red or amber—the TV industry in mid-1940 was now destined to wind itself down and shift into war-related production. Indeed, an estimated 20 percent of all industry in the United States might soon be committed to defense, and as much as 80 percent if the United States entered the war. Already, plans for mobilization—M Day, it was called—were widespread throughout corporate offices, awaiting the actual contracts from Washington.

RCA's David Sarnoff, in fact, had quietly begun planning for military production back in September 1939, after Germany conquered Poland. As a Russian Jew, Sarnoff's desire to help the British fight Hitler and the Nazis was as personal as it was business related. Yet television also represented a major commitment for Sarnoff and RCA. Television was Sarnoff's "torch of hope in a troubled world," as he'd proclaimed only a year earlier at the World's Fair's opening, and it was not easily abandoned in mid-1940. After all, over 1,000 TV sets were already turned on in American homes and other sites, with the growing audience of viewers the base on which Sarnoff and others in the industry still hoped to build a mass medium. Sarnoff had promised, in particular, that a TV network would be set up in time to cover the 1940 presidential campaign; despite the war in Europe, that promise was fulfilled.

THE 1940 REPUBLICAN CONVENTION

In June 1940, thousands of Americans watched live on TV for the first time the spectacle of national politics in action. The Republican Party was meeting in Philadelphia to select its ticket; on June 25, Philco began televising the proceedings live from inside Convention Hall, using lights so bright that some of the delegates wore sunglasses. Americans watched the convention on TV sets in living rooms, hotels, bars, and department stores within range of Philco's own experimental TV station, W3XE.

Also for the first time, audiences in other cities watched the same program at the same time. In a rare instance of cooperation within the TV industry, RCA combined with Philco and General Electric to televise the event in New York City and upstate New York. It marked the debut of TV's first network, called the Eastern or East Coast network, which would become a mainstay of the TV industry for the next dozen years.

The first leg of the network, between Philadelphia's station W3XE and New York's W2XBS, used a coaxial cable built in 1936 by Bell Telephone; the thick tube could carry 200 phone conversations and one television signal. The second leg used the TV transmitter atop the Empire State Building to beam a signal to an antenna on Helderberg Mountain in upstate New York, where it was relayed to a station operated by General Electric in Schenectady. Added together, the three stations had a potential viewing audience of 50,000 people, based on the number of sets in operation in mid-1940.

An amazing political drama began to unfold on the convention's second night when the last Republican to have won the White House, Herbert Hoover, strode down the center aisle as delegates cheered and whistled and the band played "California, Here I Come." Among the TV viewers in New York was a *Times* reporter, who wrote, "The scene of excitement was reminiscent of an ex-champion entering the arena confident of staging a comeback."[4] Indeed, Hoover was hoping to run for President for a third time, having won in 1928 and lost to Roosevelt in 1932.

When Hoover reached the podium to speak, however, "the elder statesman appeared tired," wrote the reporter watching him intently on TV. "Delivery lacked punch. Few gestures, no table pounding or clenched fists enlivened the television picture." He concluded, "Possibly Mr. Hoover was more effective unseen; [radio] listeners were found who reported his speech emphatic and thrilling. Telegenically, however, he did not score."[5] Thus, the notion of the "telegenic" presidential candidate first entered American politics that night in June 1940.

The next day, TV viewers saw the Republicans nominate their two leading candidates, Ohio's Senator Robert Taft and New York's young attorney general, Thomas Dewey, who was leading in the delegate count and in the polls. Then, in the prime of the evening, Congressman Charles Halleck of Indiana came to the podium to face a chorus of boos as he nominated a true "dark horse," Wendell Willkie, the former director of the Commonwealth and Southern Corporation. Willkie had first caught the public's eye in 1939 when he opposed the Tennessee Valley Authority, headed then by the FCC's Larry Fly. Yet Wendell Willkie had never held a public office or even run for one, nor had he ever worked a day in government or politics.

What prompted the televised boos from the Republicans, however, was the fact that Willkie was until recently a registered, voting, and active Democrat. Halleck responded to the jeering delegates by asking, "Is the Republican party a closed corporation? Do you have to be born in it?"[6] Wrote *The New York Times* reporter, "Televiewers will long remember the waving, defiant finger of Representative Halleck as he nominated Willkie and fired back at the dissenting boos."[7] Willkie's backers had filled the galleries with young and raucous supporters, and they followed Halleck's speech with the chant, "We want Willkie! We want Willkie!" At that point, the convention's chairman, Joseph Martin, adjourned the meeting for the night. The TV broadcast ended, too, and the scene was set for the next day's balloting and a classic moment of televised American political drama.

Although TV was bringing the visual excitement of national politics into American homes for the first time, it failed to show the political maneuvers taking place. Television had no reporters on the floor or in the hotel rooms where Willkie's backers were following a plan to steal the nomination from Dewey and Taft. Viewers were thus unaware that Joe Martin, the convention chair, was secretly a Willkie supporter, and that's why he'd given the "We want Willkie" chanters the last word on Wednesday night.

After the first two ballots on Thursday afternoon, Willkie trailed far behind both Dewey and Taft. Willkie's supporters intended to keep his vote total low during early ballots, then build up the numbers and momentum so that the delegates of other candidates would suddenly see a bandwagon to jump aboard. Then, in the third and fourth ballots, dozens of delegates who had been pledged to Dewey and to "favorite sons" and other minor candidates switched to either Taft or Willkie; it quickly became a horse race between the two. At 11:20 p.m., a fifth ballot began before a packed Convention Hall, a wild gallery, and the uncounted thousands who had stayed up late to watch the drama unfold live on TV.

Willkie now took the lead, but either he or Taft could win on the next ballot by picking up delegates from Michigan or Pennsylvania. At twenty minutes past midnight, the sixth ballot began, as the TV broadcast crew posted the vote tally on camera, using a piece of cardboard that leaned against the back of a chair.

The roll call reached Michigan, and its delegation switched to Willkie. Now, the bandwagon for Willkie was hitched and rolling.

Pennsylvania shifted to him as well, and by 2:00 a.m. it was all over; history had been made. Before a TV audience that had watched up to sixty hours of programming that week, the Republican Party had nominated its first modern candidate: a political novice who was literally a product of the mass media.

Willkie's rapid rise to the top of the party, it seems, had begun when he caught the attention of a magazine publisher. "I've met the man who ought to be the next President of the United States," *Fortune*'s Russell Davenport told his wife after meeting Willkie in 1939. When she asked if the idea was "his or yours," Davenport said, "It's spontaneous. You see him and you know it."[8] Wendell Willkie was indeed an appealing character. With tousled hair, a broad smile, and a mildly plump physique, he had a boyish, likeable appearance. His speech was direct, sincere, and intelligent; he was a political moderate with views that were more pro-business than anti-New Deal.

Soon, Davenport and a group of Republican businessmen and political operatives were promoting Willkie in the media, with magazine articles and radio and personal appearances. Willkie entered a few primaries in the spring of 1940 and gathered a small set of delegates to vote for him on the first ballot. "I have no campaign manager, no campaign fund, no campaign headquarters," he'd told reporters on his arrival in Philadelphia. "All the headquarters I have are under my hat."[9] He did have Davenport and his other sponsors, and they'd crafted a plan to win the nomination that worked perfectly.

Winning the election, however, was a different story. Once Willkie hit the campaign trail in the late summer of 1940, he suffered a series of losses. First, he lost his bandwagon when Republican conservatives backed off supporting the moderate ex-Democrat. Then he lost his voice while campaigning, and the harsh tones that remained took away much of his appeal on radio. Perhaps his biggest loss came when President Roosevelt broke with a precedent set by George Washington and ran for a third term, in part because he saw in Willkie what Russell Davenport had seen in 1939—someone who could beat the Democrats.

Willkie was a fresh face in American politics, and he was photogenic and most likely telegenic. He might have contrasted favorably with Franklin Roosevelt in a modern, TV-oriented campaign, but that was not to be, given the small scale of television in 1940. In fact, Willkie's nomination in Philadelphia marked the high point of both his political career and TV's coverage of the campaign. Similar to Willkie himself, TV failed to capitalize on the excitement it broadcast during the convention. The national convention held by the Democrats a month later was a letdown. Not only did the event lack the drama of the Republican National Convention, with the only interest coming from Roosevelt's announcement that, as expected, he would seek a third term, but because the convention was staged in Chicago, there was no live TV coverage.

Chicago in 1940 had only the beginnings of a television station: an experimental TV license that had been granted to an entertainment company, Balaban & Katz, earlier in the summer. RCA had no mobile TV unit in Chicago, nor any means of relaying a signal outside the city. Instead, RCA arranged with Pathe, the newsreel film company, to purchase 1,000 feet of motion picture film shot at the convention each day. The film was flown to New York and aired on station W2XBS the following afternoon and evening in ten-minute programs.

A DISAPPOINTING FALL

As disappointing as this coverage may have been to TV set owners, especially when compared to the many hours of live TV from the Republican convention, even worse news came the following week. RCA announced that it was shutting down station W2XBS for at least the month of August. The station was moving its signal up to a higher frequency on the electromagnetic spectrum and needed time to readjust its equipment and transmitter. The press reported that W2XBS might be off the air for as many as three months, and that RCA was cutting back on programming until the FCC agreed to grant its station a commercial license.

The summer of 1940 ended with no word from RCA as to when station W2XBS would be back on the air. Nonetheless, RCA announced in October that its NBC subsidiary would build a tricity TV network linking New York, Philadelphia, and Washington, DC. Already, NBC had signed a lease for a new station and studio in the Wardman Park Hotel in the nation's capital. Why was Washington, DC, selected as RCA's second station? "It is only reasonable to assume," explained NBC president Niles Trammel, "that Washington will be an important source of interesting material for tomorrow's nationwide television network."10

A station in Washington, DC, was valued in part because American politics made for good TV programming, as the Republican National Convention had shown. In fact, when station W2XBS finally went back on the air in late October, it was to transmit another live political event: President Roosevelt addressing a packed political rally in Madison Square Garden. His speech that night was the most memorable of the campaign. Criticizing the isolationist Republicans in Congress who opposed his plans to mobilize the nation, Roosevelt gave the crowd and TV viewers a roll call of their names. He ended with what he called "a perfectly beautiful alliteration: Congressmen Martin, Barton, and Fish."11 He repeated it: "Martin, Barton, and Fish"—and the phrase was picked up by his audience at Madison Square Garden. Over the next few days, as the campaign drew to a close, Roosevelt used "Martin, Barton, and Fish" as a catchphrase to rally his audiences.

Roosevelt's speech at Madison Square Garden was his second and final appearance on television. On Election Day the following week, he was at his home in Hyde Park where he may have watched the election results on TV. The live telecast from New York began at 7:00 p.m., and NBC brought in Leo Rosenberg to add a touch of history: Rosenberg had presided over radio's first election night on the country's first station, KDKA in Pittsburgh, twenty years earlier.

This Election Day, the TV audience watched tally sheets being held in front of the camera as the latest results came into the studio, sometimes before the announcers themselves saw the numbers. "I am called upon to tell you something," one TV announcer admitted on air, "that undoubtedly you already have read, through this new marvel."12

Among the thousands of Americans watching the results that night was Wendell Willkie, seated before a TV set and a small radio in the bedroom of his suite in Manhattan's Commodore Hotel. At 9:30 p.m., Willkie saw Ohio go for Roosevelt, virtually ensuring his loss; then he heard that Cleveland's *The Plain Dealer* had declared Roosevelt the winner. Willkie told his entourage, "I can still win," and at midnight he went down to the hotel lobby to tell his supporters that he wasn't conceding.

At 1:00 a.m. the election telecast ended; Willkie waited until the next morning before he conceded. Roosevelt had won his third term, and although the final results weren't close, it wasn't a landslide either. Willkie took 45 percent of the popular vote and carried ten of forty-eight states—far better results for Republicans than in Roosevelt's two previous wins. The New Deal's hold on American government had begun to slip. The Republicans would lose twice more, however, before winning the White House with another fresh and photogenic face—Dwight Eisenhower.

As for television, the 1940 Republican National Convention was not just a highlight of the year, it remains to this day one of the most exciting political events ever televised. Years later, Tony Miner, a major producer/director of early TV dramas, described it as the first proof that "when television gets a decent chance to report an event, it is able to rise above any inherent shortcomings and establish a triumphant record."[13]

In the remaining weeks of 1940, RCA resumed a regular schedule of programs on W2XBS, but the station was on the air fewer hours than before its summer shutdown. Also, W2XBS was relying more on films and outside events—sports, in particular—which cost less than studio productions. At the same time, RCA was hiring more workers and expanding its manufacturing plants, just as David Sarnoff had promised in his testimony at the TV hearings in Washington earlier in the year. But these new workers weren't making thousands of TV sets for Americans to buy for Christmas or in the next year; instead, they were hired to fulfill RCA's new $7 million contract with the U.S. Army to produce equipment for the war raging in Europe.

RCA was one of many electrical equipment companies, including most of the TV manufacturers, now retooling in response to new military orders. "We must be the great arsenal of democracy," President Roosevelt told the nation right after the November election. England, in particular, needed America's "armaments of war," said Roosevelt, with its cities under siege for months from Nazi bombing raids. The British were "the spearhead of resistance to world conquest," the President said,[14] and that night the Nazi bombing raids on London were especially destructive, hitting the city's financial district.

DEBATING TV'S FUTURE IN 1941

Over the next few months, Congress and the American public debated whether the nation should intervene further in the war on the side of Britain. Roosevelt had followed up his Fireside Chat by submitting to Congress a military-aid bill, known as "Lend Lease." If the bill passed, the United States government could give England the weapons and tools of war without demanding payment; if it failed, the British couldn't afford the American industrial products they needed to fight the Germans.

As the issue of the United States' role in the war dominated the winter months of 1940-1941, the smaller debate over TV's future continued as well. January 1, 1941, had been an unofficial deadline for the TV industry to reach agreement on technical standards, required by the FCC before it would issue any more licenses. If a new station were built in Washington in early January 1941, thousands of East Coast viewers could watch the presidential inauguration on live TV.

Committees of engineers and other industry people met in late 1940 to set television's technical standards, but by January 1, 1941, they'd agreed only to submit reports at a public hearing later that month. In the meantime, Chairman Fly and other FCC members went to New York City for some well-publicized demonstrations by industry leaders of TV's latest innovations, including two new screens from RCA. The first was a full fifteen feet by twenty feet, and RCA displayed it at the New Yorker Theatre, suggesting it would be used to televise special events to large audiences. Their second screen was for the home set; it used a mirror to project a picture that was a relatively big at 13.5 inches by 8 inches.

Television in theaters and a bigger screen in homes—these demonstrations in early 1941 were hints of what TV might become in the near future; at the very least, the new sets would answer complaints about TV's small picture. Much more exciting, however, was a demonstration by the Columbia Broadcasting System (CBS) of color television, with a picture judged equal to that of 16-mm color movie film. Could it be that color TV sets would soon enter the market? That tantalizing prospect just added to the confusion over TV in early 1941. Would the American public reject black-and-white sets for color TV, even at a substantially higher price? If so, then why should the industry now set technical standards for black-and-white sets and promote them to the public? Black-and-white TV could become obsolete even before it became popular.

On January 27, 1941, the FCC received the industry's recommended set of technical standards for television. The months of meetings had resulted in standards that were virtually the same as the old ones RCA had been using since 1939. There were minority reports to consider, however, and the next day the FCC announced it would hold one more public hearing in Washington, DC, on March 20 before issuing its final rulings.

A matter of greater importance was settled in Washington in the weeks before the FCC met. Congress passed the Lend Lease bill on March 8, and it was immediately signed into law by President Roosevelt, who then sent a shopping list of weapons to England. Americans soon heard Roosevelt on the radio calling for hard work and sacrifices to move products "from the assembly lines of our factories to the battle lines of democracy." What was needed, he said, was "speed, and speed now, now, now."[15]

On March 20, as the final FCC hearings on television standards began, the world remained troubled. German planes were bombing London; its ships were routinely sinking or capturing other ships in the North Atlantic; and its troops were moving down the coast of North Africa, putting the Western Hemisphere within flying range.

Chapter 3

In a Troubled World

THE 1941 FCC HEARINGS

When the FCC opened its new hearings on TV in March 1941, almost two years had passed since RCA began selling sets and televising programs. The FCC was finally ready to grant commercial licenses and to let the industry support its investment in TV by seeking sponsors for programs. First, however, came the FCC's precondition that the industry agree on technical standards for TV sets and transmissions.

Instead of the 421-line picture that the industry was expected to endorse, a new number appeared: 525. According to Donald Fink, then editor of *Electronics,* the number was selected almost randomly. Before the hearing began, he was asked to find a compromise between RCA's 421 lines per image and Philco's 604. According to Fink, "I said it ought to be an odd number, it ought to be composed of a small number of odd factors, how do you like 525?"[1] The number was adopted and became the industry standard until the advent of high definition television (HDTV), with roughly twice the lines per image, as an alternative in the late 1990s.

Finally, television's commercial start was at hand—or so it seemed, until the hearings in Washington actually began. Then, to the apparent astonishment of FCC Chairman Larry Fly, RCA confessed that it was no longer eager to receive a commercial license for its New York station, W2XBS. "But a few months ago, you were ready to go ahead," Fly said, after RCA's chief engineer C. B. Jolliffe held back from asking the FCC to grant commercial licenses. "Now you seem to want to delay to let the rest of the industry catch up." Fly pursued. "Why? Haven't you more data, more information, more orders, than a year ago?"[2]

"More engineering and technical data," Jolliffe admitted, "but less information about the industry as a whole, and fewer orders."[3] It was no surprise that RCA had fewer orders for TV sets in 1941 than in 1940. The company had stopped marketing its sets and had cut down on its broadcasts. Television may have been Sarnoff's "torch of hope in a troubled world" two years before, but now the troubles of the world had erupted in a war, and Sarnoff's company was mobilizing to make radar sets and other war-related equipment. Getting a commercial license for W2XBS was no longer a priority.

In fact, a commercial license would probably hurt more than help RCA. The FCC could require as much as thirty hours of programs a week from TV stations with commercial licenses. No other company had invested the millions of dollars that RCA had in studios, mobile units, and programming. In a "worst-case" scenario for RCA, the rest of the industry would forego commercial licenses rather than spend the money needed to produce thirty hours of telecasts per week. With few shows on the air and few sets on the market, television's growth would remain stunted. Sponsors would stay away in droves, and RCA would be left holding the corporate bag and draining its budget by the week to pay for its unsponsored programs.

RCA may have surprised the FCC at the March hearings by admitting it "would like to go ahead, and would go ahead" with TV, but only "when others do."[4] Their new reluctance made sense—and it marked a turning point in the brief history so far of American television. With RCA no longer anxious to drive the industry, prod the FCC, or woo the public, TV had at least avoided the risk of becoming a monopoly. Consequently, the new medium would need more support from other companies, and it would need to enhance its own basic power to attract the public and keep them watching.

When the hearings ended on March 25, *The New York Times* predicted that the FCC would set an early date to issue commercial licenses, but not because the FCC or the TV industry expected television to grow in the near future. It was simply that "in the capital city," wrote the *Times*, "it is felt that the FCC wants to get the television problem 'off its hands.'" [5]

THE BEGINNING OF COMMERCIAL TV

In the meantime, RCA continued to transmit programs from station W2XBS to the 3,000 or more TV sets in the New York City area. Live sports events now dominated the schedule, with hockey and basketball from Madison Square Garden on Monday and Friday nights, along with boxing and wrestling matches from an arena in Jamaica, Queens.

The week after the FCC hearings, RCA transmitted a night of boxing from Madison Square Garden by cable across the street to a projector in the balcony of the New Yorker Theatre. It was TV's first closed-circuit theater telecast, and watching the fights on the theater's large movie screen was an audience of sports promoters, engineers, and journalists.

They were told by one speaker at the event that someday theaters would be linked outside the city "in Yonkers, White Plains, Coney Island, etc.," to televise sporting events to "cheering spectators." Boxing promoter Mike Jacobs told the audience, "It's worth a million,"[6] and he was eventually proven right. As it turned out, closed-circuit live telecasts of boxing matches in the 1960s and 1970s attracted big audiences and brought many millions of dollars into the worlds of boxing and broadcasting.

No longer interested in selling TV sets to the American public, RCA now saw theater broadcasting as an alternate way to profit from television, and one that required few sets, stations, and sponsors. RCA went public with its theater television on May 9, 1941, when over a thousand people watched another night of televised boxing at the New Yorker. The highlight was a lightweight championship bout in which "virtually every blow struck was visible" on the big TV screen, according to an impressed newspaper reporter.[7]

Notre Dame football coach Frank Leahy was among the panelists who spoke on live TV from RCA's studio before the bouts. Leahy predicted that the crowd of 80,000 in the stands at the annual Notre Dame-Army football games was just "a drop in the bucket" compared to the number of people who might view the game in theaters.[8] Madison Square Garden's president, John Reed Kilpatrick, told the audience that his arena already staged over sixty events a year "that would have definite television theater box-office values."[9]

Ironically, the FCC had just announced its long-awaited date for the start of commercial TV: this new era would commence in less than two months, on July 1, 1941. David Sarnoff, who had led the fight for the licenses in early 1940, now wondered publicly whether commercial TV could survive with only a few thousand sets in homes to attract advertisers. "We have lost none of our enthusiasm for television," Sarnoff told RCA shareholders, "nor our faith in its eventual success." RCA had stopped making new sets, he said, having "enlisted in the first line of America's defense on land, on sea, and in the air."[10] In fact, RCA had received almost $40 million in defense orders and commitments by mid-1941, and Sarnoff himself was serving as the broadcast industry's advisor to President Roosevelt's Defense Communications Board.

On May 23, 1941, Franklin Roosevelt declared an "unlimited national emergency" and took on new powers to set and enforce restrictions in trade, utilities, communications, and other areas of American industry. He warned Americans that the war in Europe was now "approaching the brink of the Western Hemisphere itself," with the German navy in the Atlantic creating an "actual military danger to the Americas."[11] The President vowed to keep the supply routes open to England and soon ordered more war material to be produced for the British government.

At the same time Roosevelt was taking the country one step closer to war, the TV industry was preparing to go commercial. Even RCA, despite its protests, was awaiting its new license for station W2XBS; Sarnoff had no intention of losing RCA's leading position in the industry. It seemed at first that New York City might have three commercial TV stations on the air. One of them, W2XAB, belonged to CBS and had the most spacious studio in the industry: the loft above the main waiting room in New York's Grand Central Station. W2XAB had no mobile unit, and its staff had little experience in creating programs. Nevertheless, CBS announced plans to broadcast Monday through Saturdays for several hours in the afternoons and early evenings. Du Mont Laboratories, too, had a station that was expected to begin transmitting on July 1. Although CBS had no mobile units but had a spacious studio, Du Mont had no studio but did have mobile units to cover events on location.

RCA, of course, had a station, a studio, mobile units, and two years of experience in televising a regular schedule of programs. In addition, RCA had been working with a few sponsors on a small scale for the past year. The Standard Oil Company, for example, was supporting a TV news program on station W2XBS titled *Esso Evening News* and had some positive results to show for it. A study of New York City consumers showed a much higher rate of product recognition for the company's Esso gasoline among those who owned TV sets versus those who did not.[12]

On July 1, 1941—the day commercial TV began in the United States—all three New York City stations were on the air. Only RCA's station, however, had acquired a commercial license by committing itself to fifteen hours of telecasts per week. That was the minimum required by the FCC for commercial stations, and it was half the number of hours the agency had wanted back in March. RCA's station now bore a new name, WNBT, combining the National Broadcasting Company (RCA's broadcasting subsidiary) with "television."

WNBT aired TV's first commercial at 2:30 p.m.; it was simply a picture test pattern that had been redesigned into a working clock, ticking off the seconds in front of the TV camera. The sponsor's name, Bulova, appeared on the clock, which ticked for a full minute at 2:30 and later again that night. Bulova paid four dollars for the afternoon spot and eight dollars for the evening, and afterward they signed up for thirteen weeks of similar commercials. Although the money was merely a drop in the sea of RCA's debts thus far in TV, it marked the start of the era of commercial television. The medium was now bringing in money.

The first TV program with a commercial was televised on WNBT that night: *Uncle Jim's Question Bee,* sponsored by Spry, a shortening made by Lever. *Uncle Jim's* was a radio show, described by *Variety* as "one of the innumerable audience participation programs" on the air in 1941 and "neither worse nor better" than any other.[13] The Spry commercials featured a radio character named Aunt Jenny who was, in *Variety*'s words, the "perfect prototype of the kitchen-proud American homekeeper."[14] In TV's first commercial break, Aunt Jenny opened a can of Spry; it filled the TV screen as she said, "How smooth an' satiny-lookin' with that big, snowy swirl on top. Spry looks purer, doesn't it, folks?"[15]

Later in the program, she presented to the cast a finished chocolate layer cake made with Spry. Wrote *The New York Times,* "The camera dwelt on this enthusiastic scene while every one ate his cake 'radiating enjoyment'" and then asked for seconds.[16] It was, explained *Variety,* "a clinical study in beautiful, good-selling hokum." Live TV also displayed its power to show a bit too much. "The next time she cuts a chocolate layer cake on television," *Variety* suggested to Aunt Jenny, she should "remember not to lick the cake-knife with her mouth and then offer to cut her guests another slice with the same knife."[17]

WNBT transmitted two other sponsored programs that night. A news broadcast with Lowell Thomas aired on both radio and TV at the same time, and viewers could see a few stacks of the sponsor's product, Sunoco Motor Oil. Later that same night, WNBT televised a quiz program from radio, *Truth or Consequences,* sponsored by Procter and Gamble. Viewers saw their first televised dishpan hands in a commercial for Ivory soap. The program itself, wrote *Variety,* "helped to begin television under commercial sponsorship on a pretty low level," with the "strange spectacle" of an "adult citizen" performing a hula dance and "another fat gent" wearing a large diaper and "bawl[ing] while seated on the lap of a middle-aged woman."[18]

The "low level" that *Variety* referred to in its review of the first day of commercial TV has been used to describe TV ever since. NBC, the broadcasting subsidiary of RCA, was using popular shows from its own radio network to attract viewers and sponsors. From a business viewpoint, this made perfect sense. Why shouldn't programming that was popular on radio succeed as well in television? After all, TV was a visual form of radio, and RCA and most of the rest of the TV industry were radio businesses as well.

Culturally speaking, however, this system was subject to the same criticisms that could be heard in 1941 about radio: it was too commercial and pandered to the tastes of an unsophisticated mass audience. Now, new visual evidence could be added: the "fat gent" in diapers on the NBC television show, sponsored by soaps and detergents.

THE SUMMER OF 1941

RCA's use of its radio talent didn't continue on WNBT. The station had little success in attracting sponsors and reverted back to the sports, films, and studio shows that had been on the schedule before the station went commercial. Viewers in the summer of 1941 could watch another style of programming on a second station in New York City, W2XAB. The station was owned by RCA's biggest rival in network radio: CBS. The CBS station had no commercial license on July 1 (although it soon would), but it televised a few programs that afternoon. "All easygoing, unhurried, unstiff," wrote *Variety*,[19] in contrast to the commercial programs on WNBT. The station aired, for example, a children's storytelling program and a dancing lesson with instructors from the Arthur Murray dance schools. A host served as a "roving emcee," who would "walk across the floor every now and then" to become involved in the action.[20] Viewers could see the TV equipment and technical staff in the spacious, well-lit studio.

The staff of the CBS station took a less-polished approach to TV programming because CBS lacked the resources and the experience to do more than the simplest of shows. Also, CBS had yet to show the interest in television that RCA had and was not using its radio shows and performers in the new medium. *Variety* found the CBS style appealing, however, and this casual approach to TV has survived over the decades. Talk shows, late-night and daytime TV, local access programs, and some educational shows—in these and other telecasts viewers can still experience an "easygoing, unhurried, unstiff" style of broadcasting.

The summer of 1941 remains the high-water mark of the early years of television. At long last, TV owners within range of New York City had programs to watch nearly every afternoon and evening, and they even had the option of choosing between shows on different stations. It was a sign of things to come.

On a typical day that summer—August 21, 1941, for example—the TV audience in the afternoon could view an exhibit from the Metropolitan Museum of Art and a children's story program on WCBW or a WNBT program on coaching sports. That evening, they could choose between a sports news program and a "Country Dance" on WCBW, and an assortment of shows on WNBT, including *June Boyd, Xylophone,* a news program, and a quiz and participation show called *Play the Game,* which was one of TV's earliest regular programs.

The competition in *Play the Game* was charades, with viewers able to phone in their guesses as to the phrase being acted out by the program's guests. *Play the Game* had an unlikely host: Dr. Harvey Zorbaugh, a professor of education at New York University who became one of TV's first "celebrities" when he developed a following among viewers in New York. The guests were Zorbough's wife and friends; they had brought to WNBT the idea of televising the parlor game they'd played at home and were put on the air the very next week.

Viewers that summer also became familiar with singers Joan Edwards and Harvey Harding, both of whom performed a few times a week in fifteen-minute programs, and with a pioneering female broadcast journalist, Helen Sioussat, who hosted an afternoon interview program, *Table Talk with Helen Sioussat*, on WCBW. By late summer, WNBT was televising college and professional football, horse racing from Aqueduct and Belmont, boxing and wrestling matches, some films, and a handful of studio programs.

In hindsight, TV in 1941 was clearly heading toward the path it would eventually take: offering a regular schedule of popular entertainment shows, interspersed with news and sports events and other types of shows, in competition for an audience and commercial sponsors. The mix of shows would appeal to many viewers, disappoint some critics, and be popular enough to make almost anyone on TV a celebrity. That complicated path was still beyond the range of TV in 1941. Only 5,000 TV sets had been produced thus far; with a total potential audience of perhaps 50,000, the new medium was unlikely to attract sponsors to pay for a schedule of programming.

THE BUILDUP TO WAR

Even TV's strongest initial booster, David Sarnoff, abandoned it for the time being. In early September 1941, Sarnoff launched another RCA campaign with a big splash of publicity, but this time the campaign had nothing to do with selling TV sets. From his desk at Radio City, Sarnoff tapped out the letter "B" in Morse code on a telegraph key. It stood for "Beat the Promise" and symbolized RCA's pledge to fulfill its military contracts to the government sooner than promised. While RCA industrial plants around the country held noontime rallies, Sarnoff wired a speech declaring that "defense has had and will continue to have the right of way in all of our plants."[21] RCA had clearly made its last TV set for the foreseeable future.

Nor were other manufacturers likely to make many TV sets either. Americans in 1941 were buying radios, not TVs, and listening to the ominous war news from Europe. Both radios and TV sets used aluminum and nickel, now in short supply; the metals were needed to make the weapons and items of war being shipped to Europe. The radio industry adjusted to the shortages by making fewer radios and using substitute materials in the ones they did make. Most of the TV set manufacturers also made radios, and they were not about to use their dwindling stock of metals to make TV sets that the public didn't want.

In October, officials in Washington, DC, declared that the broadcast industry was now a lower-level defense industry. That rating meant that TV and radio stations already in operation could maintain their equipment and thus remain on the air. But the industry could no longer build any new stations or improve those in existence—the raw materials were needed for the military and for industries with higher priority ratings. America's TV industry was officially stopped dead in its tracks. The government had turned the red light back on, just as the biggest national drama of the decade—wartime—was unfolding and before a TV station could be built in Washington, DC, to show it live.

Even without TV from the capitol, however, the screens of the several thousand TV sets in use during the fall of 1941 showed America preparing for war. Both WNBT and WCBW now had civil defense programs on their regular weekly TV schedule. WNBT's program, for example, demonstrated first aid and fire control; viewers were encouraged to become "television defense aids" and gather their families, friends, and neighbors in front of the TV to watch the lessons.22

In addition, a news program called *Face of the War* was airing on WNBT with commentator Sam Cuff using maps and a pointer to explain and analyze the latest developments. In mid-November 1941 came the news that Congress had repealed its neutrality laws, allowing U.S. merchant ships to travel armed across the Atlantic. In late November, Sam Cuff's maps on TV showed the German army positioned just thirty miles from Moscow.

On December 4, the Japanese government secretly sent nineteen transport ships into the South China Sea, while six aircraft carriers headed into the Pacific under the cover of heavy clouds. TV failed to bring news of this ominous event to the American public, but then so did newspapers and radio. Three days later came TV's first bulletin: the shocking news that Japan had attacked the U.S. Navy base at Pearl Harbor, Hawaii.

Television screens on Sunday afternoon, December 7, 1941, clearly showed Sam Cuff on WNBT's *Face of the War* pointing on a map to Pearl Harbor and the sites of other Japanese attacks that morning in the Philippines, Guam, Wake Island, Hong Kong, and Singapore. Of course, most Americans listened intently to their radios that day, as John Daly on the CBS network and Hans Kaltenborn on NBC told them the dramatic news. But those who watched TV could read the bulletins themselves on an Associated Press teletype machine shown close-up on the screen by WNBT.

The following day at noon, President Roosevelt's famous "date which will live in infamy" speech to Congress was televised live on WCBW—but only the audio. For its picture the station used a photograph of a waving American flag. By 2:00 p.m., Congress had passed a declaration of war against Japan, and at 4:10 that same afternoon President Roosevelt signed it. To cover this historic news, WCBW canceled its *Children's Story* and the other programs scheduled to air from 2:30 to 3:30 p.m.

Within the next few days, the United States declared war against Germany and Italy. Quickly, the darkest of times had begun. As 1941 drew to a close, many Americans enlisted in the military or worked overtime in newly converted defense industries. Tens of millions of people followed the war news on radio, in newspapers and magazines, and on movie newsreels. A few thousand Americans also watched the great drama of World War II unfold in their living rooms on *Face of the War* and other news shows being televised on WNBT and WCBW.

These stations lacked the equipment, staff, and resources to cover the war firsthand; instead, they read news reports on the air and televised newsreels. WNBT and WCBW filled the rest of their required airtime with the same kinds of shows they had televised before the war: films, sports, musical programs, and an occasional play. On New Year's Eve, for example, TV viewers watched the countdown to 1942 as Guy Lombardo and his Royal Canadians played "Auld Lang Syne" at the Rainbow Room in New York.

WARTIME TELEVISION

The new year was less than a week old, however, when TV programming itself began to change as a result of America's entry in the war. On the night of Monday, January 5, 1942, WNBT televised a special wartime instructional program, "Air Raid Protection—Fighting the Bomb." It included civil defense films and tool demonstrations, and it was sent along the same East Coast network that RCA had developed for the 1940 Republican convention, from Manhattan south to Philadelphia and north to Schenectady.

The air raid program that WNBT televised on January 5 reflected the nation's concern regarding civil defense in the early months of America's entry into the war. Civil defense agencies were established in every state by early 1942, and air-raid drills and large-scale blackouts were practiced along the coasts. Residents on the East Coast were worried about bombings by German warplanes. Their fears were fed by government officials such as New York City's Mayor LaGuardia, who said, "The war will come right to our cities and residential districts."[23]

In New York City alone, over 60,000 people volunteered as air-raid wardens, and in mid-January RCA agreed to help train them. RCA's station, WNBT, would produce and televise a regular schedule of training programs and would join forces with three of RCA's competitors—Philco, General Electric, and Du Mont—to transmit them to TV sets in New York, New Jersey, Pennsylvania, and Connecticut. For RCA and the TV industry, televising a civil defense training program brought some benefits. It was good publicity for TV, and it gave the industry a clear wartime role. It also helped fill RCA's required hours of telecasts each week, and it even offered the prospect of selling whatever TV sets were still in warehouses.

"Air Raid Warden's Basic Course: Lesson One" was televised for the first time on Monday, February 23, on WNBT in New York City, WRGB in Schenectady, and WPTZ in Philadelphia. The same lesson was repeated mornings, afternoons, and evenings during the week with eighteen showings in all, followed by a similar pattern for other lessons in subsequent weeks. Each airing was televised live from NBC's Radio City studio.

The TV lessons featured actors and actresses, sets and scenery, and props and sound effects. One lesson, for example, had an actor and actress portraying "the Browns," a city couple in whose apartment a firebomb had landed. As Mr. Brown carefully prodded the bomb on his living-room floor, Mrs. Brown prepared to put out a fire with a stirrup pump—a bicycle pump attached to a bucket of water. The same lesson also portrayed Times Square hit by an aerial bomb; other lessons covered such topics as blackouts, poison gas attacks, and decontamination procedures.[24]

Tens of thousands of civil defense volunteers and others were trained via TV sets that were placed in classrooms, firehouses, police stations, and even in private homes. Group leaders received teaching material beforehand. During the telecasts, a studio panel asked questions that were answered live on the air, and each lesson ended with a sign that read "Discussion Period" on the screen; even quizzes were given.

These air warden lessons were TV's first educational series, and they showed the medium's power to instruct. Through the magic window of TV, thousands of people in separate locations could see and hear the lessons together. Austin Lescarboura, a writer for *Radio News,* for example, claimed to have twenty-two people in his own house watching the training series. His experience led him to wonder if TV, "originally thought of mainly in terms of entertainment," would instead be used primarily in schools. He concluded, "Certainly it will make a single lecturer or instructor [and] one demonstration available to thousands and even tens of thousands of students."[25]

Although, as usual, WNBT had the most sophisticated broadcast, it was not the only TV station to televise civil defense programs during 1942. WCBW aired Red Cross programs demonstrating first aid and, in March 1942, began a series of broadcasts that promoted conservation of goods and materials, such as rubber, sugar, and tin, needed to fight the war. On the West Coast, an experimental station in Hollywood, W6XAO, televised government films related to the war, such as *Safeguarding Military Information* and *Building a Bomber.*

At the same time, most of the leading TV set manufacturers were switching 80 to 100 percent of their production to war goods. On March 7, the federal government made the changeover to war production official. Beginning April 22, no new radio or television sets could be built for the home market; even the manufacture of replacement parts for home sets was now in doubt. FCC Chairman Larry Fly quickly voiced his approval. "At every turn," he stated, "we must consider how many Germans and Japs can be eliminated with a given amount of material."[26]

As to the fate of TV programming during the war, the FCC gave the industry a chance to voice its opinions on whether stations should continue to operate. RCA argued that TV stations should be shut down for the war unless the government deemed them vital for national defense. CBS agreed and noted that the industry was losing all its engineers to the draft or to working on war contracts. The TV audience would begin dropping, said an engineer from General Electric, as soon as the tubes in TV sets burned out and replacement tubes ran out.

In May 1942, the FCC issued its ruling on the wartime status of TV in America. To keep their licenses, TV stations would have to remain on the air during the war, but they need broadcast only four hours a week. By then, WNBT had replaced most of its studio programs with the air warden training course; after transmitting the course a second time in the spring of 1942, the station cut its broadcasting schedule to the four-hour minimum.

Only three years after its bright beginning at the New York World's Fair, RCA's TV operation was now halted indefinitely. The "magic window" of television was barely open, as WNBT's weekly schedule consisted of films and slide programs that were squeezed into one or two broadcasts a week. The schedule of broadcasts for WCBW was just as empty as WNBT's by the middle of 1942, and both stations shut down the studios they had used for live programs. Another era in the brief history of American television had begun, with TV now mired in the depths of World War II.

SCHENECTADY'S WRGB

One heartbeat of television remained strong, however, throughout the war. It belonged to an unheralded station in an unlikely location: General Electric's WRGB in Schenectady, New York.

General Electric was one of the early pioneers in TV, along with RCA, and had experimented with televising programs as far back as 1928. Its station in Schenectady, New York, where the company was headquartered, had been operating as W2XB since 1939 and was part of RCA's Eastern network that televised the 1940 Republican National Convention. Now, in the middle of 1942, W2XB was licensed as commercial station WRGB, named after General Electric's television leader, Dr. Walter R. G. Baker.

Similar to RCA, General Electric had important and profitable contracts with the government during the war, but General Electric hadn't shut down its TV studio. In fact, the company kept to a fifteen-hour weekly schedule during the war, even after the FCC cut the required minimum hours to four.

WRGB also had the best equipped studio in the country, which General Electric had built just before the government restricted the use of raw materials. The studio was used, according to General Electric, to experiment in staging, lighting, and televising programs. Lighting, in particular, was a special field for General Electric, and WRGB's studio had experimental control panels and water-cooled lights.

During much of 1942, WRGB transmitted the air warden's training course from New York City to TV sets installed in such places as Union College in Schenectady. By 1943, the station was televising its own programs three nights a week. Most of the performers on WRGB were amateurs. In January 1943, for example, a community theater group from Albany performed a light opera on WRGB, and the Yale Drama Group put on a one-act play. Several other college acting groups performed plays on TV over the next two months. WRGB also aired wrestling matches, fashion shows, news programs, and war-related broadcasts, such as promotional appearances by females from the military auxiliary units—the Women's Auxiliary Army Corps (WAACS) and Women Accepted for Volunteer Emergency Service (WAVES).

WRGB televised amateur performers because they were the available talent in the Schenectady area. The station was an example of a low-scale TV operation with little connection to the larger worlds of network radio, show business, and advertising. WRGB showed how TV might develop after the war in smaller cities and towns: stations could be rooted, as were newspapers, in their communities and encourage local participation. Programs would lack the talent and professionalism of New York City's pool of performers, but they could still attract and satisfy a local TV audience.

Schenectady's most popular TV performers in 1943, for example, were the Owens troupe of puppeteers. Joe Owens was a General Electric engineer who built the marionettes himself; he was joined in operating them by his wife, two children, and a few young friends.[27] As puppeteers, they performed a type of popular arts that was visual and had entertained audiences throughout the world for centuries. As were many of WRGB's performers, the Owens were amateurs who could entertain a family audience at home. Television now provided a means for them to perform live in the homes of thousands of families.

In November 1943, the station televised a special news program to a group of newspaper and magazine executives who had been invited by General Electric to tour the studio. Wrote *Newsweek* afterward, "Most of the newspaper guests regarded the demonstration as a warning,"[28] as they watched WRGB perform many of the functions of their own print media. They saw, for example, WRGB televise what might be the next day's front-page story, using film footage shot that same morning of a speech given by Governor Dewey in Albany.

The show was described as a "living newspaper" and was probably the most diversified program televised on any station thus far. The TV program was divided into segments that matched the sections of a local newspaper. The living newspaper had films of the war and live comments from news reporters; it also showed newspaper cartoonists at work, a live fashion show, and films of sports events. The TV viewers watched an economist use stacks of play money to show what happens to the average paycheck. They saw "televised want ads," in which a baby buggy for sale was displayed and a housewife interviewed a prospective maid.[29]

PLANS FOR POSTWAR TV

With this special news telecast, General Electric was also showcasing its studio and equipment with future sales in mind. New TV stations throughout the country would need transmitters, lights, and other products made by General Electric and tested by WRGB. Of course, new TV stations wouldn't be built until after the war, but the end to the fighting was in sight by the summer and fall of 1943.

The tide had clearly turned against Germany and Japan. The two Axis powers were for the most part fighting without success to hold onto territory they had seized earlier, and now their third partner, Italy, had overthrown its fascist government and surrendered to the Allies.

In August 1943, an article appeared in *Fortune* that was the first lengthy piece written about TV's future since the war had begun. Describing TV as "one of the brightest stars in the heaven of the postwar planners," the article claimed that television now had "an opportunity given to no other industry in all industrial history. It has the opportunity to start afresh, in the hiatus of war, and soundly plan its future."[30]

A few months later, RCA made public its own plans for TV's postwar future. The occasion was a dinner speech by RCA's television manager, Thomas Joyce, to a group of advertising executives in New York. Within three years after the war, Joyce said, a network of TV stations would stretch 600 miles from Boston to Washington; in two more years, television would be reaching 72 million people in 150 markets. "The generations that come after the war," Joyce predicted, "will take home television service just as much for granted as the present generation takes the radio set."[31]

David Sarnoff also commented on TV's future in his annual review message to RCA shareholders in late 1943. "This is no one-year job," he said of RCA's plans for postwar TV. Even if the fighting ended in 1944, "there should be no expectation [that] the air will be transformed overnight to television." He predicted that retooling factories to make TV sets would "require three to six months" with more time needed to build new stations and make lower priced sets.[32] Sarnoff's words were cautious, but they showed he was still interested in TV and wanted to lower the price tag of new sets after the war.

TELEVISION AS A WAR WEAPON

David Sarnoff himself had been called up for active duty twice in 1942 to help procure equipment and supplies for the military. His company was supplying U.S. forces with electronics equipment to the extent that RCA's annual revenues tripled from 1942 to 1944 and its profits more than doubled. "This is not to suggest that RCA behaved in an improper or unpatriotic fashion," explains the author of *RCA,* Robert Sobel, "but rather that like all the other defense contractors, its profits rose substantially during the war."[33]

Among the weapons of war used by the Allies to defeat Germany's fleet of U-boats was television. With radar, the technology of video transmission displayed its power to see the enemy at great distances. By 1943, however, TV technology was being used to guide explosives into striking and destroying enemy targets. The TV-guided system was called Block and was an outgrowth of RCA's research in television. During the war RCA built 4,000 of the Block units for both the Army and the Navy to use in unmanned bombers and other flying weapons.

David Sarnoff had been interested in TV-controlled weapons since 1934 when his chief television engineer, Dr. V. K. Zworykin, outlined such weapons in a memo. "I was so impressed," Sarnoff later recalled, that "I went to Washington and presented his plans to the War and Navy Departments."[34] The military failed to act until the late 1930s. By then, RCA engineers and scientists had developed and tested some of the necessary technology, such as relatively lightweight TV cameras that could fly aboard weapons. In 1940 the government began funding RCA's work, now cloaked in secrecy and given such code names as "Dragon" and "Pelican."

The first use of TV-guided weapons came in late 1943. Unmanned and expendable B-17 bombers were dropped on Nazi submarine bases in Helgoland, an island off Germany in the North Sea. Each bomber carried a TV camera mounted in front, a TV transmitter, and a big load of explosives. A pilot on board another plane used a TV screen and receiver to see through the "windshield" of the B-17 and moved a remote-control joystick to direct the plane to crash into its target and explode.

In the Pacific, TV-guided planes and bombs were used in and around the Solomon Islands to the north and east of Australia. These weapons bombed Japanese shipping vessels in the South Pacific and destroyed a lighthouse at Rabaul Harbor, after attempts using more traditional bombs had failed.

In the climactic naval conflict in the South Pacific, the Battle of Leyte Gulf, the Japanese added their own new weapon of war: the kamikaze airplane. As with the TV-guided weapons of the United States, the kamikaze had one purpose: to drop on a target and destroy it with explosive power. However, the Japanese used human pilots, not TV cameras, to guide these planes; the power of the kamikaze to strike their targets cost the lives of these pilots.

The Germans, too, developed new airborne weapons during the war: the V-1 and V-2 rockets. These unmanned missiles flew from German-occupied Europe across the English Channel to crash and explode in Britain. The V-1 and V-2 were deadly and frightening new weapons, but they had no TV camera system to guide them; without it, their accuracy was limited. In 1944 the United States tried to destroy the V1 and V2 launching sites in Europe with bombers that used

RCA's TV-guided system. These missions met with little success, although one of them had, in hindsight, a profound effect on postwar American history.

In August 1944 a TV-guided U.S. Army airplane packed with 20,000 pounds of explosives took off from England to strike at V-1 bases in France. The plane's crew of two planned to parachute into the English Channel as another crew in a nearby plane took control via RCA's remote TV system. However, while the two crewmen were still on board the plane, it exploded in midair and scattered its fragments over the English countryside; no bodies were recovered. The pilot was Joseph P. Kennedy Jr., who was being groomed for the Presidency by his father; this goal now passed to the family's second son, John. The circumstances of the death of Joe Kennedy Jr. were kept secret. In fact, RCA's use of television to guide flying weapons was publicized only after the war.

Joe Kennedy Jr. was only one of almost 300,000 Americans who lost their lives in World War II; the worldwide casualty number approached 60 million. It's been labeled as the "Good War," but World War II involved a staggering amount of devastation, tragedy, and brutality in the military and general populace alike. The halting pace of TV technology and the workings of business and government kept true images of the war off living-room TV screens. Instead, Americans heard sounds of war on the radio and saw photographs and newsreel clips of it in newspapers, magazines, and movie theaters. One of the intriguing questions that remains is what the effects might have been of televising this war to thousands of American homes for over three years.

THE STUDIOS REOPEN

The void that NBC and CBS created when they shut their studios in 1942 was now partly filled by Du Mont's experimental station, W2XWV. This station had never shut down completely during the war. "For even in the darkest hour of war," Du Mont boasted in a 1943 advertisement, "when television activity has dropped to its lowest ebb," W2XWV transmitted live programs.[35]

Station W2XWV suffered in 1943 and 1944 from a lack of adequate facilities. In December 1943, for example, W2XWV aired a TV version of *A Christmas Carol* performed on a stage no bigger than a small living room. "The Marx Brothers troupe in a phone booth," wrote *Variety* of another telecast from Du Mont's tiny studio.[36] The station had been built on a much smaller budget than those belonging to RCA, CBS, and General Electric. Its founder and president, Allen B. Du Mont, believed that "a good start" in TV broadcasting could be made "for as little as $25,000. And that figure can be shaved if need be."[37]

In fact, Du Mont had started the company back in 1934 with a far smaller sum, using his own money and the garage of his suburban New Jersey home. His company, Du Mont Laboratories, made cathode-ray tubes and other TV equipment, and it was one of the first to make TV sets for the public. Station W2XWV was built mainly to help sell Du Mont tubes, sets, and other TV equipment, although Allen Du Mont did invite potential sponsors to use his studio and airtime for free during the war. In January 1943, for example, the tobacco company Liggett and Myers staged commercials on a variety program that featured bandleader Fred Waring, who had a daily radio show on the NBC network. Liggett and Myers had Waring ask at a cigar counter for Chesterfields, and a female clerk held up a carton while a voice offstage gave the sales pitch.

Although W2XWV provided programs for TV viewers and potential sponsors in 1943 and 1944, the Du Mont station alone wasn't likely to pave the way for a postwar TV industry. RCA could, however, and by late 1943 its station WNBT was again televising live shows. In October the station aired its first live program since 1942—a rodeo from New York's Madison Square Garden. Two months later WNBT televised an evening of boxing, followed in early 1944 by basketball, more boxing, and the Ringling Brothers circus—all from Madison Square Garden. In February, WNBT even reopened its Manhattan studio briefly while televising a college basketball doubleheader from Madison Square Garden. During halftimes and the break between the two games, the station displayed an intermission sign while college pep tunes were sung in the studio.

WNBT's live telecasts were promoted by RCA as entertainment for wounded servicemen, hospitalized in the New York metropolitan area and around Philadelphia and Schenectady. Indeed, RCA had placed TV sets in some thirty hospitals and arranged for the programs to be picked up by WRGB and by WPTZ in Philadelphia. RCA executives were speaking publicly now of RCA's plans for the medium.

Coming soon were live telecasts from the WNBT studio and more hours of programs, NBC president Niles Trammell told an audience of radio executives. As soon as the war ended, he said, RCA would build a TV station in Washington, DC, and link it by cable first to New York in 1945, then north to Boston and south to Charlotte in 1946.

This postwar Eastern network, Trammell said, would be matched by a Midwest network linking Chicago to Minneapolis and Cleveland and a Pacific Coast network that would link San Francisco to "the great talent center of Hollywood."[38] The three regional networks, said Trammell, would "gradually stretch out over wider areas, and will themselves become linked together. Thus, city after city, across the continent will be brought into network operation, until finally complete nationwide networks will become a reality."[39] By the end of the decade, he said, television would stretch from coast to coast.

"Bathers splashing in the surf at Miami in the winter, and beautiful maidens sporting in the snow at Sun Valley"—these were some of the images conjured up by a second RCA manager, Thomas Joyce, at a meeting of the Sales Executive Club of New York in March 1944.[40] A thousand salesmen, their largest gathering in a decade, heard Joyce laud the power of commercial TV to sell Americans on everything from vacations to vacuum cleaners. The medium could be used, he said, to "show consumers the advantages of the new postwar products and services and to bring about rapid buying of those goods and services on a large scale."[41]

Joyce's pitch for commercial TV came in the midst of an economic boom in the United States that was heavily slanted toward buying war products. The government was spending $300 million a day to fight the war, with much of it going into the paychecks of Americans and from there into savings bonds and accounts. By the end of 1944, Americans were predicted to have over $100 billion in savings. In a postwar economy these billions of dollars would be up for grabs.

To demonstrate how TV could generate sales, Thomas Joyce had an actor read a radio commercial describing "a cool foaming glass of Ruppert beer," followed by a second actor who actually poured one, let it foam, and drank it with a satisfied look. "In television," Joyce told the sales executives, "you don't have to take some announcer's word for it. We can see the enjoyment Ruppert's brings."[42]

Joyce also described TV programs that would sell products from start to finish. If a "progressive department store" sponsored a program on infant care, he suggested, "everything used on such a program would be a commercial." As a result, "the desire of these mothers to give to their babies the advantages of all the things shown" on the TV program would stimulate purchases and help spark the postwar economy.[43]

A month after Joyce's speech, on April 10, 1944, RCA officially reopened its New York TV studio to televise FCC Chairman Fly introducing the broadcast of a new short film, *Patrolling the Ether,* on the wartime activities of the FCC and the broadcast industry. With its TV studio now officially back in business, RCA placed its first large advertisement in four years in *The New York Times,* stating that "more and more of the world's happenings will come under television's gaze" after the war. "The need will be great for sets at prices millions can afford. Watch for them."[44]

TV'S FIRST CENSORED PROGRAM

Later in May 1944 RCA received some unwanted publicity when one of its live studio telecasts was censored. On the evening of May 25, show business veteran Eddie Cantor was to perform on TV a song he'd introduced on Broadway, titled "We're Having a Baby, My Baby and Me." Forty minutes before airtime, NBC officials ordered Cantor to eliminate the song because its lyrics were offensive. Cantor argued that he hadn't enough time to prepare another number. Apparently the NBC staff relented and allowed him to begin the song on the air, performed with a female partner, Nora Martin.

But part way through the song, NBC's engineers shut off the audio signal during the following lyrics:

MARTIN: Thanks to you, my life is bright. You've brought me joy beyond measure.

CANTOR: Don't thank me. Quite all right. Honestly, it was a pleasure.

Then, the NBC cameras televised Cantor only from the waist up as he performed what *The New York Times* called "a modified hula-hula dance,"[45] an act of censorship that predated by twelve years a similar incident with Elvis Presley on the *Ed Sullivan Show.*

Immediately after the show, Eddie Cantor said he was "blazing mad at fellows who tell you it's all right and then sneak around and cut you off," according to *The New York Times,* which printed an article detailing the incident. NBC did have the right to cut lyrics, Cantor said. "But when little Hitlers tell you you can't do it just as you're going on, that's tough." Besides, "it's a straight song," Cantor said, "and I sing it straight." He further claimed, "No man can be in the business for thirty-five years and do any vulgarity and last. I've been at it longer than NBC or television."[46]

The truth was that Cantor had often performed songs in vaudeville, on Broadway, and even on the radio that were risqué, if not vulgar. A trademark Cantor song, for example, suggested, "If you knew Susie like I know Susie—oh! oh! oh! what a girl!"[47] And one of his most famous numbers, "Makin' Whoopee," the title song to a Broadway show and motion picture in which he starred, was about sex and pregnancy.

It's quite possible that Cantor's song, had it gone out over the airwaves, might have offended some of the TV viewers that night. That was the reason stated by an NBC vice president in response to Cantor's complaints. It was "the obligation of NBC to the public," he said, "to keep from American homes material which the audience would find objectionable."[48] The NBC executives may have worried even more about a special audience they'd assembled to watch the program: a dinner crowd of Philadelphia businessmen. RCA and Philco were using the telecast to publicize the opening of an improved relay link between New York and Philadelphia.

In fact, the program itself hadn't been listed on WNBT's schedule that week and was seen only by viewers who happened to have turned on their sets. Those who did tune in saw TV's first censored program, and they also watched one of the few top show business stars to appear thus far on TV. Both were signs of television's future.

The spring of 1944 also saw the rebirth of live studio telecasts from CBS, beginning with a show on May 5 that had fifteen minutes of news, a harmonica quartet, interviews of returning servicemen who'd seen combat, and a quiz show with composer Richard Rodgers and publisher Bennett Cerf. Just before the broadcast, however, CBS announced that the show was purely "experimental" and not intended to induce anyone to buy a TV set. According to *Variety,* CBS needn't have worried: the quality of the program was too poor to promote TV. "Tele audiences," wrote their reviewer, "come post war, won't stand for it."[49]

Chapter 4

The Winds of Postwar

THE HOMEFRONT TV WAR

As the real war moved into its final stages in the spring of 1944, a homefront war over TV broke out between the two rivals in radio broadcasting, CBS and RCA. Both sides had their allies. RCA was backed by a new trade group, the Television Broadcasters Association (TBA), headed by Allen B. Du Mont and supported by Philco and General Electric. This faction wanted to keep the status quo, i.e., keep TV transmissions in the lower frequencies of the broadcast spectrum and not wait for color TV sets before selling new sets after the war. The TBA claimed that the images on new TV sets would be "equivalent or better . . . than 16 millimeter home movies," with the public "agreeably surprised at the picture quality."[1]

Any new TV set built under existing standards would soon be obsolete, charged E. F. McDonald, the president of Zenith, one of the country's leading manufacturers of radio sets and equipment. Facing a troubled future if Americans abandoned radio for TV after the war, McDonald backed the CBS proposal to wait for better sets. RCA's TV sets, McDonald said, would soon become "just so much wood and wire, inoperable unless rebuilt at great expense."[2] Siding as well with CBS and Zenith was Edwin Armstrong, the chief inventor and proponent of FM radio. FM's growth as a new medium had been stalled, along with television, during the war. Now, as the postwar approached, Edwin Armstrong wanted the FCC to move TV upward to the higher frequencies on the broadcast band so that FM radio could move onto the lower frequencies and build a bigger audience.

Also siding with CBS, Zenith, and Edwin Armstrong was FCC Chairman Larry Fly, who wanted the TV industry to wait until technical improvements from the war could be adopted. "Why talk of freezing television standards at their present level of efficiency," he asked during a seminar in May 1944, "below that achieved by the military and to be made known to industry?"[3]

THE 1944 CONVENTIONS

As chairman of the FCC, Larry Fly had proved to be an ardent New Dealer who had tried to influence big business to act in the public interest, but the times were changing in the spring and summer of 1944, and being an ardent New Dealer was not the political asset it once was. The upcoming presidential campaign was signaling a major change in American politics and society.

Roosevelt and his New Deal government had set the national agenda since 1933, and the needs of wartime had governed life since 1941. Both Roosevelt's presidency and World War II were heading toward conclusions in 1944. Roosevelt was running for a fourth term, but a fifth term after the war ended was unlikely. New leaders and issues and policies would govern the upcoming postwar period.

Not only might TV be an important new product and industry, it might give Americans new images of the postwar era. As an RCA advertisement for TV in May 1944 promised, "More and more of the world's happenings will come under television's gaze."[4] The first of such "happenings" was in Chicago that summer, as the Republicans and Democrats met to nominate their wartime presidential candidates for the upcoming November election.

The day the Republican National Convention began, June 26, 1944, an RCA advertisement on the back cover of *Broadcasting* showed a TV camera facing a sea of delegates and state placards. The ad's copy promised, "When Peace comes, a greater and more widespread television audience—expanding into millions of homes equipped with RCA television—will see as well as hear Democracy in action."[5] In fact, TV viewers that day actually saw democracy prior to action: California's Governor Earl Warren was filmed in advance delivering the keynote address. That film was broadcast the first night of the convention, slightly before the speech was actually delivered.

The problem with televising a national event in Chicago hadn't changed since the 1940 Democrat convention was held there: TV in Chicago still lagged behind New York. Chicago had one station with a commercial license in 1944 and another that was still experimental, but neither had the equipment to televise from inside Chicago Stadium, where both parties were meeting. Instead, a new TV division of RKO Pictures in New York arranged to film the proceedings and fly the reels of film back east for RCA and NBC to televise.

Each night that week TV viewers within range of WNBT in New York, WRGB in Schenectady, and WPTZ in Philadelphia saw highlights of the previous day's proceedings. Those viewers who could still find an operating TV set to gather around in June 1944 saw the first Republican convention held in wartime since Lincoln was renominated in 1864. Unlike the party's previous meeting in Philadelphia, this convention took only one ballot to select its candidate, New York's Governor Tom Dewey.

On Wednesday, however, TV viewers saw one of the most controversial speeches of the era made by an exceptional public figure in her prime, Congresswoman Clare Boothe Luce. The forty-one year old Clare Luce had the qualities that later propelled John Kennedy into the White House: intelligence, wit, youth, connections, and the looks of a movie star. Married to Henry Luce, the founder and publisher of *Time, Life,* and *Fortune,* Clare Luce was Connecticut's first woman in Congress.

Clare Luce made her first national speech at the Chicago convention, facing microphones linked to 675 radio stations across the country and under the bright, scorching lights needed for RKO's cameras. After paying tribute to America's "G.I. Joe" fighting overseas, she described the image of a "G.I. Jim," representing all the war's dead American men, including those remembered by the "many gold stars" worn by their mothers at the convention. Could the deaths of those sons have been averted, she asked, through "skillful and determined American statesmanship" by Franklin Roosevelt during the 1930s?[6]

Then Clare Luce publicly raised the charge that has tarnished the reputation of Franklin Roosevelt ever since. She claimed the President knew back in 1940—the year before Pearl Harbor—that America's entry in the war was inevitable, but that he kept this information from the public. Instead, Roosevelt had "promised in this very city twelve years ago that 'happy days are here again,'" and he'd "promised peace, yes peace, to [G.I.] Jim's mother and father."[7]

It was a historic moment in American politics, signaling the restart of Republican attacks on the foreign policy of Democrats that would continue and grow after the war ended. Watching Luce's speech on

TV, a *New York Times* reporter wrote that "the addition of sight had multiplied the dramatic value . . . at least tenfold."[8]

As for Luce's charge that Roosevelt had lied to the American public, "it was not the first time," said writer Quenton Reynolds at a rally for Luce's own opponent that year, that "a person named Boothe treacherously assaulted the President of the United States."[9] Even Clare Luce herself expressed some regret for the speech. "Lying," she later said about Roosevelt and America's entry in the war, "was clearly the only way to get us there."[10]

When the Democrats met the next month in Chicago, they renominated Franklin Roosevelt as expected. Viewers who watched the proceedings on film the next day witnessed a classic political fight over the choice for Vice President. The incumbent Vice President, Henry Wallace, was yet another ardent and controversial New Dealer. His supporters were the noisiest in the convention hall, as Willkie's had been in Philadelphia in 1940. They erupted before the cameras as Wallace gave an impromptu and impassioned speech at the podium, defending himself and the New Deal.

Wallace didn't win on the first ballot, however, because his opponents had outmaneuvered him. On the second ballot, the nomination for Vice President went to a candidate who'd been selected behind closed doors by party leaders, Senator Harry Truman of Missouri. Probably few of the delegates or TV viewers realized the significance of what they had just witnessed. If Roosevelt won reelection—and he was favored to win—his running mate in 1944 would likely run for the Presidency in 1948. As one of the speakers that night said, "In this year of destiny, it is more than ever necessary to select a Vice President possessing all the qualities and all the qualifications desirable and necessary for a President of the United States."[11]

Roosevelt was a sick man in 1944, as his aides, his family, his physician, and probably the president himself could see. He made no appearance at the convention, nor did he appear in public more than a few times during the campaign and not at all on TV. His deteriorating health never became the campaign issue it might have been in other circumstances. As it turned out, the party's choice in Chicago for Vice President was to become President sooner than anyone, except perhaps Roosevelt's doctor, suspected.

In the campaign of 1944, television for the first time became an issue, although a minor one, mentioned by both candidates. Republican Tom Dewey used TV as an example of how New Deal bureaucracy had gone awry with overregulation. Dewey claimed that the TV industry had "great potentials for service to the public and stimulation of business," but only if the government took the role of "cooperation and encouragement" and "reasonable regulation. But when government steps in to decide who is going to develop what and how," Dewey charged in a reference to the FCC, it has stepped "outside the province of the government."[12]

President Roosevelt never answered Dewey's charge that the FCC was overregulating the TV industry, but he did mention television in one of the few campaign speeches he gave in 1944. Speaking from the White House on national radio, he said he looked forward to a postwar "era of expansion and production and employment to new industries, to increased security. I look forward to millions of new homes fitted for decent living"—including, he said, "television and other miraculous new inventions and discoveries made during this war, which will be adapted to the peacetime uses of a peace-loving people."[13]

TV PROGRAMS BLOSSOM AGAIN

That both candidates mentioned TV during the 1944 campaign was another sign that the medium was returning to the promising status it had in 1939 and 1940. Regular programming, kept alive during World War II by General Electric in Schenectady and Du Mont in New York, had bloomed again in the middle of 1944 with RCA and CBS both reopening their New York studios. Now, a postwar American TV schedule was starting to take shape; some of programs being transmitted were the first in a long line of similar programs that would continue unbroken for decades.

Live drama, for example, became a regular feature on television in New York City, on Du Mont's WABD and on the CBS station, WCBW, which reopened its studios in mid-1944. On June 30, WCBW aired its first live drama, "The Favor," a fifteen-minute play adapted from the stage version put on by the American Theatre Wing to sell war bonds. In the story a soldier on leave talks a young woman out of spending $275 on a fur coat; instead, she buys war bonds. He then vanishes suddenly while making a phone call, and she discovers that he had been killed months earlier in France.

Tony Miner had worked in various theaters in New York City, and he brought to WCBW artists and performers from the stage. As Miner recalled later, "The theater had fallen on harder times" in the 1940s, due in part to the popularity of radio. To some young actors and actresses, "the siren song of television sounded sweetest," according to Miner. These stage performers either couldn't find work on radio or felt that the medium pandered too much to popular taste. Yet they saw the new medium of TV "as an extension of theater, a way to capture a vast, new audience, and to imbue it with a taste for something better than the inane jollities on radio."[14]

The "inane jollities" of radio, however, could be seen by TV viewers on another new CBS program in the summer of 1944. *Missus Goes A-Shopping* was a quiz and audience-participation show that featured a duck named Pierre and visual, physical humor, such as a big, burly truck driver pulling a girdle on over his clothes. *Missus Goes A-Shopping* was a televised version of a network radio program, hosted by a veteran of radio quiz shows, John Reed King.

In September 1944, NBC brought back a schedule of sports programming, transmitted from Madison Square Garden on its three-station network in New York, Philadelphia, and Schenectady. On Friday, September 29, featherweight champ Willie Pep successfully defended his title in a televised bout that was sponsored by Gillette razors. Titled *Cavalcade of Sports,* the Friday night fights stayed on the air for sixteen years. As with its other programs in 1944, NBC publicized *Cavalcade of Sports* as being intended for wounded servicemen in local hospitals, but its biggest audience crowded into the living rooms and bars with TV sets in 1944; out of their numbers would come the first wave of postwar set buyers. Working with Gillette, NBC nourished this sporting crowd several nights a week with boxing from Madison Square Garden and both wrestling and boxing from St. Nicholas Arena.

That fall WNBT added broadcasts of college football games, with such prominent teams as Army and Notre Dame playing in Yankee Stadium or the Polo Grounds. In Philadelphia, WPTZ was in its fifth season of transmitting college football from the University of Pennsylvania's Franklin Field, home of the annual Army-Navy game and its crowd of over 70,000. WPTZ had already built TV's first sports transmission facility at Franklin Field, suspended below the upper tier of seats along the 50-yard line, holding two cameras and a crew of seven. With its setup WPTZ could mix play-by-play coverage on the field with "human-interest" shots on the sidelines and in the stands, as well as close-ups of the broadcaster.

The biggest contest that fall, however, was for the Presidency. Neither Roosevelt nor Dewey made use of TV during the campaign, and the 1944 presidential election would be the last one in which television played no role. It was also the first in which a candidate booked time on TV to speak to the public. He was Senator Robert Wagner; running for reelection in New York he gave a short campaign speech on Sunday night, November 5, 1944, on Du Mont's WABD. Wagner won the election, as did Clare Luce and President Roosevelt—the latter by the smallest margin of his four victories. The results of the election were transmitted live by New York's three stations, on the air all night, and by WPTZ and Chicago's station WBKB.

WBKB had been on the air sporadically since October 1943 and was now putting together a regular schedule of programs. As with WRGB, the Chicago station reached out into the community for local talent—so much so, in fact, that *Variety* wrote in November 1944, "[The] Majority of shows televised here every Tuesday-Friday are so amateurish that reviewing them week-by-week is a needless task."[15] But WBKB's production staff—all females during the war—had found a few sponsors for their programs, and by early 1945 the station was paying on occasion for professional talent.

DOCKET NO. 6651

Before WBKB could show much improvement and before more stations similar to WBKB could begin operating in other cities, the government had to lift its wartime restrictions on the industry. The FCC took an important step in that direction on January 12, 1945, when it issued a set of rulings on the electromagnetic spectrum, titled Docket No. 6651, to be implemented after the war. This thick, brown document was issued without the signature of Larry Fly, who had resigned his post at the FCC in November 1944. In his parting words to the TV industry, Fly expressed his "hope that some day, somehow, it would be possible for government and industry to sit down together, go over the entire spectrum, channel by channel, and devise a plan that would seem fair to all parties."[16]

Docket No. 6651 was a step in that direction: a compromise between those who wanted to produce and sell TV sets as quickly as possible and those who argued for a pause to improve the technology. The FCC now agreed to allow two types of TV to exist alongside each other on the electromagnetic spectrum. One type (VHF) would continue using the lower frequencies of the broadcast band, which would allow the TV industry to make new sets and build new stations as soon as wartime restrictions were lifted.

The second type of television (UHF) would use higher frequencies on the spectrum, as recommended by CBS, with the FCC asserting that the development of the upper portion of the spectrum was necessary for the "establishment of a truly nationwide and competitive television system."[17] The FCC restricted the TV industry to using these frequencies solely on an experimental basis for the near future, and the agency had little to say about CBS's proposal for color TV.

Winners and losers were implied in the FCC rulings. The winners were RCA and its allies who wanted to restart TV in the postwar using prewar standards, although the FCC made it clear that its ban on building new sets and stations was still in effect. One loser was CBS, with the FCC not willing to hold back the industry for the sake of higher-frequency and color TV. The biggest loser, however, was the FM radio industry, which was being pushed up to higher frequencies by the FCC. Now the FM industry would have to do what RCA and other TV manufacturers had feared would be required of them instead: discard all existing sets, sold and unsold.

In hindsight, Docket No. 6651 was a milestone in the history of American communications. With few exceptions, it established radio and television as the country knew it for the next forty years, until cable and satellite broadcasting came into their own. It gave an edge to lower-frequency television (VHF) over higher-frequency television (UHF), as well as an edge to AM radio over FM radio, that would last for decades. It opened up American culture to the future technology of personal communications—pagers, beepers, CB radios, and portable phones—by setting aside a portion of the airwaves for the public to use the "walkie-talkie" communications that had been developed for the military during the war.

With the release of the FCC docket, the TV industry could now foresee its base of operations expanding in postwar America. Nine TV stations were broadcasting in early 1945, with all but two located in just three cities: New York, Chicago, and Los Angeles. Fifteen other stations had licenses from the FCC but had yet to begin broadcasting, and another eighty stations were waiting for the FCC's approval of their license applications. Added together, they created the potential for over 100 postwar TV stations—from Boston to Jacksonville, from Minneapolis to New Orleans, and from Detroit to Spokane and Salt Lake City.

These postwar stations would benefit from improvements in TV technology, including new cameras that would put an end to the brightness and heat problems that had plagued studio programs thus far. Postwar TV sets, too, were likely to have bigger, brighter, and sharper pictures—and maybe soon in color; some new sets might sell for under $200.

But would the American public buy TV sets when the war ended? Not necessarily, said the vice president of a newly formed business group, the Television Broadcasters Association, at their first national conference in December 1944. Lewis Allen Weiss of station W6XAO in Los Angeles believed that predictions of "six out of ten persons . . . waiting to buy sets" were far off target. Instead, Weiss said, postwar TV would "face bright competition in the consumer market against new model refrigerators and indoor plumbing," and he predicted that "not more than 10 percent of people in the foreseeable future" were likely to buy TV sets."[18]

A survey that was published in 1944, however, showed that many Americans were indeed likely to buy TV sets after the war. A Long Island bank had begun a savings program with its customers, with the idea of saving for a "big ticket" postwar item. The depositors were asked what they were saving for, and the highest number said a TV set. Television was out-polling automobiles, refrigerators, and washing machines as a postwar item to be desired.[19] Another survey from 1944 showed that many of these potential buyers were the friends and neighbors of TV owners. According to *Electrical Merchandising,* these viewers were swelling the audience size in homes with TV sets to eight viewers per set, twice the average family size. They "openly angle for return invitations" and are "anxious to purchase television receivers as soon as the new sets arrive on the market."[20]

TV AND THE END OF THE WAR

On the same day that the FCC issued its new ruling, January 15, 1945, the Third Fleet of the U.S. Navy for the first time sent its carriers into Japanese-controlled waters; there they launched air strikes against Japanese-held ports in China. On that day, Russian troops advancing through Poland were now fifty miles from the German border. Also on that day, the armies of the United States and Great Britain had all but ended the "Battle of the Bulge" in Belgium and Luxembourg, which was to be Germany's last offensive against the Allied forces that had invaded France on D-Day.

A week later, Franklin Roosevelt was inaugurated for a fourth term as President. The low-key ceremony was held at the White House, and his short remarks ended with a prayer for "the vision to see our way clearly."[21] The inauguration was the last one not to be televised, so the viewing audience missed seeing clearly that their President looked thin and drawn. In the early afternoon of April 12, 1945, Franklin Roosevelt collapsed as he sat for a portrait at his vacation home in Warm Springs, Georgia; two hours later, he was declared dead. Over the previous twelve years, Roosevelt had led Americans out of the Depression, then into, through, and almost out of World War II. Radio captured for the mourning public the powerful emotional experience of his death and funeral, but from now on television would bring such national events into America's living rooms—beginning with V-E Day, less than a month later.

May 8, 1945, had been designated in advance as V-E Day by America's new President, Harry Truman. When crowds gathered in Times Square to begin celebrating on the afternoon of May 7, WNBT sent its mobile camera there and interrupted a test pattern to broadcast the emotional moment as it happened. Like the nomination of Wendell Willkie in 1940, the V-E celebration on May 7 was an unexpected national drama captured by TV and televised to an audience of thousands.

The next morning WNBT went on the air earlier than ever before, at 8:45 a.m., to transmit the V-E Day speech recorded in advance by Truman. WNBT stayed on the air all day, switching among its mobile unit covering live the celebration, films of the war, and interviews, commentaries, sermons, and discussions in the RCA studio. One of those interviewed live on TV was Eleanor Roosevelt, now the widowed former First Lady. Sitting before a backdrop of flags from countries in the newly formed United Nations, she cautioned the public not to become apathetic or too weary of war. WNBT's coverage of V-E Day continued nonstop until the closing strains of Verdi's "Hymn to the Nations" on film with Arturo Toscanini and the NBC Symphony Orchestra, at 10:54 p.m.

In Schenectady, WRGB sent its own mobile unit out to televise reactions in this war-industry city and also brought local officials into the studio for interviews, all interspersed with WNBT's coverage relayed from New York. Together, WNBT and WRGB made V-E Day in May 1945 a milestone in American television. For the first time, television went on the air to cover a major news event—and stayed on the air, filling the hours with live coverage, background films, and studio commentary. With V-E Day television journalism was born.

Although the war continued in the Pacific, the postwar process of demobilization had begun in Europe, sending servicemen back home to America. One of those who returned in the spring of 1945 was Burke Crotty, an NBC television producer who had specialized in covering sports on location. Another returning serviceman was General Dwight Eisenhower, and their paths crossed on June 19, 1945, at the Polo Grounds in Manhattan.

General Eisenhower had been given a hero's welcome that morning, including a ticker-tape parade, but now he was having his one request for the day fulfilled: he was attending a Major League Baseball game—the New York Giants versus the Boston Braves. WNBT had its mobile unit at the stadium not just because Eisenhower's presence made it a news event, although the station had been airing his visit to New York on programs sponsored by Esso Gasoline, but because WNBT had added baseball to its schedule of sports programming, ostensibly for wounded servicemen in area hospitals. Beginning with a Memorial Day doubleheader at Yankee Stadium, Burke Crotty and an NBC crew were transmitting live at least one game a week.

The viewers who tuned in on June 19 for either baseball or General "Ike" Eisenhower thus saw both together. At one point, Eisenhower was asked to face the TV camera positioned on the mezzanine level above first base, about 150 feet from his first-row box seat. "Would he wave a greeting to the hospitalized veterans?" he was asked, according to *The New York Times*. "He did, vigorously, demonstrating again the famed Eisenhower smile."[22] The likeable Ike, his smile, his wave, the baseball game, the Esso Gasoline—and of course the TV camera: if any of those watching had the premonition that they were seeing America's postwar future, they were right. It was the 1950s in America—just a decade too soon.

The war in the Pacific ended after the United States dropped two atomic bombs on Japanese cities, and television played a role in those events as well. Back in June 1942, the United States and Britain decided to build an atomic weapon; two months later, the secret Manhattan Project began. The scientists and engineers working at the project's site in Los Alamos, New Mexico, needed to observe the reactions of radioactive material with safety; for this, they used television cameras and receivers.

On July 16, 1945, shortly before dawn, the first test bomb was exploded on Air Force land at Alamogordo, New Mexico. As described in the official report from General Leslie Groves, the Army engineer in charge, "For a brief period there was a lightning effect within a radius of 20 miles equal to several suns at midday; a huge ball mushroomed and rose to a height of over ten thousand feet before it dimmed."[23] The general's deputy, Thomas Farrell, had a simpler version of what the two men had witnessed that morning: his first words to Groves were, "The war is over."[24]

One month and two atomic explosions later, the war was indeed over. With the destruction of the cities of Hiroshima and Nagasaki by the two atomic bombs dropped by the United States, World War II ended and the ominous threat of nuclear war began. World War II had introduced to civilization the use of rockets, atomic bombs, and television as weapons of death and destruction; joined together, these technologies would put the chill of mass annihilation into the Cold War years that followed. Of the three, only television has thus far become a basic instrument of war around the world—in radar and sonar, spy planes and spy satellites, Airborne Warning and Control System (AWACS) and cruise missiles.

On August 14, 1945, an estimated half million people gathered in and around Times Square anticipating the surrender of Japan. WNBT's mobile camera atop the marquee of the Hotel Astor had been televising since midmorning as the crowd swelled, anxious and noisy and finally overcome with rejoicing when the Times Square moving news sign proclaimed at 7:00 p.m., "Official—Truman Announces Japanese Surrender." A writer for the trade publication *Television,* Mary

Gannon, watched the celebration on TV in an NBC viewing room. She later described how "the mob excitement became contagious. Individual expressions picked up by the close-up lens used gave an intimate note—took you right into the crowd, made you feel part of it. If people all over the nation could have seen it," she wrote, they would have been "glued to the video screen."[25]

It would be another three or four years, about as long as the war itself had lasted, before TV would truly catch on with the American public. In the meantime, the industry would continue to struggle with internal conflicts and with FCC hearings and rulings that would slow its progress. But to anyone paying attention, television's coverage of the end of the war was a clear preview of the medium's potential to keep postwar America "glued to the video screen."

Chapter 5

Turning the Corner

THE CAMERA WITH THE EYES OF A CAT

Two months after V-J Day, the first postwar product in the TV industry was unveiled by RCA. It was the "Image Orthicon" TV camera, developed for the military to be 100 times more sensitive to light than prewar TV cameras. The camera had "the eyes of a cat," proclaimed RCA in its trade advertisements. "Television broadcasts will no longer be confined to brilliantly illuminated special studios, nor will outdoor events fade as the afternoon sun goes down."[1] RCA planned to market the new camera to TV stations in six months.

In the meantime, RCA used its own Image Orthicon cameras, beginning with a dramatic show for the press and industry on October 25, 1945, in its WNBT studio. First, the new camera televised a scene in the studio lit only by the flame from a single matchstick. A second new camera then televised live images of a rodeo show in Madison Square Garden; wrote *The New York Times* reporter watching a TV set in the studio, "Most of the arena and performers in action could be seen vividly without a hint of the shadows or blackouts" that were typical of previous telecasts.[2]

On December 1, 1945, WNBT used the Image Orthicon camera outdoors to televise the annual Army-Navy football game from Philadelphia's Franklin Field. The game had special significance this year, since the Army and Navy had, after all, won a world war since their previous battle on the playing fields. Crowds of viewers gathered around sets in homes and bars as the telecast attracted the biggest TV audience thus far. For the first time, press reports mentioned "television parties." Wrote *Variety*, "Viewers saw the entire game from a fifty-yard line seat in the warm comfort of their own homes,"[3] including live, close-up pictures of President Truman among the 100,000 fans at the stadium.

The close-up images were courtesy of the new Image Orthicon cameras, which were operated by the experienced technical crew of Philco's TV station WPTZ. It was the sixth Army-Navy game televised by WPTZ from Franklin Field, using platforms that held cameras, operators, an announcer, his assistant, and a spotter all above the fifty-yard line. In a control room right behind them, the program's director ordered the movements of the cameras, then chose which images to send along the cable that linked Franklin Field to a Philco transmitter a half mile away. Just as today, the director mixed play-by-play action on the field with human interest shots on the sidelines and in the stands, as well as close-ups of the announcer.

RCA next took their Image Orthicon camera to Washington, DC, to televise President Truman's first State of the Union speech to Congress, but Truman changed plans and instead had his message hand-delivered to Capitol Hill. RCA chose to televise the Lincoln Day ceremonies in its place on February 12, 1946, which showed General Dwight Eisenhower placing a wreath at the Lincoln Memorial. RCA promoted its Lincoln Day program with full-page advertisements in New York papers that read, "If you own a television set, invite your friends to enjoy this historical television broadcast with you."[4] TV viewers saw General Eisenhower emerge from his limousine and walk up the steps and into the shadows of the monument. It was indeed a historical broadcast, but one whose significance wasn't clear at the time. RCA's new TV camera had shown America clear pictures of a wreath being placed on the statue of its first Republican president by the man who would become its next.

TV BEGINS IN WASHINGTON

The Lincoln Day telecast was the first public event to be televised live from Washington, and it began TV's postwar expansion into new areas of the country. Television's growth had been halted in 1941 in Washington, DC, after both RCA and Du Mont had announced plans to build stations there. In early 1946, the only television station in Washington was Du Mont's experimental station W3XWT in the Hotel Harrington. However, the FCC had already picked Washington as the first city to be awarded new commercial TV licenses out of the scores of American cities that had applied.

The postwar TV industry coveted the Washington market, where many residents had above-average incomes and could afford to buy TV sets and the products that might be advertised by TV's potential sponsors. Washington's viewers could be linked with the Philadelphia and New York audiences to lure more sponsors into advertising on TV. In fact, AT&T was offering usage of a new coaxial cable between New York and Philadelphia free to TV stations, in its own effort to build a postwar business in relaying TV signals.

In March 1946, the FCC granted licenses to operate commercial TV stations in Washington to four companies: RCA's subsidiary NBC, Du Mont, the *Washington Evening Star,* and Bamberger Broadcasting. All but Du Mont also owned radio stations in Washington. Philco had wanted to build a TV station in Washington, but the FCC held back on granting it a license outright. Philco then withdrew its application and complained about the process by which the FCC was selecting TV's new licensees.

Although television's portion of the broadcast band allowed for thirteen channels, the FCC had limited the actual number available in each city. The federal agency was, in part, preventing signals from stations in neighboring cities from interfering with each other, but the FCC also wanted to save channels 12 and 13 for what it labeled as community use.[5] The agency envisioned small low-powered stations that would bring local TV to areas not served by bigger stations in nearby cities.

Community television was rooted in a public interest principle from the Communications Act of 1934, written early in Roosevelt's Presidency, to ensure that broadcast stations would be equitably distributed throughout the country, but the FCC plan for community stations would result in two fewer channels available for bigger commercial stations. The agency had an answer for those companies, such as Philco, vying for the few channels allocated for commercial licenses: wait for the upper frequencies of the spectrum to become available and for the new TV sets that would be able to receive the UHF signals.

Most of the TV industry, however, was eager to begin marketing sets to the public. They united behind a proposal to keep channels 12 and 13 for commercial stations and to give America's cities an extra fifty-nine stations, all on the lower frequencies. The industry argued that community stations were less likely to be built. "If the public is going to be hurt by having a channel allocated and then left vacant," said an industry spokesman, "then that's not in the public interest."[6]

In late 1945, the FCC adopted the industry's proposal and dropped the idea of using channels 12 and 13 for community stations. Their decision also reduced the urgency for TV stations in the upper frequencies. In effect, the federal government was now permitting the lower TV frequencies, up through channel 13, to be dominated by commercial stations in American cities. Postwar TV had lost the potential to take another shape, in which small-scale TV stations rooted in local communities would coexist with big-city commercial TV.

THE LOUIS-CONN FIGHT

At the same time the FCC dropped its plans for community stations, the agency called on the TV industry itself to follow its public interest guidelines. All commercial TV stations, said the FCC, should air programs in the public interest, and the more local these programs, the better. When the agency began taking applications for commercial TV licenses in Washington, DC, it asked for a sample weekly schedule of programming from each applicant. The tentative schedules filed by NBC, Du Mont, Philco, and the others were filled with public interest programs—news, current events, cooking, travel, etc.—and almost empty of popular entertainment, other than sports.

The trade magazine *Television* wondered if viewers really wanted "their television screens to play the role of 'teacher' up to 70 percent of the time."[7] Public service, wrote Mary Gannon in an article on the proposed weekly schedules for Washington, "is a service to the public," which clearly included entertainment. She noted that "in the final analysis, the public is always the determining factor in what makes a hit and who hits the skids"—not the government.[8] Gannon's words were prophetic. A few months later, in June 1946, the TV industry aired its first "hit" program. It was a sports event—the first heavyweight title fight in four years—and it captured not just the public's interest but, ironically, the government's as well.

Boxing was at a peak of popularity in the 1940s, and the sport's biggest draw was Joe Louis. Since 1937, Louis had been heavyweight champion, but he'd spent the previous four years in the Army and outside the ring. Now he was back for a rematch in Yankee Stadium with Billy Conn, who had been winning their previous fight in

1941 until he tried to knock Louis out late in the fight and lost by a knockout instead. The Louis-Conn rematch was a promoter's dream, with ringside seats selling for $100 and scalpers reportedly charging $500. The fight's promoter was Mike Jacobs, who'd already worked with RCA in televising sports from Madison Square Garden. Jacobs sold RCA the rights to televise the bout, and RCA in turn charged the Gillette Razor Company $125,000 to sponsor it.

In New York City, tens of thousands of Americans gathered around TV sets in bars and restaurants the night of the fight. A trio of RCA Image Orthicon cameras gave them clear, vivid pictures of the fight. "Along about the fifth round," wrote a reporter for *The New Yorker,* "some of the audience were carried away by the illusion that they were actually at the Stadium." He was standing with a noisy crowd of about 300 watching a twenty-inch Du Mont TV set perched on the wall of a Greenwich Village bar. "Hit him, Billy!" he described a viewer shouting at the TV set, as another answered, "G'wan, you think he can hear you?"[9]

The boxing match itself was a disappointment. Billy Conn showed little of the desire to fight that boxing fans had expected from him, and Joe Louis knocked him out in the eighth round. Yet an estimated 140,000 Americans had watched the fight on TV that night—enough for the *Philadelphia Daily News* to declare, "The winner—Television!"[10] In Washington, an audience of 800 members of congress, cabinet members, FCC commissioners and staff, and other government officials watched the fight on TV with David Sarnoff at the Statler Hilton. "Is this acceptable television?" he asked at one point, "obviously alluding," wrote *Broadcasting,* to RCA's disagreement with CBS as to whether TV was ready to be marketed to the public. "He said the answer was evident—practically all concerned wanted to know when and how they could buy television sets, and most of them didn't ask how much."[11]

HOUR GLASS

Another breakthrough for TV in mid-1946 was a series that fore-shadowed many of TV's most popular programs in the 1950s and 1960s: a big-budget, one-hour variety series called *Hour Glass.* The big budget in 1946 was $4,000 a week, allotted by the sponsor of

Hour Glass, Standard Brands, makers of Chase and Sanborn coffee and Tender Leaf Tea. Only $250 went to the show's regular host; the rest of the budget went to an assortment of guest talent each week. They included the radio star Edgar Bergen with his wise-cracking dummy, Charlie McCarthy, and other popular performers from radio and show business, such as comedians Bert Lahr and Jerry Colonna, and singers Peggy Lee and Dennis Day.

The host of *Hour Glass* during much of its run was an attractive young actress, Helen Parrish, who became the subject of TV's first publicity campaign, managed by the sponsor's advertising agency. She might have become TV's first star performer, but instead she became pregnant and, even though she was married, it was a social "taboo" for a pregnant woman to display herself in public. She was forced to leave the show.

After televising *Hour Glass* weekly for ten months at a total cost of $200,000, Standard Brands dropped its sponsorship and the program ceased to exist. Nonetheless the format and style of *Hour Glass* anticipated the countless similar TV shows that followed it. In fact, TV historians Tim Brooks and Earle Marsh have cited *Hour Glass* as "one of the most important pioneers in the early history of television."[12] It had intermixed popular stars from radio and film with its own fresh talent to perform music, skits, and comedy, in between short commercials for a few household products. That style of variety show hit its stride in the 1950s and 1960s with top-rated network programs hosted by Milton Berle, Ed Sullivan, Dinah Shore, Perry Como, Carol Burnett, Dean Martin, Flip Wilson, Sonny and Cher, and others, before running out of steam in the mid-1970s.

THE NEW POSTWAR SETS

In hindsight, television had finally turned the corner to success by the middle of 1946, after seven years of starts and stops. When 140,000 people crowded around TV sets in June to watch the Louis-Conn fight, the medium's power to attract and to please a mass audience was proven. Similarly, when Standard Brands paid $4,000 a week to sponsor *Hour Glass,* it was clear that TV could attract the money it needed to thrive.

Television in 1946, however, still couldn't hold onto either the mass audience or the generous sponsor. A crucial ingredient for success was missing: new TV sets to sell to the public. The few thousand prewar TV sets still working in 1946 could capture a mass audience for the truly big event, e.g., a Louis-Conn fight. For a schedule of daily programming to attract so many viewers, it would take tens of thousands of TV sets in America's homes, bars, and restaurants.

Although wartime restrictions on building new sets were lifted in 1945, the industry took another year to retool its factories from making radar screens to TV sets. Slowing the process, too, was the "homefront war" between RCA and CBS over shifting the TV spectrum to the ultrahigh frequencies. Finally, on September 17, 1946, America's first postwar TV set rolled off the assembly line of the RCA plant in Camden, New Jersey. At long last, new TV sets were headed back on the market.

RCA's new TV set had a ten-inch picture tube made in an industrial plant in Lancaster, Pennsylvania, built for the government by RCA during the war. After the war, RCA bought the plant back from the government and converted it to make picture tubes for the thousands of home TV sets that were now being assembled in Camden. RCA was not alone: over a dozen companies including General Electric, Philco, and Du Mont were now making their first postwar sets.

Estimates in the trade press were that 20,000 to 30,000 new sets would be on the market by Christmas 1946. However, when Mary Gannon of the trade magazine *Television* went shopping for the new TV sets in New York City that fall, she found the department stores mostly out of stock. "RCA ran a big campaign with absolutely nothing to back it up," one salesman complained to her. "They promised me five sets before the end of the year—five and I could sell 500 if I had them."[13]

Gannon also found that some of the salesmen knew little about the current status of TV in New York City—not the number of stations, for example, or their hours on the air. "I think there's about two stations in New York . . . let's see, either two or three," explained a salesman. "They don't operate much."[14] In fact, New York had three TV stations operating in late 1946 with several hours of telecasts most afternoons and evenings. Television's weekly schedule had now surpassed the industry's previous high-water mark in the summer of 1941.

Sports dominated the airwaves in late 1946. A typical Monday night had boxing on two stations, WNBT and Du Mont's WABD, and

Friday night had boxing from Madison Square Garden on NBC's Gillette *Cavalcade of Sports* and wrestling on WABD. On Thursday and Friday nights, college basketball doubleheaders were telecast from Madison Square Garden, sponsored by Ford on WCBS—the new call letters for WCBW. On Wednesday nights, WCBS aired professional hockey from the Garden, competing with more boxing on WABD.

On Sunday afternoons in late 1946, TV viewers could choose between two professional football games on WNBT and WCBS. On Saturday afternoons they could watch some of the final games of the college football season, including one of the most thrilling ever played: the 1946 Army-Navy game. Over 100,000 spectators—including President Truman—saw the game in Philadelphia's Municipal Stadium, but at least twice as many watched it on TV.

When the second half began, TV viewers saw that Truman was now sitting on the opposite side of the stands—a traditional move for the President, who was Commander in Chief of both services. By then, Army's Doc Blanchard had already raced sixty-four yards for a touchdown and his team was leading 21-6. This was expected: Army hadn't lost a game in three years, and Navy had won only once all season. Then Navy scored twice in the second half and was just a field goal away from tying Army with a minute left to play. By now the crowd was "standing in a turmoil of excitement," according to *The New York Times,* "cheering, pleading, urging its heroes on, or to stand and hold that line."[15]

NBC was using four Image Orthicon cameras to televise the game, giving TV viewers a fifty-yard line view as Navy made its final drive. *Variety*'s reviewer watched on a new table-model RCA set and described the pictures as "amazingly clear and sharp."[16] Close-up images of the players and coaches were mixed with the action on the field, as Navy elected to go for the touchdown—for "the upset of the ages,"[17] according to the *Times*. With the ball pushed to just five yards from the goal line, "the 'brave old Army team' stood fast," according to Army's coach, "like the Federals of General George Thomas at Chicamauga."[18] The clock ran out on the Navy team just five yards from victory, and Army remained undefeated.

Once again, a big event on television had captured a mass audience. The 1946 Army-Navy game showed TV's magic at its best: allowing viewers to see a piece of life transpire from a great distance, with each new moment dramatically revealing itself as it happened. At the same time, thousands of new TV sets were slowly heading to appliance and department stores; the pieces were finally in place for TV's emergence in American culture.

THE BIKINI BOMB EXPLOSION

Also in 1946, news programs of five to fifteen minutes in length were scheduled four nights a week. WNBT's *Esso Reporter* was airing film footage of news events, including the weigh-in for the Louis-Conn fight, sessions of the newly formed United Nations, a nine-alarm fire on Staten Island—all on the same day they happened. Other than the rare news event that had been covered live on TV (the V-E Day and V-J Day celebrations in 1945, for example) the *Esso Reporter* was the fastest that news had ever been shown to the public—faster by days than the movie newsreels.

Televising news so quickly was no small feat in 1946. Videotape and video recorders had yet to be invented; instead, the *Esso Reporter* used motion picture film, which took several hours to develop. The show's producer and commentator, Paul Alley, thus had little time to spare. Alley wrote his narration as the film was being edited; sometimes he watched the film for the first time as it was being televised and improvised his narration on the air.

In the summer of 1946, the *Esso Reporter* aired the first controversial TV news broadcast, involving a film that had been flown to New York from the Bikini Atoll in the western Pacific's Marshall Islands. The word *bikini* later became popular in American culture as the skimpy two-piece bathing suit that symbolized new sexual values in 1950s America. The bikini was first called the *atome* in France, thus named because of its small size—like an atom; the switch to *bikini* in naming the swimsuits came from the site of the first atom bombs exploded in peacetime at the Bikini Atoll.

The first of the Bikini atom bombs was exploded by the United States on July 1, 1946, and was viewed live on TV screens by scientists, journalists, and military men who were less than twenty miles away on the USS *Mount McKinley.* Two TV cameras and transmitters were mounted beforehand on the Bikini Atoll to send pictures to the *McKinley* as the bomb exploded offshore. The nuclear blast was "an awesome, spine-chilling spectacle," wrote a reporter watching it live on TV, "a boiling, angry, super volcano struggling toward the sky, belching enormous masses of iridescent flames and smoke and giant rings of rainbow."[19]

"Tele Beats Newsreels Showing A-Bomb Films," headlined *Variety* when, a few days later, motion pictures of the Bikini bomb were televised on WNBT's news programs. The next week a controversy flared over whether the bomb had been a dud. Floating in the test zone for the explosion were seventy Navy ships, and the Bikini bomb was intended to prove that the new, powerful weapon could destroy a nation's fleet. Yet the TV monitors aboard the *McKinley* showed that most of the ships escaped heavy damage, and some of the reporters who watched the telecast wrote this in their stories. They suggested that either the bomb had missed the target or was weakened intentionally to support the U.S. Navy's own claim that its ships could survive a nuclear blast at sea. RCA was soon asked to turn over all available films of the explosion to a military censorship board, and the nuclear tests that followed were held under tighter security.[20]

With the Bikini bomb explosion, TV had displayed its power to televise images in conflict with those painted verbally by the military and the government. In this case, the public controversy was small; few Americans had watched the blast on TV. For the mass audiences of the 1960s and 1970s, big controversies would, however, erupt over TV images of war and other national issues. In this respect, the rise in public skepticism about the government and military that fueled the Vietnam War protests can be traced back to the Bikini bomb telecasts of 1946.

SURVEYING THE TV VIEWER

Television was also showing clear signs in 1946 of its power to change the daily lives of Americans. A CBS survey that year reported most families with sets were watching TV at least five nights a week, and a third of them watched every night. Ninety percent said they missed TV "very much" when the New York City stations went off the air temporarily in 1946 to switch to new frequencies; only 3 percent missed it "not at all." The viewers in the survey liked TV's basic ability to transmit live pictures, so that "[you] can see things that happen right before your eyes that you couldn't visualize with the radio."

Half of the TV viewers said there were "no regular radio programs they listen to in preference to television," and they reported attending movies less often. They cited the "freedom, comfort and convenience" of television as a means of entertainment: as one viewer said, "When it's over all you have to do is shut it off and go to bed."[21]

Another survey in 1946 focused on Newburgh, New York, the town where RCA had test-marketed television in 1939-1940. Hundreds of Newburgh's families had lived with TV for seven years now, prompting Hal Borland to ask, "What has television done to Newburgh home life?" in an article on the survey in *Better Homes and Gardens.* "Several families say it has strengthened home ties," wrote Borland, "that home is the entertainment center once more," with children inviting their friends to visit and with relatives, neighbors, and other friends who "drop in for 'the show.' "[22]

Borland described Newburgh as a "picture of tomorrow," when TV is commonplace and "radio is old stuff" throughout the country. "It's worth noting," he wrote, "that seven years later you can't buy a secondhand (TV) receiver in Newburgh; the owners won't part with them, at least not until they can get postwar sets." Borland noted in particular that Newburgh's youth were accustomed to TV in their lives. They lacked "a very clear memory of the time when there wasn't a television set in the living room. They walk out on a good many routine telecasts, but they seldom miss sports events," Western movies, or their favorite quiz programs.[23]

THE EMERGING GENRES

Several of the quiz shows that aired in 1946 had an extra twist to lure viewers and keep them watching: they were interactive, using the phone system to make the home audience part of the telecast. *Cash and Carry,* for example, was a quiz show—on Du Mont's WABD, sponsored by Libby's foods, and set in a grocery store—that phoned viewers at home. Those who knew the answers to questions taped to cans of the sponsor's products, or who guessed the secret item hidden under a barrel, could "carry" away the "cash"—from five to fifteen dollars. *King's Party Line* on WCBS had a radio game-show host, John Reed King, calling viewers at home to guess the answers to questions about studio audience members. The prizes included tubes of Ipana toothpaste and bottles of Vitalis hair cream—both products of the sponsor, Bristol Myers. On WNBT's *Face to Face,* viewers were phoned to guess the famous face being drawn by the resident artist.

Other TV shows in 1946 encouraged viewers to play along with panelists in the studio. On *Junior High Quiz,* students from two public schools competed each week, and, as the reviewer in *Television* noted, "Problems are tricky enough to keep an adult viewer interested in guessing too."[24] Families watching at home could also play along with the panelists on the charades program *Play the Game,* hosted by New York University professor Dr. Harvey Zorbaugh. *Play the Game* was first televised before the war, had survived during the war by moving upstate to WRGB, and was now back in New York City on WABD.

Other TV programs in 1946 were instructional, following in the footsteps of the civil defense lessons televised in 1942. Friday nights on WNBT, for example, instructional shows filled the airtime prior to the boxing matches on Gillette's *Cavalcade of Sports.* Viewers could learn to cook a meal from chef James Beard on *I Love To Eat,* draw a landscape from Jon Gnagy on *You Can Be an Artist,* or dance the ranchero from D'Avalos on *Let's Rhumba.*

Sunday nights on WNBT offered live drama on *NBC Television Theater.* Along with *Hour Glass,* WNBT's landmark variety show on Thursday night, this weekly program was TV's best attempt in 1946 at entertainment that was scripted, rehearsed, and performed at a high professional level. *NBC Television Theater* premiered back in April 1945 with a three-part adaptation of Robert Sherwood's Pulitzer prizewinning *Abe Lincoln in Illinois.* By 1947, NBC's drama series had acquired a sponsor, Kraft, and a new night, Wednesday, where it was televised weekly for the next eleven years as *Kraft Television Theater.* NBC alternated between three production teams for its *Television Theater,* giving each one nearly a month to create and rehearse their show. Often, three plays were in rehearsal at the same time, putting NBC's Studio 3-H in Radio City in constant use. In less than a month, for example, NBC televised *The Front Page, You Can't Take It With You,* and *Winterset,* using actors and actresses from the New York theater scene just as Tony Miner was doing ten blocks away at WCBW.

Another form of drama, the soap opera, was making an early TV appearance on Wednesday nights in 1946 with Du Mont station WABD's *Faraway Hill*. Soap operas were popular on radio during the 1930s and 1940s; *Faraway Hill* simply brought the genre to television, where real arms were embraced, real tears shed, and where a card reading "Continued Next Week" was held before the camera at each episode's climax. In *Faraway Hill,* Broadway actress Flora Campbell played Karen St. John, a wealthy Manhattan widow who moved to the country and fell in love with a farmer. The farmer, however, was engaged to a local woman, and from that premise the plot thickened and twisted and turned for the show's twelve-week run.

DRAMA IN WASHINGTON

TV viewers in late 1946 and early 1947 could also watch a real-life drama unfolding in Washington. The Democrats had controlled Congress since Roosevelt's election back in 1932, but the Republicans tapped into a mood of the times in the midterm election of 1946 with a new campaign slogan—"Had Enough?"[25] Enough American voters stopped supporting enough Democrats to give the Republicans the majority in both houses of Congress. This shift of power was one of the biggest of the century. It was captured on live TV on January 3, 1947, the day television for the first time transmitted from inside the U.S. Capitol.

The 80th Congress opened with a vote, along party lines, to elect its speaker. *The New York Times* described the TV images as "so clear that a bandage could be seen on a finger of the House tally clerk,"[26] as Democrat Sam Rayburn, now the former Speaker of the House, relinquished his place on the rostrum to a Republican. "If it had to come," Rayburn told Congress and the TV audience, it was a "high privilege" and "great personal pleasure" to introduce Congressman Joe Martin as the House's forty-fifth speaker.[27]

Four days later, President Harry Truman delivered his State of the Union speech to Congress in person, on the radio, and, for the first time, on television. Those watching him on TV on the East Coast saw Truman's grin and the "sparkle in his eyes" as he looked at the Republicans, now sitting as the majority party on the other side of the aisle. He began, "It looks like a good many of you have moved over to the left since I was here,"[28] but he was joking, of course; Truman knew this Republican Congress would be the country's most right-wing since before the New Deal.

TV viewers could see Truman turning the pages of his speech as he called for better housing, civil rights, and national health care, but the New Deal was now old politics, and viewers could see firsthand the disinterest of the Republicans. "One of them held in his lap what appeared to be a comic book," observed *Broadcasting,* while others "twiddled their thumbs."[29]

Truman's televised speech that day signaled a new era for the United States. This was Postwar America—this gathering, its first Congress—and this President, its first leader. Most of his speech dealt with America's economy, its postwar readjustment problems, labor issues and strikes, and its production and standard of living. Truman also warned Congress and the public of a new foreign threat to national security—that "an unforeseen attack could come with unprecedented speed. We must be strong enough to defeat, and thus to forestall, any such attack."[30] His words here were a clear preview of the Cold War and anti-Communist rhetoric that would be preached by America's presidents for the next forty years.

THE FIRST COLOR TELECASTS

Three weeks after Truman's speech to Congress, another telecast launched a war within the TV industry. This special program featured Patti Painter, a model, as she walked and talked, applied lipstick, smoked a cigarette, and waved a scarf. The transmission was brief and traveled only a short distance, from a CBS laboratory in New York to an audience of FCC officials, TV executives, and journalists gathered nearby. The images they saw on their TV screens of Patti Painter were sharp, clear, and—most significantly—in color.

The occasion was a public hearing called by the FCC to assess whether color TV was ready to be sold to the public, as claimed by CBS. Other TV manufacturers were allowed to raise questions about the CBS color TV system, and they did—concerning the lighting, the amount of frequencies needed to broadcast, and other technical matters.

Their biggest objection went to the very heart of the CBS color system. Like the earlier Jenkins TV system that had failed, the new

CBS system was partly mechanical: three disks of different colors spun rapidly inside both the cameras and home sets. If the CBS system were adopted, all TV sets, cameras, and transmitters sold thus far would instantly become obsolete. The industry would be stopped dead in its tracks once again—or pushed back, argued Allen Du Mont. He claimed at the hearing that twenty-inch color TV sets would need spinning disks that were five feet wide, and they'd be rejected by the public.

The FCC met the next day at a country club in Princeton, New Jersey, to view color pictures televised by RCA from their nearby laboratory. RCA's color system was still in the experimental stage, yet it had one big advantage over the CBS system. It used electronics, not spinning disks, to send and receive its images. RCA claimed that its color TV system was five years away from being marketed; instead, RCA told the FCC, Americans should continue buying black-and-white sets. RCA's color system was compatible with black-and-white TV, so the public could gradually trade in their old televisions for new color sets.

When the hearings ended, the trade publication *Radio News* predicted the FCC would side with CBS because the agency "favor[ed] competition and new developments."[31] Instead, the FCC ruled in March 1947 against CBS beginning commercial color telecasts. CBS hadn't field-tested its system adequately, said the FCC, and, in a nod to RCA, added that "there may be other systems of transmitting color which offer the possibility of cheaper receivers and narrower band widths that have not been fully explored."[32]

The decision was a shock to some at CBS. "We felt we had been dealt a foul blow," said Dr. Peter Goldmark, the inventor of the CBS color system.[33] Six months later, the FCC chairman who announced the decision, Charles Denny, resigned to become a vice president of the NBC subsidiary of RCA, and this was "noted cynically" by "everyone in the CBS camp," according to Goldmark, who viewed the job as a payoff for the FCC ruling.[34]

But one of Goldmark's colleagues at CBS, director Tony Miner, later came to suspect that a few CBS executives had raised the color issue simply to delay television, in order "to enhance CBS's primacy in radio." Miner claimed that his bosses at CBS had made him "a prime patsy," in charge of producing CBS's public showings of the color system that were secretly intended, he said, to "cripple television."[35] Indeed, CBS had little to lose by slowing down the sales of TV sets in 1947. CBS was first and foremost a radio network; it wasn't a manufacturer of TV sets or equipment, nor had it invested much capital in its TV studios and programs.

CBS responded dramatically to the FCC ruling: it shut down its WCBS studio, dismissed its production team, and disbanded its research laboratory. All that remained of the CBS television operations was its New York City station, still on the air, but now claiming to be "concentrating our efforts for the time being on actuality broadcasts, such as sports and special events."[36] Ironically, one of the first "actuality broadcasts" that CBS aired after closing its TV studio marked a turning point in the history of American society.

INTEGRATION ON TV

On April 15, 1947, WCBS brought its cameras to Ebbets Field in Brooklyn, New York, to televise the first Brooklyn Dodgers baseball game of the season. For the TV industry, the game was noteworthy as the first baseball telecast to be sponsored. For American society, the game became historic the moment the Dodgers took the field at the top of the first inning. Running out from the dugout to play first base was an African American, Jackie Robinson; in that instant, witnessed by 26,623 at Ebbetts Field and thousands more watching on TV, an American racial barrier fell.

The United States was still a decade away from the Supreme Court rulings on integration and two decades away from the landmark Civil Rights Acts of the 1960s. But on that afternoon in April 1947, Jackie Robinson and Dodgers owner Branch Rickey integrated one of America's great institutions, Major League Baseball, and generated a backlash that lasted all season.

On Opening Day all was calm; Robinson was hitless in three at bats as the Dodgers beat the Boston Braves. Before Opening Day, however, baseball's team owners had voted fifteen to one to exclude Robinson (they were overruled by the sport's commissioner, Happy Chandler) and several Dodgers asked to be traded. After Opening Day, Robinson received death threats against himself and his wife and a kidnapping threat against his child, and he was taunted, spiked, and thrown at by players on other teams.

The Brooklyn Dodgers added a second black player during the season; eventually, the other teams followed suit. Baseball was ahead of American society, however, in becoming integrated—and ahead of American broadcasting as well. WCBS may have shown Jackie Robinson playing on an equal footing with his white counterparts, and the many Dodgers games that were televised during the 1947 season were a breakthrough for African Americans, but such equality was the exception on either radio or TV. In radio comedy programs, for example, blacks played subservient roles or had their parts performed by whites using comic voices and dialects: the very popular *Amos 'n' Andy* was the best example. Only a few African Americans had appeared thus far on TV, with Jackie Robinson by far the most prominent.

Later in 1947, a black male student in the Katherine Dunham dance school raised a stir merely by dancing on TV with a white female student. When the show was televised by Du Mont in New York and Washington, *Variety* reported that "more than 100 objecting letters and phone calls" were received. The industry was worried, according to *Variety,* about the near future when TV expanded south of Washington, DC. "If a sponsor is afraid that scenes like this will affect his sales in the southern states," predicted *Variety,* the sponsor might threaten to drop the program. The station would be forced to choose between integration and sponsorship.[37]

THE SECOND WAVE OF TV STATIONS

Although TV's window hadn't yet widened south of Washington, DC in 1947, it had expanded beyond the East Coast. The new region for TV in 1947 was the Midwest, with stations opening in St. Louis, Detroit, Milwaukee, and Cleveland, added to Chicago's WBKB which had been on the air since 1943. They marked the start of America's second wave of TV stations.

However, these new stations weren't founded by the pioneers in TV and radio, such as RCA, General Electric, or Philco as the first wave had been; instead, they belonged to big-city newspapers. In Detroit, it was the new TV station WWJ owned by the *Detroit News*—in St. Louis, station KSD owned by the *St. Louis Post-Dispatch.* The *Milwaukee Journal* started television station WTMJ, and in Philadelphia the *Inquirer* owned WFIL. In Ohio, the Scripps-Howard newspaper chain, owners of both the *Cleveland News* and the *Cincinnati Post*, opened station WEWS in Cleveland and acquired a license for a TV station in Cincinnati.

In each case, the newspaper company that owned and operated the new TV station also owned and operated a leading local radio station. This was cross-ownership, a form of monopoly that was allowed under FCC regulations, and it had its advantages. For one, cross-ownership gave the new TV stations a solid financial base. When the *Milwaukee Journal* built station WTMJ in 1947, for example, the firm spent $375,000 of its capital on equipment and $2,000 on its first telecast—money that a less wealthy local business might not have available to invest.

These parent companies could also fill a schedule of TV programs with staff from their newspapers and radio stations: e.g., announcers, reporters, fashion and home experts, cartoonists, etc. Here, they followed in the footsteps of Schenectady's WRGB, the station that during the war had televised daylong programs making use of local newspaper staff.

Cross-ownership in local markets also hurt the rival media in town. In Milwaukee, for example, the *Journal* was by far the leading paper among readers and advertisers; just as dominant was the paper's own radio station. The *Journal*'s TV station WTMJ easily attracted sponsors even before it aired its first telecast. There was, however, only so much advertising money to spend in one market; the sponsors supporting the *Journal*'s WTMJ used money that had been going to other local radio stations. One sponsor in Milwaukee, reported *Variety*, dropped a $200 a week contract from another radio station to help defer a new $500 a week contract with WTMJ.

Throughout the country in 1947, this pattern of cross-ownership was becoming the norm. The FCC had granted TV licenses to other newspaper publishers in New York, Los Angeles, Chicago, San Francisco, Philadelphia, Baltimore, Washington, Portland, Memphis, Louisville, and Fort Worth. In nearly every other city acquiring a new TV station, a radio broadcaster was building it. Television wasn't becoming RCA's monopoly, as the FCC under Larry Fly had once feared. Instead, TV was now joining with America's urban newspapers and radio stations in an economic oligarchy, in which a few companies dominated the media in each major market.

THE "SPLIT" TV AUDIENCE

The new TV stations that began operating in 1947 as well as those preparing to open were clear signs that television was finally expanding, as were the increasing numbers of TV sets being watched in the cities that already had stations. By mid-1947, there were roughly 60,000 TV sets in operation—still located mostly from New York to Washington, but with growing numbers scattered in the Midwest and in Los Angeles. New TV sets were also being produced in record numbers, rising from 5,000 a month in early 1947 to 11,000 in June.

These figures were just a fraction of what the industry hoped to produce, but not until it had satisfied a big public demand for radio sets. Sixty million American families had radios in 1947, and many were now replacing old sets with the new postwar models or buying a radio for another room, to listen to their favorite programs and performers. Once these demands were met, however, the manufacturers were likely to see their sales figures drop. At that point, they hoped sales of TV sets would be great enough to compensate for any decrease in sales of radios.

Most American families in the early postwar years had some disposable income; in general, workers were earning twice the income they made from 1940 to 1945. A survey conducted in New York in early 1947 showed that nine out of ten people wanted to purchase a TV set, but only one in four intended to buy one within the year. The survey also reported that the price the consumer was willing to pay for a TV was still less than the cost of the average set.[38] Clearly, the public needed to feel more compelled to watch TV before a boom in the sale of new sets could begin. An improved TV schedule, with popular shows filling more hours each day, was likely to boost the attraction of buying a set. But creating such a schedule was complicated in 1947 by what *Business Week* described as "the 'split personality' of the television audience."[39]

Most TV sets were in America's homes, but many were in bars, being watched by bigger audiences. The bar crowd loved sports, and television gave them plenty of it in 1947: football, boxing, basketball, wrestling, hockey, horse racing, tennis, track and field, and especially baseball. By the summer of 1947, nine Major League Baseball teams were on the air regularly in the East and the Midwest.

In June 1947, a *New York Times* reporter spent a midweek night with the "regulars" at a neighborhood bar in the Hells Kitchen district of Manhattan; the newspaper ran a feature story on their banter as they watched TV. During a Brooklyn Dodgers baseball game, for example, the group argued umpire calls and cheered their team's home runs: "I knew that was tagged right. Could tell as soon as the wood was hit."[40]

Between rounds of a televised boxing match, the crowd "discussed the merits of each fighter, digging back into memory of fights they've seen or read about. They laugh at commercials," noted the reporter, "chuckle at lame puns by the announcer," and between bouts talk about their families and neighbors. The writer described the "warm, festive spirit" of watching TV with the group and concluded, "Television is the best thing that's happened to the neighborhood bar since the free lunch."[41]

Another favorable account of watching TV appeared in *The New Yorker* that summer—in this case, focusing on one family's experience. The writer, Robert Rice, spent parts of a week with the Dubins of Manhattan, who had owned a TV set for six years. Harry Dubin saw his first TV set back in 1941 and was struck that "all this movement and flesh could be carried into my living room through the invisible air. I knew right then I wanted to have a set of my own."[42] Now, the TV set was the focus of the household on weekday nights and on Saturday afternoons. When the set was on, the Dubins invited friends, rearranged chairs, ate snacks, and chatted, especially about what they were watching.

One night Rice watched the Dubins watching one of their favorites, the quiz program *Cash and Carry,* in which the home audience had a chance to win by phoning in and naming what was hidden under a barrel. The Dubins had won the contest three times in the past; this time, Harry Dubin dashed off several times to the phone and won tickets to the show. On another night Harry Dubin and Rice alone watched a one-hour live NBC version of Shakespeare's *Twelfth Night*. Dubin said, "This is the first time television has risen to a professional level. I think it is coming of age."[43]

On Saturday afternoon, fourteen-year-old Ronald Dubin and eight friends gathered to watch a baseball game between the Dodgers and the Philadelphia Phillies; they had each bet ten cents on the final score. The group snacked and joked and roughhoused as they watched, their excitement growing when the game went into extra innings. In the bottom of the tenth, the Dodgers were behind by a run with two outs and a runner at first base, at which point "there was an unceasing uproar in the living room," wrote Rice, as the group begged and groaned and chanted for each batter at the plate. At last, the TV showed "a fine closeup of the Philadelphia first baseman reaching into the box seats" to catch a foul ball, and the game was over. Almost as suddenly—"within a few minutes"—Ronald Dubin's friends paid off their bets and filed out of the apartment.[44]

TELEVISION AND WOMEN

Another program the Dubins watched with their guest from *The New Yorker* was NBC's *In the Kelvinator Kitchen,* sponsored by a kitchen appliance company. They saw the host of a women's radio show, Alma Kitchell, broil a steak she took out of the big Kelvinator refrigerator in the WNBT studio. This show was typical of a "homemaker" genre on TV in which a housekeeping skill was demonstrated, often using the sponsor's products. On NBC's *The Wife Saver,* sponsored by General Foods, host Allen Prescott showed an assortment of homemade labor-saving gadgets. Similar kitchen-based shows aired in 1947 in New York, Chicago, Philadelphia, and St. Louis.

The homemaker shows were designed to attract the women in the TV audience; so were fashion programs and talk shows, often with interviews of celebrities. Most of them were televised at night. "Ad agencies are experimenting with such packages after dark," wrote *Variety* in May 1947, "hoping the experience gained will give them sufficient know-how [for] the time when there's a large enough daytime audience to make such shows pay off."[45] During the day, TV sets at home were turned off, as radio still held the American housewife in its grip with soap operas, talk shows, and quiz and game programs. TV sets in bars and local department stores were either turned off during the day or showed a test pattern; there were usually no programs on the air.

In 1947, however, NBC created a new daytime TV show that blended the homemaker, fashion, and talk shows. *The Swift Home Service Club* featured a married couple, Tex McCrary and Jinx Falkenberg, who had been hosting talk shows on radio. Tex and Jinx were ideally suited for television. Both were bright, attractive, and educated; they were world travelers with connections among the rich and famous, and they were experienced at conversing over the airwaves.

Jinx Falkenberg garnered the most attention. She was a former actress and model—New York's "Miss Rheingold" Beer in 1940—and a new mother who'd been a Long Island homemaker just a year earlier. But on television in 1947, Falkenberg was one of a small group of women who didn't sing, dance, model, pose, or display homemaking skills. Instead, she hosted a program that exhibited her intellect and knowledge. In her category as well was Millicent Fenwick, then an editor of *Vogue* and later a congresswomen from New Jersey; she was a panelist in 1947 on *Americana,* a quiz show about American history and culture. When the public affairs show *Meet the Press* began airing on TV as well as radio in 1947, its first moderator was a woman, Martha Rountree. She stayed with the program—the longest-running in TV history—for six years.

More women held jobs in TV as producers and directors, and many worked behind the scenes in the industry's studios, offices, and factories. One woman who worked part-time on the air in 1947, Dorothy Wootton, was the focus of a full-page photograph in the June 16 issue of *Life,* in a long article titled "American Woman's Dilemma." *Life* used Wootton and her job in TV as an example of how part-time work served as "one solution for a bored housewife or an idle woman," and the magazine's photo of her showed her husband and young child watching her from off the studio set.[46]

The next month Dorothy Wootton also appeared on a new TV program, NBC's *Author Meets the Critics,* based on a popular radio show. On this particular night, the show focused on the *Life* article. Wootton told her viewers that she was satisfied with her life; so did a second woman on the show, housewife Marjorie McWeeny, who had been the subject of four pages of the *Life* article. McWeeny had a "nice husband," wrote *Life,* and "three fine children." *Life* printed photos of her standing by a week's worth of beds to make, food to cook, dishes to wash, etc., and dressed in the various outfits of the roles that "keep her busy 100 hours a week [as] laundress, cook, expert nurse-governess, seamstress, chauffeur, and housemaid . . . [and husband] John's glamour girl."[47]

The author on TV that night on *Author Meets the Critic* was Dr. Marynia Farnham, whose best-selling book in 1947, *Modern Woman: The Lost Sex,* was summarized in the *Life* article. Dr. Farnham wrote of the "20 million women, nearly half of all adult female Americans," who she claimed were "essentially idle. They do not have children under 18, they are not members of the labor force. . . ." Quoting from Dr. Farnham's book, *Life* described these women as "functionally little more than wastrals seething into afternoon movies, tea shops, cocktail lounges, expensive shopping centers." These were the women who "escape[d] too readily" into radio soap operas.[48]

In its review of the TV show, *Variety* chose to quote Wootton and McWeeny and not Dr. Farnham. Instead they dismissed Farnham as a "specimen of her sex who dresses in the severe garb it seems to behoove a woman doctor to wear," unlike the show's panelist Eloise McElhone, who was "fetching . . . in an off-the-shoulder dress."[49] This tone was typical of *Variety,* which described in many of its reviews the physical appeal of the women on TV. The tone was typical, too, of American culture at large and the value placed on a woman's appearance and the support she gave the men and children in her life. America's working woman and her daily life had no place on TV's schedule; instead, the housewife—busy or "idle"—had taken over. On television, the working woman was the "lost sex."

MIDDLEBROW TELEVISION

Author Meets the Critic was one of several book-chat shows on TV in 1947, in which authors such as Dr. Marynia Farnham faced a panel of critics, both pro and con. *Books on Trial* had a similar format, and these shows were among TV's early efforts to air intellectual programming. They belong to a category labeled middlebrow culture, where the ideas and works of the intellectual elite are packaged for the general public. Middlebrow culture is part of America's tradition; it has appeared in the form of lecture tours, discussion groups, book-reading clubs, and radio shows that began in the 1930s to repackage these older forms on the nation's airwaves.

Televised versions of radio's middlebrow shows appeared in 1947, including *Author Meets the Critics, Americana,* and *Juvenile Jury,* which, as did *Quiz Kids,* used children for its intellectual panel. Because TV sets were still a luxury item in 1947, the home audience was skewed toward the upper and upper-middle classes. The middlebrow TV shows gave these viewers, in the words of Joan Shelley Rubin, the "opportunity to declare one's home a center of refinement and distinctiveness."[50]

The most successful middlebrow show on radio was *Information, Please,* in which questions sent in from listeners were submitted to a panel of witty experts; their humor and the comments of the moderator, Clifton Fadiman, were basic to the show's popularity. The program was cited by *Saturday Review* for "Distinguished Service to American Literature," yet its "display of personality," according to Rubin, always competed with "the educational features of the broadcast."[51] That mixture of entertainment and education was at the heart of middlebrow culture.

On TV in 1947 the *Information, Please* format was copied by three programs: *Seven Lively Arts, Let's Pop the Question,* and *Americana.* The latter was hosted by a popular middlebrow figure, John Mason Brown, who once described other TV shows as "so much chewing gum for the eyes."[52] A Harvard graduate, professor of drama, theater critic, and busy lecturer, Brown performed as a critic in the public arena. He hosted *Americana* for just a few months, then moderated and performed on other middlebrow shows through the mid-1950s.

By then, however, the middlebrow genre had fallen off television's nightly schedule. *Author Meets the Critic* and *Juvenile Jury* survived until 1954; *Americana* and the other middlebrow shows of 1947 ceased earlier. Yet some of their formula of education mixed with entertainment lingered; for example, two of TV's most popular quiz programs, *What's My Line?* and *Jeopardy!,* had that same mixture. The middlebrow TV show today remains a staple of public broadcasting stations and on such cable networks as CNN, Bravo, and the Discovery Channel.

The TV industry aired both homemaking shows and middlebrow programs in 1947, hoping to broaden television's appeal as new stations opened and new sets were marketed. But could anyone predict in mid-1947 that TV was finally on the brink of mass popularity—that, in fact, an incredible boom in sales of new sets was about to begin? No; not unless their crystal balls also foresaw the paths of baseballs, bats, and gloves that summer. Just as young Ronald Dubin and his friends were on Saturday afternoons in June 1947, millions of Americans would be swept up in October by the drama of televised baseball.

Chapter 6

From Boom to Berle

THE 1947 WORLD SERIES

As baseball's 1947 season entered its final weeks in September, one of its two pennant races was still unsettled. So, too, was the role TV would play in the upcoming World Series. The New York Yankees had already clinched the American League pennant, ensuring that part of the series would be played in TV's biggest market and televised on the East Coast. However, either the Brooklyn Dodgers or the St. Louis Cardinals could win the National League pennant. Should Brooklyn win, of course, all games could be televised along the Eastern network. A Yankees-Cardinals series would present a problem. Although St. Louis now had a TV station, KSD wasn't on a network; it could neither receive games from New York nor transmit games out of St. Louis.

On September 21, 1947, Jackie Robinson was named Rookie of the Year for the National League; the next day St. Louis lost to the Chicago Cubs and fell too far behind Robinson's Dodgers to win the pennant. Now the Brooklyn Dodgers would play the New York Yankees in the 1947 World Series, and all games would be televised live from New York to Washington, DC—or maybe none would be. Baseball Commissioner Happy Chandler had already turned down an offer of a million dollars from the Ford Motor Company to buy the TV rights to sponsor the World Series for the next ten years.

That a company in 1947 offered so much money to sponsor TV programs and that such an offer was rejected was surprising, given TV's small audiences thus far: both Ford and baseball had their eyes on TV's future, when a World Series might easily attract an audience in the millions. After all, 300,000 Americans had watched the 1946 Army-Navy game on TV; estimates were that half a million might watch the Yankees-Dodgers "subway" World Series in 1947. That audience alone was worth $100,000 to potential sponsors, figured baseball's Commissioner Chandler, and so he turned down Ford's long-term offer to hold out for a better one-year deal.

Chandler never got the offer he'd hoped for and instead settled for $65,000, split between Ford and Gillette, for the rights to sponsor the 1947 World Series. Even that sum was a gamble for the two sponsors, with no guarantee that the Series would last more than four games or attract half a million viewers. After the Yankees—who were favored—won the first two games, the chances for a long and exciting World Series decreased.

The Dodgers won the third game, however, and by then bars with TV sets from New York to Washington, DC, were reporting up to a 500 percent increase in business, with crowds of men watching the games in the afternoons. Bartenders, reported *Variety*, "complained their saloons were so crowded they couldn't reach customers on the fringes of the crowds to serve them drinks."[1] The fourth game, played on Friday afternoon, October 3, in Brooklyn's Ebbetts Field, attracted TV's first audience in the millions.

All along the Eastern network, TV viewers who'd left work early became transfixed by one of baseball's classic, dramatic games. They watched Floyd Bevens of the Yankees pitch a no-hitter through eight innings and retire two more batters in the bottom of the ninth. Bevens was now one out from pitching the first World Series no-hitter, but he had only a one-run lead and a runner on second base. He intentionally walked the next batter, hoping now for a ground ball that would end the game. Instead, as a million TV viewers in bars and homes held their breaths, pinch-hitter Cookie Lavagetto of the Dodgers hit Beven's second pitch out to the right field wall. The runner on second quickly scored to tie the game. The runner on first raced home, too, and beat the throw from right field. In that instant, the no-hitter was gone and the game was over. Bevens and the Yankees were suddenly losers, and the Brooklyn Dodgers had tied the World Series at two.

Only TV, wrote *Variety*, "could have given viewers the thrill that came when Cookie Lavagetto hit his pinch double. . . ."[2] In the locker room, Lavagetto said, "That's the top thrill of my life, without a doubt. Nothing else could happen."[3] In fact, a second thrill happened two days later, on Sunday afternoon, and this time an estimated 3 million Americans saw it live on TV.

The Yankees had already won the fifth game of the Series and were a victory away from the championship. The Dodgers were leading by a run in the sixth inning of the sixth game, when the great Joe DiMaggio stepped to the plate with two Yankees on base and two outs. DiMaggio hit a pitch for a sure home run, headed beyond the bullpen fence in left field, and destined to put the Yankees in the lead. But the Dodgers had just sent in Al Gionfriddo from the bench to play left field. "I looked over my shoulder once," he said later, "and I could see the ball was still coming, and I put my head down again, and I kept running and running, and when I got to just about where I thought the ball would come down, I reached out with my glove like I was catching a football pass over my shoulder, and I caught the ball."[4]

Three million TV viewers saw DiMaggio's ball flying over the fence; they saw Gionfriddo hit the fence himself, reach and snag the ball, barely keep his balance, and hold onto the ball for the final out of the inning. Halfway home, Joe DiMaggio kicked the dirt in disappointment; in later years, he called it the greatest catch he had ever seen.

The Dodgers won that game and tied the Series again, but the Yankees won the next day and became baseball's champions. The biggest winner of the 1947 World Series, however, was television. TV had "proved conclusively," wrote *Variety* on October 8, 1947, "that it's better than radio—and even better than a seat on the first base line—when it comes to dramatic moments."[5] Television had indeed given an audience in the millions the chance to watch two of baseball's most exciting plays right as they happened, in the midst of an unfolding sports drama.

As it turned out, neither Al Gionfriddo, Cookie Lavagetto, nor Floyd Bevens ever played in another Major League game after October 1947; the World Series was both the climax and finale of their careers. The next month, however, 25,000 more Americans bought TV sets, and a television boom had begun.

PUPPET PLAYHOUSE

Thousands of the newly acquired TV sets were put to good use during the last weekend of 1947, when a blizzard struck the Northeast. Over two feet of snow fell in New York City in sixteen hours, setting a record, crippling traffic, and keeping everyone at home. Late in the afternoon on Saturday, those parents with TV sets and restless children found some respite in a program premiering on WNBT called *Puppet Playhouse*. For an hour, the children were captivated by the puppets on strings, by the smiling host who sang and played the piano, and by an imaginary character with a funny laugh who said he was too bashful to come out of the desk drawer. The character's puppet had yet to be fashioned, but he did have a name—Howdy Doody.

America's first wildly popular TV series was born in a blizzard that afternoon. The paralyzing storm had created a big and eager audience for *Puppet Playhouse,* later known as *The Howdy Doody Show.* The program would soon usher the country—especially its postwar and "baby boom" children—into the age of television.

Similar to the marionette shows performed by the Joe Owens family troupe on Schenectady's WRGB during World War II, *Howdy Doody* used a form of theater—puppetry—that can be traced as popular entertainment back to the ancient world. One of the best puppeteers of the time was Frank Paris, Howdy Doody's creator. Paris came to TV in late 1947 when NBC hired him to create and operate puppets for a new show based in part on a children's radio program, *The Triple B Ranch.*

The host of *The Triple B Ranch* was a young man from Buffalo, Bob Smith, who did the voices for an imaginary set of rural characters he had created. Smith was adept at performing before children in the studio and in personal appearances, and his show quickly won a young following. In late 1947, NBC executives decided to add a children's TV show weekdays at 5:00 p.m., "to keep the kids occupied while Mom makes dinner,"[6] according to Stephen Davis, who wrote a history of *Howdy Dowdy.* They chose Bob Smith to host it and Frank Paris to add puppets to Smith's voices and music.

Children's programs were an important feature of network radio and were especially popular among sponsors. A research study earlier in 1947 had shown that four out of five children could name the sponsor of their favorite radio program. The study was published in *Broadcasting* under a big headline, "Child Listeners Recall Product Names," and it noted that a peak listening time for kids was from 5:00 p.m. to 6:00 p.m., the time slot NBC chose for *Puppet Playhouse.*[7]

Du Mont was already attracting children in the late afternoon with its own TV show, *Small Fry Club,* in New York on WABD and in Washington on WTTG. *Small Fry Club* was the TV version of a radio program that had been on the air since the early 1920s, hosted by "Big Brother" Bob Emery. The show promoted good behavior and healthy habits, and included short sketches performed by actors in animal costumes, but *Small Fry Club* was also a real club. Its young fans were encouraged to join, write, enter contests, and submit their artwork. By the end of 1947, TV's *Small Fry Club* had over 10,000 members and its own sponsor.

With its successful debut on the day the Northeast was snowbound, *Puppet Playhouse* became NBC's answer to Du Mont's *Small Fry Club.* The show was soon airing three times a week but with no regular sponsor. In March 1948 the show's writer, Eddie Kane, had the puppet Howdy Doody announce his candidacy for President and ask viewers to send in ideas for his platform. Those who wrote in, Howdy promised, would receive an "I'm for Howdy Doody" campaign button. NBC ordered 10,000 buttons and hoped they hadn't overstocked; instead, they received 20,000 letters in just the first three days. In a few weeks, the total was 60,000.

Immediately, NBC bought a front-cover advertisement in the trade publication *Television,* picturing Howdy and the button and proclaiming, "That means nearly one request for each set,"[8] based on a survey that showed roughly one-third of the region's sets were tuned in to the program. With those numbers, NBC quickly found sponsors for *Puppet Playhouse.* First, Colgate toothpaste signed up; then, Wonder Bread, Ovaltine, and Mars candy. Soon the show became the first in TV history to be fully sponsored two years in advance.

THE EXPANDING NETWORK

The success of *Puppet Playhouse* climaxed a period of great progress for American TV that had begun in mid-1946 with *Hour Glass* and the Louis-Conn boxing telecast, and continued in 1947 with the dramatic World Series. These programs were milestones in the history of American television.

A smaller milestone occurred on November 7, 1947, when NBC televised its *Swift Home Service Club* daytime program on the two stations it owned, WNBT in New York and WNBW in Washington, and on Philco's WPTZ in Philadelphia. NBC had been transmitting programs from New York to other stations since the 1940 Republican convention. This time, however, the Swift company was paying to sponsor the program in all three cities, which was a first for a non-sports event on TV. It hinted at the day when TV broadcasters might charge a national sponsor thousands of dollars for airing its commercials on a single program, coast to coast. As an NBC vice president predicted on the *Swift* program that day, "within two years' time we should be seeing this program in Hollywood as well as on the East Coast."[9]

In early 1948, NBC added Baltimore and its new station WBAL to the network, and by April new stations in Richmond (WTVR) and Boston (WBZ) were included as well. The United States now had its first big regional TV system, the Eastern network, transmitting to roughly 150,000 sets within a population of 20 million people. CBS, too, created a TV network in early 1948, using its own WCBS in New York and affiliated stations in Washington and Philadelphia, as did Du Mont, with its own stations in New York and Washington and an affiliated station in Philadelphia.

This system of affiliated stations was already resembling the network structure of the radio industry in America. NBC, CBS, and ABC dominated radio broadcasting in the late 1940s. They owned radio stations in America's major cities and had agreements with scores of other stations around the country—their affiliates—to air their programs and commercials. The radio networks also had many of the top names in entertainment under exclusive contracts, along with multiyear sponsorship deals with leading corporations. This system brought profits to the radio networks, some of which had been used by NBC and CBS to pay for their TV programming thus far.

There were a few weak spots in TV's network system in 1948. In Baltimore, for example, WMAR-TV was affiliated with both CBS and Du Mont and also aired programs from WMAL in Washington and WFIL in Philadelphia. The trade magazine *Television* described this situation in January 1948 as a "fluid state of network arrangements," and suggested that "general thinking . . . seems to be against definite tie-ups" with any one network. Instead, stations were "angling for the best programming they can get off the line before making any definite commitments."[10] Were this "fluid state" to remain, it might keep the TV networks from attracting national sponsors for programs that weren't being carried by all of their affiliates.

THE "ORIGINAL AMATEUR" NETWORK

Also complicating TV's economics in early 1948 was the possibility that more than just a few companies might build networks. Already, ABC was in the process of getting licenses and affiliates, while the theater company Paramount owned stations in Chicago and Los Angeles. Newspaper chains, too, could build TV networks by linking together stations they owned.

There was also the special case of Du Mont, a pioneer in the industry that now had its own network of three TV stations. Du Mont was a "deviation from the old radio guard," according to *Television*.[11] Du Mont had no radio network and no prior experience in airing popular entertainment or attracting national sponsors.

In January 1948, Du Mont began televising a show that had once been the top-rated program on radio. The *Original Amateur Hour* featured amateur and semiprofessional talent, from singers and comics to people who did birdcalls, all competing to win the studio audience's approval. Back in 1937, the radio version of the *Original Amateur Hour* had introduced a vocal group called "The Hoboken Five" to the public; their lead singer was a twenty-year old unknown named Frank Sinatra.

When the program's creator and host, Major Edward Bowes, died in the mid-1940s, the *Original Amateur Hour* dropped off the airwaves. But the show's production staff revived it on TV with Bowes' assistant, Ted Mack, as its new host. They kept its basic format and its popular "Wheel of Fortune," which was spun by Mack to determine the cash prizes paid to the winning contestants. Du Mont televised the program from its New York City studio every Sunday night at 7:00 p.m. on WABD and transmitted it live to stations in Philadelphia, Washington, DC, and Baltimore.

Later in 1948 the Du Mont network picked up more affiliates among new TV stations, sending them filmed versions of the *Original Amateur Hour* to televise later in the week. The films were made by focusing a motion picture camera on a TV screen as the program was being televised live from the studio. The result was a 16 millimeter motion picture of the live broadcast, called a "teletranscription" at first, then later a "kinescope." The kinescopes weren't as crisp and clean as the original telecasts, but they could easily be copied and shipped to other stations around the country that were not wired directly to Du Mont's network. In the long run, Du Mont's *Amateur Hour* kinescopes would change the very nature of American TV by pointing the medium away from live broadcasts and toward edited, "professional" films.

In the short run, the *Amateur Hour* telecasts shook up a few notions about the TV industry. The first was that NBC and CBS—the two powerhouses of network radio—were bound to dominate the TV airwaves as well. In March 1948, two months after Du Mont began televising the *Original Amateur Hour,* the TV industry's first official ratings were released by C. E. Hooper, Inc., the company that compiled the ratings for network radio programs. Atop the list was Du Mont's *Original Amateur Hour:* the network with no experience in radio had itself the most popular TV show in the country.

Not only was the ratings success of the *Original Amateur Hour* a coup for Du Mont, it challenged a second notion that TV's audience was skewed toward the wealthier upper classes because home sets were luxury items. The *Amateur Hour* was decidedly popular entertainment that appealed to America's middle classes. Its place atop the ratings list, as opposed to televised drama, for example, suggested that many of the Americans who'd bought TV sets since the 1947 World Series were of average income and social status.

"The majority TV audience is folks who stay home nights so they can go to work in the morning," proclaimed a new TV station in New York, WPIX, in a full-page advertisement that spring.[12] The ad cited a recent survey reporting that only 12.5 percent of new TV owners in the New York area belonged to the upper class, compared to 60 percent who were middle class. Two more surveys later that year gave the same results, and in Philadelphia as well as New York.

The TV sets being purchased by middle-class Americans in early 1948 were still expensive: RCA's lowest price model, for example, cost about $385 to own and install, but banks and department stores in 1948 were encouraging consumers to buy the new TV sets and other postwar household items on credit. According to the Federal Reserve Board, the public used credit for over half of their big-ticket purchases. Typically, a new TV owner made a down payment of about $75 and then paid $10-20 per month for another twelve to eighteen months.

The economic climate had clearly changed by early 1948. Postwar America was consumer oriented, putting the TV industry finally in the right place at the right time. In fact, in just the few months between the 1947 World Series and early 1948 the TV industry sold twice the number of sets that had been bought in the previous eight and a half years.

By the spring of 1948 the TV boom had become national news, with long articles appearing within weeks of each other in *Time, Fortune, The American Mercury,* and in a whole section devoted to TV in the Sunday, June 13 edition of *The New York Times.* Television "is upon us with a rush," wrote *Fortune*—a common theme to all the articles.[13] They predicted that TV would soon become a major American industry, a serious competitor to radio and motion pictures, and probably a basic part of American life.

"MISS TELEVISION OF 1948"

The *Time* article on the TV boom featured a photograph of a pretty young singer, Kyle MacDonnell, described as "already becoming television's No. 1 pin-up girl."[14] Kyle MacDonnell's background in show business was scant. She had left Kansas in 1946 to become a model, had a small part in a Hollywood movie, and then sang in a Broadway musical revue, *Make Mine Manhattan.* While still appearing nightly in the revue, MacDonnell became the featured performer on a fifteen-minute NBC television program, *For Your Pleasure,* that began in April 1948. Quickly, she became a favorite of TV reviewers such as Jack Gould of *The New York Times,* who called her "television's first truly new and bright star."[15] She was also on the cover of *Life* in 1948 and was named "Miss Television," the outstanding female performer on TV that year.

Kyle MacDonnell's rapid rise to the top on TV signaled in part an important change in programming in 1948. For several years, a labor dispute involving the musician's union had kept singers and musicians from performing live on TV. The dispute was settled in April 1948; instantly, TV was bursting with musical performances. Short variety programs featured relatively unknown singers—"a nice kid with a good voice," was one description in *Variety*[16]—singing current tunes and backed by a few musicians. With the addition of a little movement, a set and props, and perhaps a comedian or dancers as a break from the singing, the mixture became a basic show format on TV in 1948.

Variety described this change in programming as simply "the added fillip of watching live musicians on the set."[17] Viewers could now see and hear the actual live appearance and performance of the singers and musicians, almost as if they were all in the living room together. "In full close-up," wrote Jack Gould of the *Times* in his review of Kyle MacDonnell in May 1948, "she projects a warmth and friendliness which capitalize to the hilt on the factor of intimacy that is video at its most effective."[18]

"Call it personality," suggested Gould of the sense of "warmth" and "friendliness" that TV projected with "intimacy" from Kyle MacDonnell to her viewers in 1948.[19] That "personality" would be conveyed later by other performers; Perry Como and Dinah Shore, for example, seemed relaxed and casual on their own TV variety shows in the 1950s and 1960s. On the other hand, live musical performances on TV by Elvis Presley and the Beatles were so intense that they sent shock waves through American culture.

As for Kyle MacDonnell herself, she appeared on TV until becoming pregnant in 1951. By 1953, "Miss Television" of 1948 had retired from show business and moved to Santa Fe with the young man from back home she'd married. What about her male counterpart—"Mr. Television" of 1948? His fate was altogether different. Television made him a household name, and he in turn helped make TV a basic household fixture. "Mr. Television" of 1948 was Milton Berle, and the intersection of his career with television's boom that year was truly explosive.

"MR. TELEVISION"

When the ban on live musical performances ended in April 1948, the Texaco gasoline company decided to sponsor a big-budget variety show on TV—the first since *Hour Glass* aired on NBC in 1946. The *Texaco Star Theatre* took its name from a popular radio show and took its format from vaudeville. The program's director, Eddie Sobol, had worked in vaudeville and had also been one of NBC's first TV studio directors. Sobol refashioned one of NBC's big radio studios for Texaco's new show; it had room for three sets on stage and enough seats for a big audience.

Texaco budgeted $10,000 for the show's premiere, and Sobol used it to hire singer Pearl Bailey, comedian Al Kelly, ventriloquist Señor Wences, as well as dancers, an orchestra, and even a few circus acts. As with vaudeville, the acts were arranged to create variety and build to several high points. Holding the program together on stage was a "host" performer, as Helen Parrish had been on *Hour Glass,* and Texaco and its advertising agency hired comedian Milton Berle to preside over the first few shows.

Berle was a show business veteran who had worked in silent films with Charlie Chaplin as a child, and in vaudeville and the Ziegfield Follies in his twenties. He'd failed to become a star in radio and motion pictures in his thirties. Now in his forties, Milton Berle was the right person in the right place at the right time.

Berle had hosted variety shows before live audiences in the days when he'd played the top theaters in vaudeville. He'd learned to keep the audience laughing throughout the show by telling short jokes and by interacting comically with the other performers on the bill. When the *Texaco Star Theatre* premiered on June 8, 1948, Berle told jokes and played off his audience and fellow performers, just as he'd done in vaudeville. His facial gestures, body movements, and pratfalls were all well-rehearsed, but to the big, laughing audiences in the studio and in bars and homes along NBC's East Coast network, they seemed fresh and spontaneous.

"Register Mr. B as television's first smash!" hailed *The New York Times* after the first show,[20] while *Variety* called the program a "milestone in television" and "the greatest single hypo, from a strictly show biz standpoint, yet given the medium."[21] Despite the obvious success of Milton Berle on June 8, Texaco made no immediate commitment to keep him as host. Instead, the next week another comedian presided over the show, and the following week the *Texaco Star Theatre* was off the air, preempted by an even bigger live show: the Republican National Convention.

THE 1948 CONVENTIONS

In 1948, both political parties chose to meet in Philadelphia's Memorial Hall where they could be televised live on the East Coast network. For the first time since 1940, the public could watch the political parties choose their leaders live on TV. In 1940, however, only a few thousand Americans had access to TV sets; this time, the audience numbered in the millions.

NBC, CBS, Du Mont, and ABC had joined forces for "pool coverage" of the proceedings, with five TV cameras focused on the rostrum and others outside the hall and in the hotels that served as campaign headquarters. Seventeen TV stations on the East Coast, from Boston to Richmond, televised the Republican Convention live. The rest of America's TV audience in the Midwest and on the West Coast watched newsreel films and kinescopes flown in from Philadelphia and aired locally the following day.

All sorts of politicians, campaign managers, pollsters, and journalists were interviewed live on TV during the week; press conferences and public statements were covered live as well. With anyone from a state delegate to a national candidate liable to be seen by millions on TV, Republican officials had issued orders beforehand to "keep your clothes neat," "don't take off your shoes," according to *The New York Times,* and "take the toothpick out of your mouth."[22] Much of the party's advice was ignored: "Only a few had prepared themselves" for TV, noted the *Times,*[23] as the public saw delegates reading newspapers during major speeches. They saw candidate Tom Dewey looking in need of a shave; on the other hand, keynote speaker Dwight Green had used a sunlamp to acquire a tan for TV.

Television sets, too, were everywhere in sight, with hundreds installed in Philadelphia department stores. Sets were in the hotel rooms of the candidates and even in the press rooms and lounges used by newspaper reporters. "Newsmen from sections not yet reached by TV have been commenting constantly on the miracle before their eyes," noted *Variety*; some reporters even covered "the doings in the Convention hall from a comfortable armchair with a glass of beer in one hand and a plate of cheese and crackers (gratis) on end tables beside them."[24]

The big TV audience, reporters included, missed the backroom secret meetings in which the Republican ticket was debated and decided. The party leaders expected the Democrats to nominate President Truman, but Truman was unpopular and nobody expected him to win in November. Harry Truman was "a gone goose," declared Clare Boothe Luce, still the Republicans' best speaker, in the convention's most quoted speech. The next president would surely be a Republican, making the party's nomination a prize to be fought over by several serious contenders.

The frontrunner was the party's last nominee, Thomas Dewey; his opposition was split into three camps favoring Governors Earl Warren and Harold Stassen and Senator Robert Taft. In the backroom meetings, the political operatives couldn't agree on a single candidate to challenge Dewey. He held a big lead when the balloting began on TV on Thursday afternoon; he added to that lead on the second ballot, as the delegates supporting "favorite sons" began switching. Hot and weary, the convention recessed for dinner and more backroom meetings. When they came back still divided, Dewey's opponents announced one by one their support for him.

The third ballot was unanimous for Dewey, and at 9:00 p.m. he took the rostrum for his acceptance speech. The big TV audience saw a confident man addressing a confident party which had just picked, in the words of *Time,* "the kind of ticket that could not fail to sweep the Republican Party back into power."[25] Dewey's acceptance speech, in fact, seemed it could be the draft of an inaugural address as he took a lofty tone that failed to stir much emotion from the delegates.

With far less confidence, the Democrats met in Philadelphia a few weeks later. At least the Democrats could stage a convention better suited for TV, speculated the press, by avoiding the mistakes of the Republicans. Party leaders, wrote *Variety,* now understood "the necessity for timing the convention better."[26] As it turned out, however, the timing of the Democrats could not have been worse. The convention's lowest moments were televised live during prime viewing hours, and its climax came at 2:00 a.m., after most of the East Coast had gone to bed.

As the Republicans were, the Democrats too were split—not over their nominee, but on the issue of civil rights. The platform had a watered-down commitment to civil rights, but liberals led by a young Hubert Humphrey tried to add stronger planks calling for laws to end lynching and integrate the armed services. Humphrey spoke passionately on TV and for the first time the future Vice President received national attention. "There are those who say to you," he told the delegates, "we are rushing this issue of civil rights. I say we are a hundred and seventy-two years late."[27]

The Democrats were swayed by Humphrey, who would be their choice for President two decades later in 1968 in another split convention, torn over Vietnam. They approved the liberal platform on civil rights—the strongest thus far in American history. However, the next night, the delegates paid dearly for their new commitment, and their plans to televise Truman's nomination and acceptance speech during prime TV viewing time were ruined.

After the session's opening gavel, a leader of the Alabama delegation spoke against the civil rights plank, then said, "We bid you goodbye!"[28] With that, half of Alabama's delegates and all of Mississippi's walked out of Memorial Hall and up to the camera lenses outside. It was a classic piece of America's political history, seen on live TV, previewing twenty years of conflict between liberal and southern Democrats over civil rights.

The dissension continued to delay the proceedings that night, so that when Truman finally reached the rostrum to speak to America on TV, it was 2:00 a.m. and most sets were turned off. As if stood up for a date, Truman was dressed perfectly for TV in a crisp white linen suit with a black tie for the cameras. He'd prepared his speech on small notecards so he could look straight ahead at the TV cameras when he spoke.

Truman was also prepared to win in November, and his first words showed the confidence that perhaps he alone felt at that moment. "Senator Barkley and I will win this election and make these Republicans like it." He added, "And don't you forget that."[29] The delegates "howled," reported the *Times*,[30] and were awakened by Truman's feisty words. The rest of his speech was as belligerent as Dewey's had been lofty, with most of his barbs aimed at the Republican-controlled 80th Congress—"the worst," according to Truman.

One viewer who'd stayed up to watch Truman was the *Times'* TV critic Jack Gould. Truman looked "relaxed and supremely confident, swaying on the balls of his feet," wrote Gould, who claimed that Truman's performance "removed any doubt that television was going to place an increasing premium on personality in politics."[31] Yet as late as the speech was delivered, it's unlikely that a large TV audience saw it live.

THE COLD WAR ON TELEVISION

It's unlikely, too, that a big TV audience watched a third acceptance speech aired live from Philadelphia at 11:00 p.m. on Saturday, July 24, 1948. The candidate was Henry Wallace, the former Vice President from Roosevelt's third term who would have been President in 1948 had Roosevelt not replaced him on the ticket in 1944 with Harry Truman. Wallace had since broken with the Democrats and formed the more liberal Progressive or Third Party. He drew over 3,000 delegates to Shibe Park in Philadelphia for his nomination and acceptance speech, which was telecast live on the Eastern TV network.

Wallace warned his audience that night that the United States had turned in the wrong direction after the death of Roosevelt, toward a growing militarism. "The Department of State has been subtly annexed to the Pentagon," he claimed, "and the hand of the military has come to guide the hand of the diplomat." Instead of spending "twenty billion dollars a year for [the] Cold War," Wallace said, America could "wipe from the face of the earth tuberculosis, typhoid, malaria, and cholera" with just one-tenth of its military budget.[32]

Those who watched Henry Wallace on TV that Saturday night in July saw the makings of a postwar political movement. Wallace and his supporters were reacting to a shift in Washington in which America's enemies from the war, Germany and Japan, were being replaced by her wartime ally, the Soviet Union. The Cold War had begun, and nearly every TV appearance President Truman had made since early 1947 supported it.

In June 1947, for example, Truman was televised live at Princeton University calling on Congress to reinstate the draft. America had to show the world, claimed Truman, that it had "the will to fulfill our pledge to aid free and independent nations to maintain their freedoms. . . ."[33] Greece and Turkey were those "free and independent nations," and in another speech on TV in 1947 Truman asked Congress for military aid to their leaders as they faced communist opponents. The first time a President ever spoke on TV from the White House was an appeal also by Truman in 1947 for Americans to forego meat on Tuesdays and poultry and eggs on Thursday. It was part of the Marshall Plan, promoted on TV by Truman, to build the economies of the noncommunist nations of Western Europe.

Henry Wallace's televised speech in July 1948 might have sparked a national debate on this new Cold War, but it didn't. Instead, he and his supporters were branded by both Democrat and Republican leaders as crackpots and, even worse, Communists. His speech at Shibe Park turned out to be the high point of his candidacy—and an atypical TV broadcast that challenged America's anti-Communist policies.

CBS'S REVIVAL

CBS had closed its TV studio and dismissed its production staff in early 1947, after losing the fight over color television. The 1947 World Series telecasts and the TV boom that followed brought about another change in the company's thinking. In the summer of 1948, CBS management decided to jump aboard the TV train before it pulled out of the station without them. They reopened their New York studio and called upon Tony Miner, one of their experienced TV directors, to produce new programs. His orders were to create shows that would compete with NBC's most popular programs—first and foremost, the *Texaco Star Theatre.*

Tony Miner first concocted a Sunday night variety show, the *Toast of the Town,* hosted by a show business columnist from the *New York Daily News,* Ed Sullivan. Unlike NBC's *Texaco Star Theatre,* however, the *Toast of the Town* had no sponsor and only a small weekly budget from CBS. Miner and Sullivan found performers for the show's first telecasts in mid-1948 who worked for little money or for free; they were a mixed bag, described by *Variety* as "solid, so-so, and so-what."[34]

Nor was Ed Sullivan even remotely the performer Milton Berle was. Jack Gould of the *Times* expressed what others felt in his review of the first broadcast: "the choice of Ed Sullivan as master of ceremonies seems ill-advised."[35] Tony Miner later explained that he'd hired Sullivan because he wanted "a non-performing MC with a proven flair for spotting talent," and not another Milton Berle.[36] Sullivan indeed had a history of "spotting talent" that would please an audience, with a special knack for finding new and emerging stars. On the first *Toast of the Town,* for example, he introduced a comedy team on the rise from Atlantic City nightclubs to future stardom in movies and TV: Dean Martin and Jerry Lewis.

Those who criticized Miner's choice were proven wrong when Ed Sullivan and his variety program became a fixture on TV every Sunday night for the next twenty-three years. The "non-performing MC" repeatedly proved his flair for spotting talent by welcoming into America's homes the likes of Elvis Presley, the Beatles, and nearly every musical act, comedian, and Hollywood and Broadway star of significance from the late 1940s into the early 1970s. Renamed *The Ed Sullivan Show* in 1955, the program is now considered America's archive of twentieth-century popular entertainment.

Ed Sullivan credited his success in TV to his years as a reporter. "Because of my background," he said, "I developed an instinct and a sensitivity to public trends."[37] At times Sullivan seemed ahead of public trends, as evidenced in his hiring of African-American performers even in his earliest TV shows. In 1948, for example, he hosted Lena Horne, Ella Fitzgerald, Louis Armstrong, comedian "Pigmeat" Markham, and musician Louis Jordan, whose "jump band" style helped forge one of the great public trends of the 1950s— rock 'n' roll.

Sullivan showcased these performers in part because he believed that TV had the power to reshape the opinions of white Americans toward minorities. "Seeing and appreciating black talent" on TV in their living rooms, writes J. Fred MacDonald in *Blacks and White TV,* they "would be forced to reassess racist stereotyping and their own prejudices."[38]

THE BIG FREEZE

Ironically, at the same time Sullivan was ushering Ella Fitzgerald, Lena Horne, and others into 100,000 homes in 1948, the federal government was acting to keep the *Toast of the Town* and all other TV shows from entering millions of homes throughout the country.

Late in the summer of 1948, the FCC announced that it was "freezing" the TV industry in place as of September 30 for at least six months. The "freeze" had no immediate effect on the thirty-seven stations that were licensed and operating on September 30, and the other eighty-six stations that had licenses and construction permits could still open on schedule, but the FCC had 300 applications for new licenses. They'd all be put on hold; millions of Americans would remain without TV in their towns.

The FCC imposed its freeze to study a series of technical problems that had arisen among stations already operating. New regulations for transmitting TV signals were needed, with the unused UHF band of the spectrum once again a factor. In the long run, it was in the best interest of the public and the TV industry to resolve such matters, but the timing couldn't have been worse. Once again, an FCC red light had stopped TV's expansion, this time in the midst of a boom.

Issued on the same day that Milton Berle became the permanent host of *Texaco Star Theatre,* the FCC's freeze on TV expansion left vast regions of the country without even a single station. The freeze held down the size of TV's audience, which hurt the industry's ability to attract new sponsors and televise popular talent. There was much uncertainty, too, about the length of the freeze. The FCC may have set March 30, 1949, as the date that the freeze would be lifted, but the agency had a history of taking its time to issue new policies and regulations.

THE 1948 ELECTION

With the freeze on new licenses in place in the fall of 1948, the TV industry began consolidating the stations that were already licensed. By Election Day on November 2, AT&T had put in place a cable connecting TV stations in Cleveland, Toledo, Detroit, Chicago, Minneapolis, and St. Louis. That night, the new NBC-affiliated TV station in Cleveland, WNBK, transmitted its coverage of the Truman versus Dewey election results to the other stations on the cable, thus creating a Midwest network.

At 8:00 p.m. on Election Night, Du Mont, CBS, and ABC began covering the returns from their studios in New York and Philadelphia; NBC waited until 9:00, after its popular *Texaco Star Theatre.* Television had its biggest audience to date that night, with an estimated 10 million Americans watching the results along the East Coast network from Boston to Richmond. In the New York City area alone three out of four TV sets were tuned to the election news.

In New York City, too, members of the Secret Service were preparing to begin full protection of Tom Dewey and his family, convinced that Dewey was about to be elected President. That was the message they and the rest of the country had heard from journalists and poll-sters all summer and fall. Two CBS programs on the election, *Presidential Straws in the Wind* and *America Speaks,* for example, were televised weekly during the campaign; the country's leading poll-sters, Elmo Roper and George Gallup, told viewers of both shows that Dewey would win. They stayed with their prediction up through Election Day, even when the crowds along Truman's "whistle-stop" campaign route grew during the final weeks. The public never saw the growing crowds, however, because the campaign of 1948 was the last without on-location TV news coverage.

On Election Night, NBC and CBS televised some of the biggest names in political journalism—e.g., Drew Pearson, Walter Winchell, Elmer Davis—as they confirmed their predictions of Dewey's sure victory. Yet the TV audiences could see for themselves on NBC's electronic tally board that Truman was ahead in the early returns. These were city voters, explained the political pundits on TV; the rural areas would surely put Dewey ahead. Hours later, as three TV stations in Los Angeles began their election coverage, the tally boards showed Truman winning Iowa—clearly a rural state. The political upset of the century was unfolding before the eyes of TV's biggest audience thus far.

One American who wasn't watching was Harry Truman; he was fast asleep in his hometown of Independence, Missouri, which had no TV sets or stations. Television stayed up through the night elsewhere, and many Americans stayed up with it. As the surprising results came in, the TV networks televised political reporters from *Newsweek, Life,* New York's *Daily News,* and from radio. They interviewed Progressive Party candidate Henry Wallace, whose vote total was falling far below expectations. They switched to mobile camera units at Democratic and Republican headquarters and to Times Square and other street locations. Du Mont and CBS left the air for a few hours in the early morning of November 3, but NBC and a few ABC-affiliated stations stayed on, as more states from the Midwest and West went for Truman.

Shortly before noon on November 3, the TV networks switched to the Republican headquarters to televise the concession speech of Tom Dewey, who had spoken so confidently on TV from Philadelphia four months earlier. Dewey had now run for President and lost twice in a row. The majority of Americans had voted for a Democrat for President the previous four times, and they apparently weren't ready to change their habit—at least not to elect Tom Dewey.

During the 1948 campaign, neither Dewey nor Truman had used TV to reach the American public, nor had Henry Wallace and the other third-party candidate, "Dixiecrat" Strom Thurmond. In fact, the only national candidate who did use TV that year was Howdy Doody, who continued to run for President in a comedy sketch that ran on *Puppet Playhouse* for several months. One of the show's sponsors, Wonder Bread, put paper ballots in its loaves as a sales gimmick, and thousands of children mailed in their votes for Howdy. Rumors spread after Election Day that Howdy Doody had received thousands of actual write-in votes. If true, it's unlikely that Howdy's votes affected the outcome of the election. *Puppet Playhouse* was televised only on the East Coast, which Dewey carried anyhow. Truman won the election in the Midwest and West, which had few TV stations and no Howdy Doody.

SELLING SUGAR AND TOBACCO

Wonder Bread was among several companies using *The Howdy Doody Show* (NBC changed the name of *Puppet Playhouse* in 1949) to sell food to the parents of young children. Mason Cocoanut Bar, a new candy product, advertised once a week on *The Howdy Doody Show* and offered a toy lariat to youngsters who sent in two wrappers; the company received 60,000 wrappers in three months. Since then, of course, countless candy bars, sugar-coated cereals, and other sweets for children have been marketed successfully via TV, much to the dismay of health officials and parents' groups.

The one product marketed the most on TV in 1948 was cigarettes. Altogether, eleven cigarette brands competed for customers in 1948 by advertising on TV, often on sports programs; P. Lorillard, for example, promoted Old Gold cigarettes during Brooklyn Dodgers baseball games and in Chicago during both White Sox and Cubs games. Camels alone spent $800,000 advertising on TV; it ranked first among all TV sponsors. A survey in 1948 proved, at the very least, that the commercials promoted product recognition. Asked to identify the sponsors of TV programs, viewers most often named three cigarette brands—Camels, Lucky Strike, and Chesterfield.

In September 1948, P. Lorillard began airing a series of weekly live commercials for Old Gold cigarettes on Du Mont's *Original Amateur Hour,* and they became the most famous TV ads of the 1940s. They starred the "Dancing Pack," a female dancer with her head and torso inside an oversized Old Gold cigarette pack and her bare legs visible in white cowboy boots. The commercial was entertaining (the studio audience clapped as if it were one of the acts) and intriguing, since the rest of the dancer was never revealed. The "Dancing Pack" commercials aired in fifteen cities along the Eastern and Midwest networks.

A few months later, in January 1949, one of Old Gold's competing brands, Chesterfields, began sponsoring its own variety program on TV, *Arthur Godfrey and His Friends.* Arthur Godfrey was a popular radio performer in the late 1940s who was famous for the unusual and successful way that he plugged his sponsor's products. With raised eyebrows and a mischievous grin, he'd read the advertising copy provided for him, criticize the "jerks," as he called them, who wrote the words, then offer his own personal testimony as to the worth of the product. His approach added humor to the commercial and more name recognition for the product itself.

Arthur Godfrey also used his sponsor's products on the air—Lipton Tea, for example, and Chesterfields, which he chain-smoked throughout his TV show. Godfrey's smoking habit, similar to that of millions of other Americans in the 1940s and 1950s, was a success story for the tobacco industry and their advertising agencies. Their business was strong and healthy during the postwar years, in part because they sponsored radio and TV programs and aired commercials that featured models, singers, doctors, and celebrities such as Arthur Godfrey who were paid to smoke and to promote the cigarette habit.

In 1959 Arthur Godfrey became one of many American smokers to be stricken with lung cancer. He was among the fortunate ones who recovered from it, however, and he lived until 1983. By then, the United States Surgeon General had declared smoking to be a cause of lung cancer and other major diseases, and the broadcast industry no longer allowed radio and TV programs to air cigarette commercials.

The tobacco industry was the most important sponsor of television in 1948, but it was far from the only one. By the end of 1948, almost 1,000 companies had advertised on television—four-fifths of them in just the previous year. Other major sponsors included automobile makers, breweries, and the producers of food, drugs, and household goods. Most of them hired advertising agencies to plan and prepare commercials, at an increasingly greater cost. A one-minute filmed commercial in late 1948 might cost $2,000, which was often more than the budget of the show on which it aired.

One commercial for Rheingold Beer cost $5,000, but its use of stop-action photography was striking and influential. The ad featured dozens of beer bottles and cans in parade formation, marching military-like before grandstands filled with small human figures; above the parade was a flying keg of Rheingold fashioned into a blimp. Another striking beer commercial used a simple visual effect that was performed live on camera during baseball games. In a concept borrowed from Hollywood, the TV camera became the "actor"—in this case, a customer at a bar being offered a foaming glass of Schaefer beer. The customer himself was never seen; instead, the camera and the audience took his perspective. The beer was poured into the camera—or so it seemed—giving the viewer the sense of actually drinking it. According to the commercial's producer, "Even the blasé engineers drool when we stage this spot!"[39]

RADIO TAKES NOTICE

The greater attention and money now being paid to advertising on TV had its effect on radio. Sterling Drugs, for example, announced in early 1949 that it was transferring to TV a million dollars of its radio advertising budget for Bayer Aspirin, Phillip's Milk of Magnesia, and other Sterling products. The million dollars was only 2 percent of all the money spent by all the makers of drugs and toiletries in radio advertising, but Sterling's shift to TV was well-publicized. Soon afterward one of radio's biggest sponsors, Procter and Gamble, announced that it too was reassessing its commitments to advertise on radio. Before long, predicted one advertising executive, sponsors might "pull out of newspapers, magazines or radio" to advertise on TV instead.[40]

Adding weight to this shift was a study conducted by Du Mont and reported in *Variety* and elsewhere that compared the audiences for radio and TV. Within a year, the study predicted, radio's most popular programs would have lower ratings in New York City than the TV shows airing at the same time. By 1952, television would be pulling in 60 percent of the New York audience; radio only 12 percent. The nation's other big cities were "less than eight months behind the N.Y. area in degree of saturation of television homes."[41] *Variety* predicted that radio's highest-rated programs would soon lose enough of their audiences that their sponsors would leave them, too.

The radio industry itself was in the midst of a dramatic upheaval in late 1948 and early 1949, in part because of the previous year's TV boom. Among the radio networks, CBS had always trailed NBC in ratings and sponsorship. Suddenly CBS president William Paley lured from NBC some of its most popular radio stars by offering to purchase their programs. This corporate maneuver allowed the radio stars to declare their own salaries as capital gains, lowering their taxes dramatically. Paley captured first for CBS the stars of *Amos 'n' Andy* and comedian Jack Benny; they jumped from NBC when Paley offered them 2 million dollars each for their programs. They were soon followed to CBS by Edgar Bergen, Groucho Marx, Red Skelton, and George Burns and Gracie Allen.

With its new roster of popular performers, CBS had armed itself to compete with NBC in network TV as well as radio. Both networks hoped that their radio stars would be just as popular on television; as examples, they need only look at the success on TV of radio's *Original Amateur Hour* and Arthur Godfrey. In fact, Godfrey had two TV programs in early 1949, *Arthur Godfrey and His Friends* and *Arthur Godfrey's Talent Scouts,* and they ranked second and third in the ratings.

On the other hand, TV's biggest success thus far, easily topping Godfrey in the ratings, was a performer who'd never done well on radio—Milton Berle. His popularity on TV showed the uncertainty of predicting how radio stars would likely fare on television. "We all knew one thing that wouldn't work," recalled George Burns: "standing in front of a microphone and reading from a script. Unfortunately, that's what we were best at."[42]

Slowly and nervously, the stars of radio began to shift their careers toward television. On September 21, 1948, the night Milton Berle became the permanent host of *Texaco Star Theatre,* NBC brought to TV one of its popular radio figures, Mary Margaret McBride. The network showcased McBride in the timeslot right after Berle. She wasn't a comedian, however, but a conversationalist, and her program was all interviews and discussion. McBride never left her seat for the entire fifty-minute program, after first telling her TV viewers that she "looks better from the table up." That was "all right," noted *Variety* with sarcasm, "as long as someone moves now and then."[43]

Variety's reviewer also predicted that in the typical American home, "Pop . . . might wait 15 minutes" before switching from McBride to a sports show on another station.[44] Apparently *Variety* was right: McBride's show was canceled by NBC less than three months later. *The New York Times* called Mary Margaret McBride TV's first major "fatality" from the ranks of the radio stars; she would not be the last.[45]

Above: The televised image of David Sarnoff at the RCA Pavilion of the New York World's Fair on April 20, 1939. Below: A clear, lucite TV set on exhibit inside the Pavilion. *The David Sarnoff Library, Princeton, New Jersey.*

Visitors to the RCA Pavilion at the New York World's Fair were among the first Americans to be televised. *The Early Television Museum, Hilliard, Ohio.*

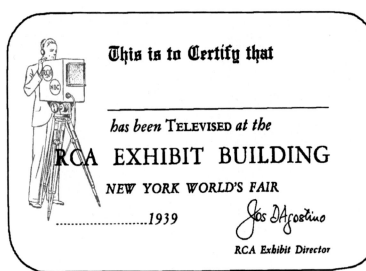

This is to Certify that

_____

has been TELEVISED *at the*

RCA EXHIBIT BUILDING

NEW YORK WORLD'S FAIR

.....................1939

Jos DAgostino

RCA Exhibit Director

You can be in two places at once with RCA Victor TELEVISION

NEWS! CARYL SMITH, FIRST TELEVISION QUEEN, CHOSEN BY HER TELEVISED PICTURES

SPORTS! WOMEN'S SWIMMING ASS'N MEET PICTURED AS EVENT TAKES PLACE

SHOWS! SPECIAL TELEVISED PRODUCTION OF "PIRATES OF PENZANCE"

Watch news events and entertainment while you sit comfortably at home before your RCA Victor Television Receiver

THE AGE-OLD WISH to be in two places at once is realized through the magic of television. You see events while they take place, and see them as well as many actual spectators.

An increasing enthusiasm has greeted RCA Television reports of special events. A baseball game, a track meet, a bicycle race, a heavyweight fight, brought growing realization of what television can do. The reception to the King and Queen proved the point still further. Now all New York knows that with an RCA Victor Television Receiver you can count on the luxury of sitting in your home and watching the important happenings of the week. And in addition, you also have available a variety of outstanding studio programs.

RCA Victor offers you a choice of three console models which combine television and radio reception in one

instrument. There is also a Television Attachment, which shows television pictures, and reproduces television sound through your radio. Your RCA Victor dealer will be glad to demonstrate these sets at your convenience.

FREE!... Interesting booklet of facts about Television. Write RCA Victor, Camden, N. J.

Listen to the "Magic Key of RCA" every Monday, 8:30 to 9:30 P. M., E. D. S. T., on NBC Blue Network

"Television certainly covers everything," says Mr. Homer B. Hand of Wycoff, N. J. "The other night we saw Gilbert & Sullivan's 'Pirates of Penzance,' and a few days later our RCA Victor Television Receiver showed us the Women's Swimming Association Meet pictures. The pictures, as we have come to expect, were clear and vivid."

Perfected by 7-Year $2,000,000 Field Test

A supreme television instrument and a glorious high fidelity radio in one, RCA Victor Television Receiver TRK-12. In addition to its magnificent reception of television and regular radio broadcasts, it can also be used with an RCA Victor Record Player to reproduce recorded music **$600***

See exhibit of all RCA services—including Television—in RCA Bldg. at New York World's Fair

In Radio and Television . . . It's RCA All the Way!

All prices f.o.b. Camden, N. J., subject to change without notice. Installation and antenna extra. You can buy RCA Victor Television Receivers on C. I. T. easy payment plan. For finer radio and television performance—RCA Victor Tubes. Trademark "RCA Victor" Reg. U. S. Pat. Off. by RCA Manufacturing Co., Inc. All RCA Victor Television Receivers provide superlative foreign and domestic radio reception also.

RCA Victor
A SERVICE OF THE RADIO CORPORATION OF AMERICA

This 1939 newspaper advertisement features RCA's TRK-12 set, in which the image is seen as a reflection in a mirror mounted on the open lid. *The David Sarnoff Library, Princeton, New Jersey.*

RCA and NBC Present

TELEVISION

November 28, 1939

TELEVISION PROGRAM SCHEDULE

(WEEK OF DECEMBER 3-9)

STATION W2XBS   (Video frequency, 45.25 mc.)   NEW YORK CITY
                 (Audio frequency, 49.75 mc.)

SUNDAY (December 3)   2:00-4:30 - Professional football: New York
                                   Giants vs. Washington Redskins, at
                                   the Polo Grounds. Bill Allen, tele-
                                   vision announcer

                       8:30-9:50 - "Broken Melody", film feature, with
                                   Merle Oberon, John Garrick, Margot
                                   Grahame and Austin Trevor

WEDNESDAY (December 6) 2:30   - film, "Wild Innocence"
                        2:55   - film, "Music In The Air"
                        3:20-3:30 - film travelogue, "Cuba"

                        8:30-9:45 - "Jane Eyre", by Helen Jerome, with
                                    Flora Campbell, Dennis Hoey, Carl
                                    Harbord and Olive Deering. Anton
                                    Bundsmann, director

THURSDAY (December 7)   2:30-3:40 - "The Quitter", film feature, with
                                    William Bakewell and Emma Dunn

                        8:30-9:30 - Wrestling at the Ridgewood Grove
                                    Athletic Club. Sam Taub, announcer

FRIDAY (December 8)   2:30   - film, "War, Peace and Propaganda
                        2:50   - film, "Throne of the Gods"
                        3:20-3:30 - film, "Night Lights of London"

                        8:30-9:30 - "Another Language", by Rose Franken,
                                    with Ben Smith, Anne Revere, Dorothy
                                    Mathews and Kendall Clark. Donald
                                    Davis, director

SATURDAY (December 9)   2:30   - Raymond Loewy on Interior Design
                        2:45   - Ernest Jones, golf instructor, dem-
                                    onstrating "Swingtest", a new prac-
                                    tice device

                        2:50   - film, "Horizons"
                        3:20-3:30 - film, "NBC Tele-Topics"
                        9:00-11:00- Boxing at the Ridgewood Grove Ath-
                                    letic Club. Sam Taub, announcer
                                    - - -

In December 1939, TV viewers in New York City could watch a few hours of shows on most days. *The Early Television Museum, Hilliard, Ohio.*

During World War II, General Electric's WRGB in Schenectady, NY, helped keep TV alive. Above: Training civil defense workers. Below: The Owens Family marionette show. *The Schenectady Museum.*

The first great American political drama to be televised live was the nomination of "dark horse" candidate Wendell Willkie at the 1940 Republican National Convention in Philadelphia. *KYW-3, Philadelphia.*

In 1946, *Hour Glass* and other live programs were televised from the WNBT studio in New York City's RCA Building. *The David Sarnoff Library, Princeton, New Jersey.*

Postwar television sets made TV affordable to the average American family. Above: a DuMont set from 1946. Below: an Emerson set from 1948. *The Early Television Museum, Hilliard, Ohio.*

Chapter 7

Conflicts in the Air

KUKLA, FRAN AND OLLIE

On the morning of January 12, 1949, NBC ran an advertisement in East Coast newspapers announcing the premiere of " 'Kukla, Fran and Ollie'—The greatest family show . . . Tonight and every night, Monday thru Friday."[1] This puppet program wasn't new to TV. *Kukla, Fran and Ollie* had been televised weekdays since October 1947 on Chicago's WBKB, where it originated, and for the past few months on NBC's Midwest network. What was new on January 12, however, was an AT&T cable connection between Cleveland and Philadelphia, via Pittsburgh, that for the first time linked together the Eastern and Midwest networks. Now, a live TV program could air simultaneously from New England to Virginia and west to the Great Lakes.

NBC's choice of a puppet show to inaugurate its new Eastern-Midwest network might seem unusual, but *Kukla, Fran and Ollie* was an unusual puppet show. The "Kukla" in the title was an innocent boy puppet with a big red nose, white gloves, and a round, mostly bald head. "Ollie" was a puppet dragon with a single, striking front tooth—an extrovert, who loved to sing the pep songs of his alma mater, Dragon Prep. Both were creations of puppeteer and genius Burr Tillstrom, who by himself operated and did the voices of Kukla, Ollie, Fletcher Rabbit, Madame Oglepuss, Buelah Witch, and the other members of his "Kuklapolitan Players."

Fran was Fran Allison, a Chicago actress and singer who played a rural character, "Aunt Fanny," on Don McNeil's popular network radio show, *The Breakfast Club.* She began working with Tillstrom and his puppets in 1946 on *Junior Jamboree,* a children's show on local Chicago TV. When the Midwest TV network began in late 1948, Tillstrom's puppet program, now titled *Kukla, Fran and Ollie,* became popular with children and adults throughout the region. And when the Midwest and Eastern networks linked up in January 1949, its loyal following quickly blossomed.

For a half hour live every weeknight, Tillstrom, his puppets, Allison, and composer Jack Fascinato created a charming fantasy world that was childlike yet adult, gentle yet satirical. Surprisingly, *Kukla, Fran and Ollie* was always improvised live on the air, from a story outlined earlier in the day. "They asked me if I wanted a writer," Tillstrom once said. "I'd always adlibbed, and the only thing I could think of, quite frankly, was how could I turn the pages of a script with both my hands busy?"[2]

Among the show's prominent new fans was *Times* TV critic Jack Gould. He liked *Kukla* from the start, describing it in January 1949 as "really imaginative and whimsically humorous."[3] By March 1949, Gould was claiming that "without any question whatsoever it is the most charming and heart-warming excursion into pure make-believe that is to be found in television today."[4]

Jack Gould was far less pleased with another puppet program, *Lucky Pup,* that began airing weekdays on the CBS network in September 1948. He complained in print that *Lucky Pup* focused on the "evil ways" of one of its puppets, Foodini, and "his plotting and his trickiness" as he tried to steal the fortune inherited by the show's hero, Lucky Pup. Gould explained that TV, unlike radio, attracted "tots of 3, 4, and 5," and that "certainly it is very dangerous practice to put on programs which can scare them seriously."[5]

Gould's attack on *Lucky Pup* roused a flurry of letters to the *Times* in the first public debate over children's TV programming. One parent suggested that Gould focus instead on "the old, cheap, stupid cartoons which are used on so many children's programs," while another agreed with Gould and suggested, "I think 'Kukla, Fran and Ollie' follows a wiser course."[6]

THE CULTURAL BACKLASH BEGINS

Jack Gould's criticism of *Lucky Pup* appeared in a longer piece he wrote, headlined "Video Standards: Recent Lapses in Taste and Judgement Underscore Need for Watchfulness," for the Sunday, January 30, 1949, *Times.* Television's boom in 1948 and the publicity that resulted had stirred up a backlash of opposition; Gould's piece was just one of a series of public attacks on TV in January 1949.

On January 2, a spokesman for a book publishers' group described television as a "devastating competitor" to reading and culture. J. Raymond Tiffany, the general counsel of the Book Manufacturers Institute, cited surveys that showed families with TV sets were reading less. "Unfortunately," Tiffany said, "the majority of our people are mentally lazy" and chose to watch TV because it required the least effort among leisure activities. He argued that TV was no substitute for reading: "You can't fondle a TV set as you can a good book." He called upon the "best brains" of the publishing and broadcast industries to work together so that TV could "be turned to good advantage to promote the cause of books and culture."[7]

A few weeks later, a Syracuse University dean claimed that TV was turning the United States into a "sit-down nation." He told a conference of 1,200 physical education teachers, "You want people to do things, but they just want to sit and watch a television screen." The result was "less and less exercise" among Americans.[8] His speech echoed a letter printed earlier in January in *The New York Times* from a father who regretted bringing a TV set into his home. "We are becoming a myopic family of sitters, of do-nothings, of silent beings," he wrote, who watch TV all night and are "left with a disturbing sense of lack of accomplishment."[9]

Probably the most respected voice to criticize TV in January 1949 was also one of the harshest. Dr. Reinhold Neihbuhr, a leading theologian, warned Americans in a magazine article that "much of what is still wholesome in our life will perish under the impact of this new visual aid before it will become a servant of true culture." Neihbuhr claimed that TV was already having an "immediate effect" on American society: the "further vulgarization of our culture."[10]

CENSORING TV'S CONTENTS

Vulgarization was the subject, too, of Jack Gould's column on TV in the Sunday, January 30th, *New York Times*. He cited a series of "lapses of taste" he'd recently seen on TV, such as Arthur Godfrey holding "a toy toilet before the cameras" as he made "a series of ad libs which were, to use the mildest possible word, embarrassing." Among other "suggestive or unpleasant" moments on TV for Gould were the "series of gestures" made by a musician to a female singer and "more than isolated use" of sexually suggestive jokes.[11]

These incidents recalled Eddie Cantor's performance on TV in 1944 which was censored on the air by NBC. Cantor had been a risqué stage performer, and his appearance on TV in 1944 brought his act visually into American homes for the first time. Gould, in fact, traced some of the vulgarisms on TV to those Broadway and nightclub performers "who are now working before the family audience for the first time. No matter how hard it may be," Gould wrote, they will have to revise both their material and their actions accordingly." He concluded, "It is the final responsibility of the broadcasters to see that they do."[12]

Jack Gould was legally correct in noting that the responsibility for TV's content belonged to the broadcasters. The FCC had no power to censor telecasts in advance, nor did other government officials. So ruled a U.S. District Court in 1949, when the state of Pennsylvania attempted to censor films that were being televised in Philadelphia and Pittsburgh. The case was brought before the district court by Pennsylvania's movie theater owners, who were banned from showing objectionable films by the state board of censors. The theater owners claimed it unfair that they were subject to censorship while TV stations weren't. When the board of censors tried to impose the same system on TV programming, the station owners objected and the district court ruled in their favor. Under then-current FCC guidelines, said the court, only the TV industry itself could censor TV broadcasts.

It appeared in 1949 that TV broadcasters were indeed censoring some of their programs. For example, when the song lyrics to a current Broadway musical, Cole Porter's *Kiss Me, Kate,* seemed too suggestive for a family audience, the words were changed before being performed on a TV variety show. When actresses or singers wore dresses on TV with the low necklines that were part of 1949's "new look" in fashion, costume designers added lace or other material to make them less revealing.

Not only were TV network executives concerned in 1949 about offending the public, they learned that what was acceptable to an East Coast audience might be disturbing elsewhere. When an actor drank a cocktail on TV in 1949, for example, viewers from the Midwest wrote to complain; similar scenes had been televised before in the

East without complaints. Television had recently come to a number of smaller cities and towns in the Midwest, although its growth was now restricted by the FCC's freeze on new licenses. The more people watching TV, the more likely it was that somebody, somewhere, would be upset by something appearing on the living-room TV screen. Thus, the network executive in midtown Manhattan worried about whether a costume or joke might offend the Sunday school teacher in St. Louis.

But network executives worried even more about ratings, sponsors, and money. By 1949, television had become a business striving to gather big audiences to watch programs and commercials. TV networks and stations were competing for viewers because more viewers brought in more sponsors and higher revenues. This "bottom line" of the industry was often important enough to outweigh the concerns about offending some of TV's viewers.

In early 1949, for example, NBC dropped its own ban on broadcasting crime, mystery, and suspense programs before 9:30 p.m. The ban had been in effect on both network radio and TV since 1947, after parents, educators, and social service officials complained that such shows were adding to a rise in juvenile delinquency. "Just as thoughtful parents refrain from putting mystery novels on their children's bookshelves," NBC stated in 1947, "so they are able on NBC to regulate their children's listening in this respect."[13]

Imposing the ban, however, forced NBC to reject "several advertisers who wished to place crime shows on the air in the prohibited hours," reported *Broadcasting*.[14] When other networks aired these programs in the early evening, NBC and its affiliated stations found their ratings headed down and some potential sponsors heading elsewhere. NBC's ratings declined even more after the raid by CBS on its most popular radio stars, and one of NBC's solutions was to lift its self-imposed ban and return to televising crime and suspense shows before children's bedtimes.

THE "GOLDEN HOPE" AND THE GOLDBERGS

When NBC responded in 1947 to public concern about juvenile delinquency, the results were lower ratings and fewer sponsors. The company then chose to disregard the public concern, deciding that it simply wasn't worth the loss in revenue. That any TV executive would likely do the same was the lament in early 1949 of Gilbert Seldes, who'd been director of television for CBS from 1939 to 1945. Writing in *Atlantic,* Seldes warned that television "will be used as a weapon in the war between rival networks."[15]

At the same time, Seldes held out what he called a "golden hope" for the medium. Television had the special ability, he wrote, to appeal "simultaneously to various levels of interest, to people in all their complex groupings, to the many minorities. It does not have to appeal exclusively to the mass." If TV focused on developing good, diverse programs rather than gathering big audiences for its sponsors, Geldes hoped, it could "create a total program schedule that will be at the same time popular and democratic."[16]

As the article by Geldes went to press, a program that fulfilled his "golden hope" began a five-year run on network TV. The program was *The Goldbergs,* and it was TV's first weekly series about an American family—in this case, a family of Jewish Americans. *The Goldbergs* was the creation of Gertrude Berg, an actress and writer who had begun the series on radio in 1929. Berg was college educated and wealthy, but she imbued the character she played, Molly, and the rest of the Goldbergs with the words, accents, humor, and values of first- and second-generation ethnics struggling to succeed in America.

The Goldbergs was heard for fifteen years on radio, on a daily basis for a time. However, as Berg herself said, "I always felt that the Goldbergs were a family that needed to be seen,"[17] and so she staged a theater version of the show as well as a single airing on prewar TV. In early 1949, *The Goldbergs* became a weekly TV series, showing Americans a working-class Jewish family who lived in a small apartment in the Bronx. The show's scripts were warm and humorous—and often sensitive to social issues. In one 1949 episode, for example, the tenants in the Goldbergs' building united against poor housing conditions by staging a rent strike. Another episode in 1949 had the Goldbergs celebrating Passover with a seder, the traditional Jewish dinner.

The seder episode bothered the TV critic for *Variety,* and another episode that focused on anti-Semitism upset the reviewer for *Television.* In this case, the Goldbergs were snubbed and scorned while visiting an upper-class Park Avenue apartment—which "made for uneasy viewing for the TV audience."[18] The Goldbergs belonged "in their own element in the Bronx," wrote the reviewer, where "the TV audience gets the benefit of a warm and fascinating segment of American life. Certainly there could be no objection here." When contrasted with "another pattern" of Americans, the reviewer explained, "the results can be confusing, and a hindrance to the cause of better understanding."[19]

This unease among some TV critics over *The Goldbergs* was ironic, considering the pivotal roles played by Jewish Americans in the growth of television. One of TV's inventors, Vladimir Zworykin, was Jewish, and so was his boss, David Sarnoff, and the chief rival of his boss, CBS's William Paley. "Mr. Television"—Milton Berle— was Jewish, as were many of the medium's performers and writers. American culture itself, however, was uneasy about Jewish and other subcultures in its midst, and TV in general steered clear of any controversy by rarely portraying them.

Gertrude Berg was clearly the exception here, and the success of her program gave some substance to Gilbert Seldes' "golden hope" that TV could become "popular and democratic." Yet of the hundreds of TV series featuring American families that followed *The Goldbergs,* only a handful ever dealt with the problems of a specific ethnic group. As for Gilbert Seldes, he never returned to the production side of the TV industry. As his daughter later explained, "When television became this money-making machine, it lost people like my father."[20]

THE ADMIRAL BROADWAY REVUE

The same month that *The Goldbergs* premiered on TV, January 1949, another Jewish American brought to TV a show with roots in his subculture. He was Max Liebman, an immigrant from Austria, and his show, the *Admiral Broadway Revue,* came to TV via the Borscht Belt—the resort hotels in the Pocono and Catskill Mountains where families of American Jews from the cities and suburbs vacationed each summer. The Borscht Belt hotels had entertainment—singers, dancers, comedians, and novelty acts—and during the 1930s Max Liebman assembled and directed a Broadway-style variety show at the Tamiment resort every weekend.

"For all that period before television," Liebman later recalled, "I was really preparing myself for that medium at Tamiment. I was doing what you might call television without cameras. Our big show was Saturday night—one performance before a very tough audience."[21] He left the Tamiment in 1940 for New York City and then Hollywood, but he returned in the summer of 1948 to develop a show to bring to television. He believed that the current TV variety shows, like the *Texaco Star Theatre*, needed "an element of sophistication" found in Broadway revues: better sets and lighting, and more satire and artistic production numbers.

Liebman found a sponsor, Admiral Television, willing to commit $15,000 a week for a variety program called *Friday Night Frolics*, and he had two networks, NBC and Du Mont, anxious to air the show both live and on kinescope throughout the country. On January 28, 1949, Liebman's TV show premiered from a newly renovated theater in Manhattan. It was now called *Admiral Broadway Revue*, and it combined some of the best features of TV programs thus far: a variety of fresh and appealing talent, attractive sets and costumes, good comedy writing, plus a studio orchestra and a small dance troupe. Liebman hired and kept the same talent from the first show together, from cast to crew, through the run of the series, which was unique among TV variety series thus far.

From January to June 1949, Liebman and his staff and performers televised a live hour every week of comedy, music, and dance, loosely tied to a changing theme such as "Hollywood" or "County Fair." The *Admiral Broadway Revue* had both high ratings and good reviews. Wrote John Crosby in the *New York Herald Tribune*, "For an hour's entertainment, I can't think of anything better in New York's expensive nightclubs. Come to think of it, there isn't anything much better on Broadway, either."[22] Unfortunately, Admiral dropped the *Broadway Revue* after its commitment for nineteen weeks ran out, claiming that the program had increased sales orders for new TV sets beyond the company's ability to make them. According to Max Liebman, "They paid us off and now we were afloat."[23] Several of the show's performers quickly found work elsewhere on TV; actor Judson Laire, for example, was signed within a month to play the father in a new series about another family of ethnics, the Norwegian-American *Mama*.

Liebman and the rest of his team and cast later regrouped to face a bigger challenge: producing a ninety-minute TV show every Saturday night. With this new show, Max Liebman and his writers would be acclaimed as the best in the business. Two of the young and largely unknown performers from the *Admiral Broadway Revue,* Sid Caesar and Imogene Coca, would also become major TV stars.

THE BERLE PHENOMENON

In the meantime, however, the biggest attraction on TV in 1949 was the show that Liebman had hoped to improve upon: the *Texaco Star Theater,* now by far the highest-rated show on either TV or radio. Milton Berle was now a national celebrity. In fact, on May 16, 1949, Berle performed a rare feat for an entertainer by appearing simultaneously on the covers of both *Time* and *Newsweek,* in a vaudeville costume with dozens of eyes watching him on the *Time* cover and dressed as the Brazilian singer Carmen Miranda for *Newsweek.*

Inside, both magazines reported the "strange new phenomenon," as *Time* put it, taking place in the East and Midwest on Tuesday nights. "Business falls off in many a nightclub, theater-ticket sales are light, neighborhood movie audiences thin. Some late-hour shopkeepers post signs and close up for the night."[24] In other words, when Milton Berle was on the air in 1949, most people with access to TV sets stopped what they were doing to watch him. Enough TV sets had been sold by 1949 for this "phenomenon" to affect life in America.

Why had Berle become so popular so quickly? One explanation was negative: America watched Berle because so far nobody better was on TV. Tony Miner of CBS claimed that Berle was only a "third-rate talent" who borrowed liberally the routines and jokes of other comedians.[25] Show business veteran Ed Wynn told *Time* that Berle had stolen his "life's work"—in particular, Wynn's "whole format of introducing all the acts and playing a buffoon in each of them."[26] Ed Wynn had his chance later in 1949 to challenge the *Texaco Star Theater* with his own TV variety show, however, and his ratings were nowhere near what Berle's were.

The truth is that Berle and the *Texaco Star Theater* had a level of professionalism unusual for TV in 1949. For example, Berle typically made five costume changes per show. But this was live TV, after all, where every second counted, so each costume was carefully planned to be easy to take on and off. Each week his viewers could expect Berle to wear his funniest costume—a wedding dress, for example, or a loincloth—when he first walked out from backstage after being introduced.

The entrance and costume changes were part of the constant air of excitement and spontaneity on *Texaco Star Theater* in 1949, which was actually planned and practiced by Berle and his team all week. At 9:00 a.m. on the day after his Tuesday night telecast, Berle and the staff would begin working on the following week's show, staying focused on it through the week and weekend until airtime.

Berle himself was a hardworking perfectionist, devoted to making his show successful. His total involvement was infamous, and he was often portrayed as tyrannical. As *Time* noted, "He calls the camera shots, directs the acts, plans the continuity, bosses the booking, writing, lighting and costumes, dictates the musical arrangements (and frequently hands them out to the musicians), approves the scenery (and sometimes helps shift it) and, in rehearsal, often leads the band over the head of its conductor."[27]

Yet because he knew what he was doing—and worked himself and his staff hard at getting it done—Milton Berle and the *Texaco Star Theatre* remained enormously popular on TV throughout 1949 and into the early 1950s. In fact, Berle became known as the person most responsible for popularizing TV in America, although that's hard to prove. In reality, sales of TV sets boomed following the 1947 World Series, well before Berle's show premiered; the sales boom probably would have continued without him.

On the other hand, the appeal of Milton Berle and his *Texaco Star Theatre* made Americans watch TV in 1949—at home, in a bar, at their neighbor's—and then the following day talk about what they had seen. "Did you see what he was wearing when he came out?" they would ask each other. With Berle, television became a shared cultural experience, and many Americans may have bought their first TV set to participate in it directly. By June 1949, an estimated 2,150,000 Americans owned TV sets—even the Goldbergs bought one on their show—and the TV industry was now one of the great success stories of the postwar period.

A MIDSEASON SLUMP

The spring and summer of 1949, however, brought an unexpected downturn in sales of TV sets, and the whole industry went into a slump. Prices of sets fell dramatically as many manufacturers and distributors tried to cut back on their inventories. Employees were laid off throughout the industry—not just in factories but among stations and studios as well. The TV industry may have simply been hit by an economic "shakedown," in which it shed the excess labor and facilities acquired during its two-year boom. Others were claiming in mid-1949 that the American public had lost some of its fascination with TV. In fact, one survey showed that families who'd owned TV sets for more than a year were cutting back on their viewing hours.

Another possible cause of the sales slump was the warnings again being issued about buying the current models of TV sets. In March 1949, Zenith charged in newspaper advertisements that the FCC was about to make current sets obsolete by issuing licenses for ultra-high frequency (UHF) stations. Only Zenith made TV sets that could receive both types of signals, the ads claimed, while its competitors were marketing VHF-only sets that would soon be outdated. Two weeks later, the other manufacturers filed a million-dollar lawsuit against Zenith for discouraging potential buyers with misleading public statements.

The FCC soon entered the dispute, calling it a "tempest in a teapot" and assuring the public that the VHF channels would remain in use.[28] The next month, however, the FCC was much less assuring when it announced plans to issue new rules for TV channels. In July 1949 the new rules were issued, and they called for forty-two new TV channels—all in the upper frequencies, beyond the range of sets made thus far. Apparently, Zenith was right after all. Despite assuring the public that current TV sets could still be used, the FCC was now promoting new UHF channels; the agency claimed that the new channels would add another 1,700 stations throughout the country. As to ending its freeze on building any new stations, either VHF or UHF, the FCC scheduled another round of hearings to help make a decision.

In the meantime, the TV industry began its eleventh year of broadcasting with most of its top-rated shows taking the summer months off. In later years, the networks would fill these summer nights with reruns of shows aired earlier in the year. In 1949, though, most TV shows were broadcast live, with no attempt to record them on film; thus, no summer reruns were possible. Unlike 1948, there were no political conventions to televise in the summer. Instead, the networks and local stations introduced new TV programs, fully expecting their audiences to dwindle anyhow, as the hot weather pushed people outdoors at night.

WRESTLING AND ROLLER DERBY

Many Americans who did watch TV in the summer of 1949 tuned to professional wrestling. Televised matches from New York City, Chicago, and Los Angeles had boosted wrestling's popularity and made national celebrities out of "Gorgeous George" and other wrestlers, including females and "midgets." *Television* reported in 1949 that in Los Angeles "wrestling rates three-to-five times higher than boxing or baseball."[29] In Washington, DC, WMAL's wrestling show was the most popular sports program on TV.[30]

Business Week wrote that a wrestling match on a local New York station had higher ratings than a "big boxing match" on network TV from Madison Square Garden. After all, explained *Business Week,* a boxing bout can end in a few minutes or endure for fifteen dull rounds. But with wrestling, "you're always sure of a good show which will almost always go on for the specified period of time: the winning fall seldom comes too early."[31]

Wrestling was reliable entertainment on TV in part because the matches were staged, and the wrestlers had by 1949 learned to play to the viewers at home. "The men cooperate willingly," admitted Du Mont's wrestling announcer, Dennis James. "They put on their most spectacular holds where the camera can best pick them up." Thanks to their exposure on TV, Dennis explained, the wrestlers "never had it so good. When they walk into a bar these days, people say, 'There's So-and-So. See him get thrown out of the ring last night?' "[32]

Dennis James and other TV announcers made wrestling more entertaining for the home viewers through their enthusiasm and the sound effects they added to fit the action. James, for example, would slap down a rubber dog bone when a wrestler's body thumped on the canvas. Add to this the mythical appearance of the wrestlers, acting in the roles of "good" and "evil" strongmen, and the result was very popular TV programming that cut across boundaries of class and culture. Even the country's most distinguished orchestra conductor, Arturo Toscanini, was reported to be a wrestling fan who entertained his guests with it on TV after dinner.

A second sport made popular by television at that time was the Roller Derby. Two competing teams—each comprised of five men and five women—together roller-skated around and around an indoor track, scoring points when they gained a lap on their competitors. Men raced against men, women against women, each for four fifteen-minute periods.

Roller Derby was as much a creation of modern American culture as wrestling was of ancient times. Roller Derby was invented in the 1930s by Leo Seltzer, who had already made dance marathons a national craze during the Great Depression. Similar to dance marathons, the Roller Derby was a bizarre test of pain and endurance that featured both men and women. Though skating skill and agility were important in the Roller Derby, so were aggression and roughness. According to *Business Week,* "It looks more like a gangfight than a sport."[33]

As with wrestling, however, many of the physical confrontations in the contest—the body blocks, hair pulls, fistfights, etc.—happened conveniently on camera. As with wrestling, too, television brought recognition to some of the Roller Derby skaters, such as Midge Brashun of Brooklyn, known as "Toughie." The appeal of television, however, wasn't enough to create a national Roller Derby league; instead, just a few teams actually existed, and they had to wear shirts from different cities on different nights.

Jack Gould of the *Times* wrote in 1949 that Roller Derby "represents television at its most narcotic," and that its "disruptive effect on the household is virtually absolute. . . ." Because "the action is almost continuous," he wrote, it made for better television than most other sports.[34] It's true that in later years, long after the Roller Derby passed from the American scene, sports filled with continuous action, such as basketball and football, became popular on television. As for wrestling, its popularity on TV lasted through the early 1950s and then died off, only to be revived again in the 1980s by the World Wrestling Federation and other groups of TV wrestlers and enthusiastic announcers.

THE 1949 WORLD SERIES

In 1949, the popularity of the slow-paced game of baseball in America could not be contested; it alone was the national pastime. Although the 1949 World Series didn't spark a TV sales boom as the 1947 Series had done—the boom was already taking place in 1949—baseball's "Fall Classic" that year did mark yet another TV milestone. For the first time, every city with a Major League team had live telecasts of all the World Series games. The cities were linked on the Eastern and Midwest networks, reaching an audience of over 10 million people. As judged by Red Barber, who broadcast both the 1947 and 1949 World Series on radio, television for the first time had as great a pull on baseball fans as radio did.[35]

The right to sponsor the 1949 World Series on TV belonged to the Gillette Razor Company. Baseball's owners charged Gillette three times the price paid in 1947 for the World Series, but hoped to reach ten times the number of homes. In addition, movie theaters in Brooklyn, Boston, Chicago, Milwaukee, and Scranton (PA) bought the rights to broadcast the games live on large screens. Thousands of Americans watched the games this way, paying between one and two dollars for their theater seats. In New York City, hotel rooms with TV sets were in great demand and served as the sites of many afternoon World Series parties, and, just as in 1947, local bars became the ideal spots to watch the games. "In New York," reported the *Times,* "it was a poor bar that did not have video, and every one was crowded."[36]

The best game of the 1949 Series turned out to be the first, played on October 5, a weekday afternoon. Allie Reynolds pitched for the Yankees against Don Newcombe. Neither pitcher had given up a run through the bottom of the ninth inning, when Tommy Heinrich stepped to the plate to face Newcombe. Heinrich was called "Old Reliable" because of his knack for hitting in clutch situations and driving in the winning run late in the game.

As millions watched on TV—"businessmen taking a late lunch," described the *Times,* "restaurant workers in aprons, 'greasy monkeys' from filling stations, delivery boys in zipper jackets"[37]—Heinrich hit Newcombe's third pitch into the right field stands and the game was suddenly over. Don Newcombe had already walked off the field by the time Heinrich crossed home plate; Newcombe had just lost what he later called the best game he had ever pitched. In the bars, wrote the *Times,* "the beer nursers shouted once and fled to the street as though an alarm had sounded."[38]

An alarm *had* sounded with Tommy Heinrich's home run, although nobody that afternoon knew it. The Dodgers won the next day, but the Yankees won the third game and the fourth and fifth, to win the final World Series of the 1940s. The Yankees would continue to win, five World Championships in a row, then four more pennants and two more Championships before the 1950s ended.

For baseball, the 1950s belonged to the New York Yankees. Powered by money and led by big hitters, they dominated their world and were worshiped by many, and feared and hated by others. They symbolized America in the 1950s, as the nation, too, was wealthy, strong, and dominant, as well as worshiped, feared, and hated. Reflecting the larger culture they epitomized, the Yankees also balked at integration. They waited until 1955 to put their first African-American player in the lineup, then another four years before adding a second.

An alarm had sounded, too, with the first game of the 1949 World Series, that the new decade beginning in three months would belong as well to television. From that game on, TV audiences would peak in the tens of millions; television's competitors—radio and movies, newspapers and books—mighty as they may have been, would lose to TV in the contest to capture the American public. Television in the 1950s would be rich and strong and the winners, too, of their world—the mass media.

THE CHICAGO SCHOOL OF TELEVISION

By late 1949, entertainment writer Harriet Van Horne had cited *Kukla, Fran and Ollie* as the "best example" of TV programs that "fitted snugly to the medium," that were "meant for small groups, gathered in a warm circle a few feet from the 'stage.' They are intimate. They belong in the home, never in a theater. They are pure video."[39]

This intimate style of TV soon had a name, the "Chicago School of Television," picked up by critics and industry people. The creator of *Kukla,* Burr Tillstrom, explained, "We made up television. There was no influence to teach us, we weren't conforming to anything." Rather than adopt other media to television, Tillstrom said, the Chicago stations produced "live television and live-type television [which] comes out through the screen and reaches the audience. I believe television should be an intimate thing—you're not playing to a lot of people, you're playing to *one—ones*—in different places everywhere."[40]

Presiding over the Chicago School at WNBQ was Jules Herbuveaux, who was the station's general manager and the network's Midwest director. Herbuveaux was a veteran of the music and radio industries, and he'd assembled a small team of young, fresh, and talented writers, producers, and performers, and encouraged them to explore new approaches.

Jules Herbuveaux was also a lobbyist for Chicago programs within the corporate walls of NBC in New York. In early 1949, he was handed the 10:00 p.m. network slot on Saturday night, which was considered a low-audience time period. Working with a small budget and a tiny studio, his Chicago team created an innovative variety program, *Garroway at Large,* hosted by a Chicago disk jockey and former journalist in his mid-thirties, Dave Garroway.

With no real background in show business nor any talent for performing, Garroway was at first glance an unlikely host for a variety show. "The fact is Dave didn't know *what* he had," explained a writer who worked with him later on TV. "He had a quality. You could see him happening on the air, and he was happening all the time—he was fascinating to watch."[41]

Garroway functioned on the show as both host and stage manager, and that dual role came about from the unusual way the program was staged. Ted Mills, the producer of *Garroway at Large,* claimed that his idea for staging came from Chinese opera, in which performers "dispense with scenery, and frankly avow that they are play-acting by employing a property man who supplies all the necessary furniture in full sight of the public."[42] In *Garroway at Large,* Dave Garroway was the property man, and he casually walked around the set, amidst the cables, lights, and cameras, introducing each singer, dancer, and comic. He also helped move sets and scenery, working on camera with the stagehands.

Garroway at Large also looked different from other TV shows. One night, for example, the program moved up onto the roof to transmit the lights of the Chicago skyline. The program also featured special effects developed by WNBQ's technical staff, including such optical illusions as a pail of water that floated and spun in space. Two of the set builders had worked previously with magicians, and, according to producer Ted Mills, "Everybody pitched in to work up creative ideas. The crew, the cameramen—whenever somebody suggested an idea, we'd try it."[43]

As with *Kukla, Fran and Ollie,* both the public and the critics liked *Garroway at Large.* Wrote *The New York Times* in 1950, "There's no better school in television techniques than Mr. Garroway's program."[44] Yet in 1951, after three successful seasons, *Garroway at Large* was canceled by NBC. Apparently the program's sponsor had been bumped off its timeslot (now Sundays at 10:00 p.m.) by the network because a bigger sponsor, Procter and Gamble, wanted it. NBC then tried to shift *Garroway at Large* to Wednesday night, but not enough NBC-affiliated stations agreed to carry it, according to *Time,* "because most of them wanted to put on boxing matches at that hour."[45]

The same article quoted a worried Burr Tillstrom: "If it can happen to Garroway, it can happen to any of us."[46] In fact, *Time* noted that AT&T would soon be operating a coast-to-coast TV relay system; they predicted that soon "Hollywood will move up to rank with Manhattan as a producing center, and the Chicago school will be in for a long, hungry recess."[47] As it turned out, Tillstrom was absolutely right, but *Time* was a bit off in its prediction. Coast-to-coast TV wouldn't mean a "recess" for the Chicago school; it would lead to its dismissal.

CAVALCADE OF STARS

As noted, Saturday night was the nation's traditional "date night," when Americans went out for their entertainment rather than staying home. It was a night for movie-going, for listening and dancing to music, and for socializing; that's why NBC was willing to give the 10:00 p.m. timeslot in early 1949 to Jules Herbuveaux in Chicago. In these postwar years, however, Americans were getting married and having babies in record numbers. Now, more Americans were settling down into homes and families—and staying put on Saturday nights. Watching television in the living room, with free entertainment on its screen, was becoming a popular way to spend "date night."

In June 1949, Du Mont began televising a variety show, *Cavalcade of Stars,* on Saturday nights at 9:00 p.m., hosted by Borscht Belt comedian Jack Carter. *Cavalcade* was a modest success, appearing at times among TV's top-rated shows. More important, *Cavalcade* proved that an audience for TV on Saturday nights did indeed exist. *Cavalcade* had also attracted a sponsor to Du Mont: a chain of drugstores.

In October 1949, the NBC network lured away from Du Mont its highest rated program, the *Original Amateur Hour,* and its sponsor, P. Lorillard's Old Gold cigarettes. Then, in early 1950, NBC again tried to take another one of Du Mont's prized possessions—the Saturday night audience watching *Cavalcade of Stars.* NBC announced it was planning to televise over two hours of variety shows on Saturday nights, competing directly with *Cavalcade of Stars.* Moreover, NBC planned to use the Midwest cable to transmit its Saturday night shows from the East Coast to stations as far west as St. Louis, but in 1950 only one TV program at a time could be relayed each way on the cable. NBC's plans would tie up the cable until 10:30 p.m. and thus prevent Du Mont from televising *Cavalcade* west of Pittsburgh, where the Eastern cable ended.

Du Mont quickly petitioned the FCC to block NBC's plan for Saturday night. The plan was "monopolistic," Du Mont said, echoing the warnings from 1940 when RCA, NBC's parent company, launched TV's first big sales push in New York City. Now, in 1950, Du Mont warned the FCC that, with only one cable link to the Midwest, NBC or any network that could "spend the most money would buy the [cable] time over most of the program period during the week and then be in a position to bargain with the sponsors."[48] This system had the makings of a monopoly.

The FCC's answer was a compromise. NBC could use the cable all night on Saturday, but the network had to televise the first hour west to east from Chicago. Du Mont could thus continue transmitting *Cavalcade* on Saturday nights east to west, from New York to its Eastern and Midwest viewers. NBC was unable to compete against Du Mont's *Cavalcade of Stars* by transmitting a variety program from New York, but the network did the next best thing. It offered the host of *Cavalcade of Stars,* Jack Carter, enough money to lure him away from Du Mont to host *The Jack Carter Show* from Chicago, which NBC was televising opposite *Cavalcade.*

Du Mont hired comedian Jerry Lester to replace Jack Carter as host. Midway through 1950, Du Mont quit competing with NBC on Saturday nights and instead switched *Cavalcade of Stars* to Friday. By then Jerry Lester, too, was gone as host, and Du Mont tried out a series of replacements. The network finally succeeded with *Cavalcade of Stars* after finding a more talented host, the young Jackie Gleason, but he too was lured away from Du Mont in 1952 by a bigger contract offer from CBS.

HOPALONG CASSIDY

The fight among networks over Saturday night and *Cavalcade of Stars* showed how competitive TV had become by the end of the 1940s. The success of the *Texaco Star Theater,* in particular, spurred the industry to create similar variety shows, with comedy, music, costumes, skits, sets, and scenery.

On the other hand, the highest-rated local TV program in the country in late 1949 was a series of old, low-budget Western films, televised as *Frontier Playhouse* by WPTZ in Philadelphia. These films had once been Hollywood B pictures of the 1930s, churned out quickly and cheaply for double features in movie houses around the country. By the mid-1940s, the pioneer TV stations were filling parts of their schedules with Western movies, and they proved just as popular on TV as they were in the movie theaters. Bob Dixon, who played "Sheriff Bob" while hosting Western movies on TV in New York, gave the *Times* a simple explanation: "I never met a man on Park Avenue, or anywhere else, who wasn't a frustrated cowboy."[49]

By 1950, one Hollywood cowboy had reemerged as a star on TV: "Hopalong Cassidy," played by William Boyd, a former romantic lead in silent films. After his early career in silents ended, Boyd began a second career portraying cowboy Hopalong Cassidy in sixty-six Western pictures in the 1930s and 1940s. In the mid-1940s, Boyd purchased the rights from his studio to televise his Western films and to make more of them for TV. Beginning in June 1949, *Hopalong Cassidy* was televised along the Eastern and Midwest networks by NBC, and aired on local stations elsewhere around the country.

Although he dressed in black, Hopalong Cassidy was the typical Western hero. He was a "puritanical figure," according to media historian Fred MacDonald, who crusaded for justice, shunned vices, and "kissed a woman only once, and she was on her deathbed."[50] The Cassidy character was popular among adult viewers as well as children, which was true of TV Westerns in general; in fact, over half the viewers of *Frontier Playhouse* were adults. William Boyd knew that Hopalong attracted both children and adults; he told *Life* in 1950, "I play to the adults. That pleases everyone."[51]

Within a year, *Hopalong Cassidy* was ranked among TV's top ten programs in ratings. A $200 million industry quickly developed around Cassidy, with toys, clothes, comics, etc., marketed that used his name and likeness. William Boyd, the former silent film actor, was now the first Hollywood figure to shift his career successfully to TV—and he made a fortune in the process.

Boyd's success on TV in *Hopalong Cassidy* opened the gates for other Western programs with similar cowboy heros. *The Lone Ranger* premiered as a TV series in September 1949, having been a popular radio show since 1933. In July 1950, Hollywood's most famous singing cowboy, Gene Autry, moved to television with a series of new filmed programs. Both TV shows had the *Hopalong Cassidy* style— "straight and simple and clean," as described in one review of *The Gene Autry Show.* Both were as successful as *Hopalong,* lasting on TV through much of the 1950s. These early TV Westerns were filmed in and around Hollywood, quickly and cheaply, as befitted their B-movie origins. In the words of actor Dick Jones, who played Gene Autry's sidekick, "They would do two shows at once. We would chase one way up a dirt road [and] when you'd get to the end, you'd get on a spotted horse that had been painted with white paint, change hats, and go shootin' the other way for the second film."[52]

The typical Western was a simple morality tale with a violent but positive ending. The Western's "good guy" rose up to face the "bad guys," often to defend his weak and powerless neighbors from the threat of domination by outlaws. One side or the other forced a showdown: weapons were drawn, shots were fired, and bodies fell in the dust. In the end the "bad guys" were vanquished, and the "good guy" was the hero who restored peace to the land.

"Hoppy operated in a black-and-white moral world," explains Fred MacDonald. "One was either good or bad, and Cassidy was uncompromising with those who were bad."[53] Reflected in the simple morality tale, however, was America's slant on the world in 1949 and

1950 and the confrontational spirit of the times. As the "good guy" was in the Westerns, the United States was arming for a possible showdown with the Communist "bad guys."

THE NEW BOMB AND THE "RED SCARE"

In July 1949—just weeks after *Hopalong Cassidy* began its network TV run—President Truman signed the North Atlantic Treaty Organization (NATO) agreement. Now, the United States was officially committed to defending Western Europe against an attack from the Soviet Union. A month later, the Soviets set off their first nuclear bomb, prompting Truman to announce that the United States was building a more powerful nuclear weapon, the hydrogen bomb. The age of the nuclear buildup—and the threat of an atomic showdown—had begun.

So, too, had begun the criticism of this new buildup. In early 1950, physicist Albert Einstein appeared on TV to warn the nation of the dangers of nuclear weapons. The occasion was the premiere of a new TV program on Sunday afternoon on the East and Midwest networks. *Today with Mrs. Roosevelt* was hosted and moderated by Eleanor Roosevelt, the former First Lady, who politely served tea to her guests. Her first show had a rare appearance on film by Einstein, whose private letter to her husband back in 1942 had led to the atomic bomb's creation in the first place.

Albert Einstein now warned his TV viewers that, with the new hydrogen bomb, the "radioactive poisoning of the atmosphere and hence annihilation of any life on earth" was "within the range of technical possibilities." Therefore, "the idea of achieving security through national armament," he said, had become "a disastrous illusion." Instead, the only path to peace for Americans was "to do away with mutual fear and distrust," then make a "solemn renunciation of violence."[54]

Einstein also warned his TV audience of government policies based on fear and secrecy. He disagreed with the "mechanistic, technical-military psychological attitude" that America now had to seek "utmost superiority" over its opponents, in case another war broke out. He spoke, too, against America's "arming and economic strengthening" of its allies, i.e., the NATO treaty. He also warned against the "close supervision of the loyalty" of American citizens, and the "indoctrination of the public" through the media and schools.[55]

Einstein was referring here to the strong anti-Communist movement that was asserting itself throughout American society at the midcentury point. A "witch-hunt" to expose Communists and their supporters was asserting itself in the government, in Hollywood, and in the arts, similar to the uncompromising "good or bad" stance of *Hopalong Cassidy* and the other TV Westerns. In particular, performers with ties or rumored ties to leftist groups had been subject to industry blacklisting since 1948, putting them suddenly out of work.

In the mid-1940s actress Mady Christians had starred as "Mama" in the Broadway play, *I Remember Mama*. When the play became a TV series in the summer of 1949, "Mama" was played by Peggy Wood; Mady Christians was blacklisted due to her involvement in pro-left causes earlier in the decade. The New York theater industry, too, refused to hire her. In 1951, Mady Christians was suffering from hypertension when a cerebral hemorrhage killed her.

In January 1950 another "red scare" case surfaced in TV when Ed Sullivan allowed a blacklisted performer, Paul Draper, to dance to "Yankee Doodle Dandy" on his *Toast of the Town* show live on the CBS network. Draper had been on TV ten years before, but now he was controversial due to his mother's links to Communist causes and his own connection to leftist groups. He'd recently had a performance canceled in Connecticut after a Greenwich housewife wrote letters of protest to local papers.

Draper's appearance on Sullivan's TV show created a much bigger storm. CBS received 350 letters and 425 phone calls; Sullivan's sponsor, Ford, received many more, all in protest. Among the angry groups were the American Legion and the Catholic War Veterans, while New York's Hearst paper, the *Journal American,* attacked Draper and Sullivan in several columns. Three days after the show, Ed Sullivan made a public apology to Ford's advertising agency. "You know how bitterly opposed I am to Communism and all it stands for," he wrote. "You also know how strongly I would oppose having the program used as a political forum, directly or indirectly."[56] Sullivan also had Draper's performance removed from the kinescope of the show that was sent to TV stations on the West Coast.

Two months later, in March 1950, another TV blacklisting case erupted, and this one involved Eleanor Roosevelt. At the conclusion of her weekly TV program, she announced that appearing next week to discuss "The Position of the Negro in American Political Life" was Paul Robeson, a well-known black actor and singer. Robeson was controversial in 1950, however, for his outspoken views on civil rights and his active support of Communist and left-wing groups.

Within a few hours, NBC received thirty phone calls in protest, and the next day the network received hundreds more—which was hardly surprising. During the previous summer, a Robeson concert in Peekskill, New York, had caused two riots. The first took place the day of the concert, which forced him to cancel it, and the second followed his rescheduled concert a week later. Over 100 people were treated for injuries after the second riot. In both cases, the rioting erupted first among Robeson's opponents.

NBC acted promptly by announcing that the Robeson appearance would be postponed "indefinitely" and probably canceled. Speaking for NBC was former FCC Chairman Charles Denny, now a network vice president. He explained that the announcement by Mrs. Roosevelt of Robeson's appearance had been "premature" and hadn't been cleared with NBC first. "We are all agreed," he said, "that Mr. Robeson's appearance would lead only to misunderstanding and confusion. . . ." Denny also promised that Robeson would never appear on an NBC telecast.[57]

The next day Paul Robeson called NBC's action a "sad commentary on our professions of democracy."[58] He also claimed that NBC hadn't wanted an open discussion on TV on the role of "the Negro in politics" (the topic was changed that week to foreign policy) and that the network encouraged racial stereotypes in its programs.

A few weeks later, the American Civil Liberties Union became one of only a few groups to criticize NBC's banning of Robeson, describing it as "censorship by private pressure."[59] They urged NBC to put Robeson on the air, but the network never did. Later in 1950, the State Department revoked Robeson's passport; he became, as described by writer Michael Barson, "a prisoner in a hostile country—his own."[60] Robeson never appeared on any network TV program; his treatment showed that television was limited as a source of diverse viewpoints for the American public.

Following the Draper and Robeson incidents in early 1950, the blacklisting controversy died down for a few months. But the same week of the Robeson banning, FCC Chairman Wayne Coy spoke out in public against certain TV performers—not left-wing supporters, in this case, but off-color comedians. He seemed to be singling out Arthur Godfrey in describing "a comedian [who] gets so big that his network can no longer handle him" and instead carries him "straight into the home without having taken the precaution to see that he is housebroken."[61]

"Clearly, there must be a day of reckoning," Coy warned the industry, suggesting that the networks "clean house before public opinion demands the more drastic remedy of governmental action."[62] Of course, criticizing TV's standards of taste was nothing new; the previous year had seen a spate of it. The difference here was that Coy could actually influence program content through the FCC's power to revoke the licenses of stations that it deemed not to be operating in the public interest.

FAYE EMERSON

The first controversy over standards of taste to erupt after Coy's speech came not from a comedian but from a talk-show hostess. Faye Emerson, in the words of columnist Earl Wilson, was "beautiful, well-read and witty."[63] She had been a model, an actress, and had been married to Elliot Roosevelt, Franklin and Eleanor's son and a television producer himself. In 1949, Emerson had become the quintessential guest on TV game and panel shows; by early 1950, CBS was transmitting Faye Emerson's own fifteen-minute talk show at 11:00 p.m. on their TV network. At one point in the spring of 1950, Faye Emerson had programs on both CBS and NBC, including the Saturday 10:30 p.m. slot on NBC, following their popular variety programs.

The format of her shows was simple: Emerson would talk about people and events in her New York social world, then chat with one or two guests—typically from the theater or the arts. Because she wore low-cut evening dresses, however, her looks became the subject of newspaper columns. In the *New York Herald Tribune* in January 1950, for example, John Crosby wrote that she "fills a ten-inch screen very adequately. Very adequately."[64] That and other comments prompted Emerson herself to ask during her TV show that her viewers write in their preference: should she wear low or high necklines? The following week, she read a number of the answers on the air, most of them favoring the low neckline.

She was the subject of an article in *Time* in April 1950, in which she responded to criticism of her low-cut dresses: "I wear on TV just what I'd ordinarily wear at that time of the night. I don't think children can be adversely affected. They're probably not up at that hour, and, anyway, have you ever seen the clothes worn by the women in comic books?"[65] Eventually, Faye Emerson ended the controversy herself by raising her necklines. Now, John Crosby wrote, "Miss Emerson was observed in a dress with the most enormous white collar seen in these parts since the days of the Pilgrims. Looked like something out of Nathaniel Hawthorne, modified by Louisa M. Alcott."[66] By the following year, the National Association of Radio and Television Broadcasters had announced plans to develop program standards that would ban TV performers from appearing with an "exposure or emphasis on anatomical details as would offend home viewers."[67]

TV'S EFFECTS ON CHILDREN

Faye Emerson's comment on whether children were "adversely affected" by her necklines reflected a new national interest in children who watched TV. In late 1949, a school principal in Clifton, New Jersey, sent home to parents a letter complaining that TV was lowering their children's grades. Their schoolwork had fallen below standards, and "the teachers and I feel that one reason for this condition," explained Principal Charles Sheehan, "is the late hours kept by the children because of the television programs" they watched at night.[68] Thus entered into American society one of the great complaints of postwar educators and parents: the idea that watching TV is harmful to children.

With TV now in some 5 million American homes, millions of youngsters were displaying the same devotion to TV that was noted years earlier among the kids of Newburgh. In early 1950, a study of 450 junior high students from the suburban town of Stamford, Connecticut, showed that watching TV had become, next to sleeping and school, the biggest activity in their lives. Half the children in Stamford had sets in their homes and watched TV at least four hours each day. Another 30 percent watched TV at least three hours a day at the homes of friends and neighbors.

A month later, in April 1950, a parents' association in New York City reported that preadolescent children spent less time studying and playing sports because of TV. They also reported for the first time that children as young as five years old watched TV at least four hours a day. Some toddlers were "throwing tantrums when sets were shut off" at dinner time and insisting that "they eat dinner in places where they could view the television sets." Their older siblings, aged ten to thirteen, were reported by parents to have TV-induced anxieties and nightmares.[69]

Who was to blame for the apparent problems caused by children's TV watching? According to the editors of *The Catholic World*, writing in March 1950, "the blame rests entirely on the parents" who should "order the children to their books when they have had enough looking for the night. Hew to the line and let Cassidy hopalong as he may."[70] Parents now used the TV set as a "baby-sitter" for their children, complained Jack Gould of the *Times*, warning that "later they may find the habit difficult to break." Gould advised parents that TV "is only something to see. It is not a way of raising children."[71]

Other fingers pointed at the TV industry. The problem wasn't watching TV itself, suggested a children's librarian at a 1950 book publishers' conference, it was the quality of the programs being aired. "It has gotten so that I never turn on the TV," wrote a Brooklyn parent to the *Times*, "unless I know what I'll see because it will be a killing Western. The children . . . won't look at anything else, only Westerns."[72]

Jack Gould and others claimed in early 1950 that the TV industry had neglected its duty to air suitable programs for children at appropriate times. Gould accused TV's "top level of management" of sweeping educational programs "into an obscure corner," to be aired only at "inferior marginal time" by staff with no real authority. "A fundamental turnabout in their policy is needed now," he demanded.[73] A station owner from Pennsylvania suggested that the TV industry should "make their facilities available without charge to non-profit organizations for an hour or two each day" for educational and cultural programs.[74]

NBC responded to the criticism by premiering in April 1950 the first network TV series intended to supplement school curriculum.

Watch the World was a current events program designed for children and endorsed by New York's superintendent of schools and by two national education groups. Its host was John Cameron Swayze from NBC's network news program: he narrated short films on science, industry, the arts, etc., and interviewed a guest each week. NBC kept *Watch the World* on its network schedule until the middle of 1951. However, only in the summer of 1950 did the show air in the prime time of early evening; its time slot in general was Sunday afternoon—one of those "inferior marginal times," noted by Jack Gould, when the network didn't expect much of an audience anyway.

NBC's *Watch the World* was aimed at America's schoolchildren who were born in the late 1930s and early 1940s, and whose daily lives were changed when TV entered their homes. A new generation of children was taking shape in 1950, however: the celebrated baby boomers, many of whom would never know life without television. Over 3 million of them turned four in 1950, the biggest number in a single year in American history.

One of them was the youngest son of Bennett and Phyllis Cerf, two literary people who were TV panelists as well and who wrote articles about their kids watching TV. Back in 1949, Bennett Cerf had described in the *Saturday Review of Literature* how his older son, seven-year-old Christopher, "stays rooted to the set until he is forcibly removed." Cerf predicted, however, that "once the novelty wears off," America's TV families "rarely will watch more than two programs, on the average, an evening" and instead might even try "picking up a good book!"[75]

Phyllis Cerf agreed, writing in a parents' magazine in 1950, "It was our hope that after a decent length of exposure to this new invention, our children would become immune." Instead, the children became "television addicts," according to Phyllis Cerf. "Their eyes were tired, they were having nightmares and nobody was having any fun." The Cerfs' solution was to impose a limit of seven hours of TV per week, with the two boys allowed to pick the shows they watched. "Our system has worked like an ancient charm," wrote Phyllis Cerf. "The boys are a little like reformed drunkards who can take television or leave it alone. They enjoy it, we enjoy them, they enjoy us. It's a wonderful rationed-television world!"[76]

Chapter 8

Comics and Communists

YOUR SHOW OF SHOWS

The Cerfs and their two children were part of an American society that at the midcentury point was changing: it now had millions of newlyweds, young couples with babies and infants, and apartments and suburban homes with televisions. This changing America also now had a TV show that pictured and satirized its modern ways— *Your Show of Shows*, NBC's flagship variety program.

Your Show of Shows followed in the footsteps of *Admiral Broadway Revue*, the TV show that Max Liebman had produced for nineteen weeks in 1949. Liebman now had a much bigger budget, which he used to stock *Your Show of Shows* with a twenty-five piece orchestra, expensive sets and scenery, and a big company of dancers and singers. More important, Liebman rehired his team of writers from *Admiral Broadway Revue*, headed by Mel Tolkin and Lucille Kallen and later to include Mel Brooks and Neil Simon. Liebman still had Sid Caesar and Imogene Coca, who were possibly the most talented young comic performers on television in 1950.

Sid Caesar was rubber-faced, athletic, and a natural mimic—he could imitate everything from a Russian general to a housefly. He was "one of the wonders of the modern electronic age," in the words of critic John Crosby.[1] Sid Caesar also had a background to fit the times. He was a World War II veteran, still in his twenties, with a bride, a baby, and an apartment in the suburbs. He'd become a comedian during the war, performing in a Coast Guard servicemen's show directed by Max Liebman and appearing in the film, *Tars and Spars*. After the war, Caesar rose quickly in show business. He performed in clubs and theaters, in a Broadway show, and then back with Liebman on television's *Admiral Broadway Revue*—all in less than two years.

On *Your Show of Shows,* Caesar starred in comedy sketches and acted out monologues that seemed to capture the moods of modern life in America. As described by Ted Sennett in his book, *Your Show of Shows,*

> Somehow a man emerged whose odyssey could be traced from show to show. From the young man terrified at the thought of proposing marriage, to the young married coping with jobs, children, and in-laws, to the proud middle-aged father watching his son graduate from medical school or his daughter being married, Caesar offered an amazingly perceptive and uproarious portrait of Everyman in the middle of the twentieth century."[2]

Much of Caesar's portrayal of the modern psyche came from the program's writers. "An awful lot of what went into the comedy writing was based on our own personal experiences," recalled Mel Tolkin. "Remember, all of us had started out very young, making small salaries. . . . So, as we began to acquire new things, we could draw on what happened to us for a good deal of the humor."[3] Most of the show's writers were or had been in psychoanalysis, but it was Caesar who gave life to the lines—and whose gestures and facial expressions were being televised in American homes, where they rang true.

Caesar's counterpart on the show, Imogene Coca, had been born into a show business family and started performing at age fourteen. She was a trained ballerina and singer who could also act, tap dance, mime, and project every type of emotion. She was shy in private—as was Caesar—but on TV, she projected warmth, mischief, intelligence, and intimacy, and the critics compared her to the great Charles Chaplin.

In the comedy dialogues they performed together, Imogene Coca and Sid Caesar often focused on the small crises of everyday life, such as taking one's children to their first day of school. They frequently portrayed a mismatched couple, the Hickenloopers. Doris Hickenlooper was the modern, upwardly mobile American woman, married to Charlie, the average American "slob."

At a seafood restaurant, for example, Doris cajoled Charlie into ordering something beyond his usual meat-and-potatoes meal. "You know what the trouble is with you?" she complained. "You have no spirit of adventure! Didn't you ever try something new, strange, unusual, a little off the beaten path, something a little weird, something you thought you'd never have anything to do with?" He stared at her a moment in reflection, then said, "Once." Wrote one fan to Max Liebman about the Caesar and Coca sketches, "You have no idea what a great service you are doing. You are showing us how silly we are when we behave that way. It's very true and it's very real."[4]

Your Show of Shows remained fresh and popular during its five-year run on NBC. It was canceled after almost 200 ninety-minute shows (all televised live) because the network expected its three leading talents—Caesar, Coca, and Liebman—to succeed as well on their own. Sid Caesar had success for three years on a similar program, *Caesar's Hour,* then fell victim to drug and alcohol problems that he'd developed under the stress of his weekly shows. Imogene Coca appeared in other TV programs and Max Liebman produced other variety shows, but it's for their collaborative work in the early 1950s that all three are most noted. *Your Show of Shows* is considered one of the high points of American popular culture.

THE "BANDIT RAID" ON KOREA

In the middle of 1950, a conflict arose that made the marriage battles of the Hickenloopers and the corporate squabbles of the TV industry pale in comparison. On June 24, 1950, troops of the North Korean army invaded South Korea, crossing a border that had been set up after World War II. Although it had taken over two years for the United States to enter that earlier foreign war, this time the nation was fighting within days. The period of peace that America had been experiencing came to an abrupt end less than five years after World War II had ended.

President Truman was asked directly at a press conference on June 29, 1950, "Are we or are we not at war?" Although U.S. planes were bombing targets in both South and North Korea, Truman told the public, "We are not at war." Instead, he agreed with a reporter who described the American fighting as "a police action under the United Nations."[5] He justified the military action with words that resembled the theme of a TV Western: "the members of the United Nations are going to the relief of the Korean Republic to suppress a bandit raid on the Republic of Korea. That is all there is to it."[6]

However, there was a great deal more. North Korean troops had routed the South Korean army and captured the capital city of Seoul. America's General Douglas MacArthur asked for U.S. ground troops to enter the war; on June 30, Truman granted his request. By mid-July, American soldiers were arriving to face the enemy troops and guerrillas and snipers on the slopes of South Korea's hills, along mountain trails, and in rice paddies and peasant villages.

On the night of July 19, 1950, President Truman spoke directly to the American public about Korea for the first time, live on TV from the White House. He spoke in front of an American flag, and he wore an American Legion pin in his lapel. He used hand gestures, facial expressions, a firm jaw, and a few taps on the lectern to emphasize his points. Truman spoke on TV that night of the "international Communist movement" and their "act of raw aggression" against Korea. "This is a direct challenge to the efforts of the free nations to build the kind of world in which men can live in freedom and peace," he said. "We must meet it squarely." He said it would "take a hard, tough fight to halt the invasion, to drive the Communists back," and to do so he asked for "more men, equipment, and supplies" to send to Korea.[7]

In his speech, televised live as far west as St. Louis, Truman also called for a much bigger military buildup, "over and above what is needed in Korea," to prepare for "similar acts of aggression in other parts of the world." Needed were more combat troops, "more steel, more aluminum, more of a good many things" to make the weapons of war. Higher taxes were needed to pay for the rearmament, said Truman, and fewer purchases of nonessential items and less consumer credit, to curb the threat of inflation. "This is a time for all of us to pitch in and work together," Truman said.[8]

Truman's speech on July 19, 1950, marked the first time that an American president used TV to rally the public behind him as he exercised his war-making powers. In later years, and with similar words, Presidents Johnson and Nixon would use television to sell another war against Communists in Asia, but with mixed results: many Americans simply did not believe what these presidents said about the Vietnam War.

With Truman and Korea in 1950, however, there's no evidence that TV viewers doubted his statements. "One would like to think that sincerity and insincerity would be distinguishable on such a screen," wrote *The New York Times* about the speech. Truman, "as seen on television instruments, was a sincere man, deeply moved by what he had to say."[9] On the other hand, *Times* TV critic Jack Gould noted that the President, "assuming he was off the air" after his speech and waiting for the national anthem to begin, "looked at the wristwatch on his left hand to check his timing. Then, as he turned to his right to leave the lectern, he could be seen smiling."[10]

Truman spoke again about Korea on TV in early September 1950, announcing a new law to mobilize American industry. The new law, said Truman, would "make sure that defense orders have top priority, that manufacturers get the steel, aluminum, copper, and other materials they need" to fulfill their contracts with the military.[11] His words echoed those of President Roosevelt a decade earlier—words that had stalled the growth of the new TV industry for five years.

Would the booming TV industry of 1950 again be stalled by an economy that was retooling for the military? In 1942, World War II had stopped the construction of new TV stations; in 1950, the FCC "freeze" on building new stations was entering its third year. The defense buildup for World War II had also stopped the making of TV sets, and there was reason to believe in 1950 that it might happen again. Already, in August 1950 the industry was predicting a cutback of 10 to 20 percent in sets available for the fall. Sales of new TVs were still booming, however, when the war broke out that summer, with the average price now reduced to below $300 for a sixteen-inch set. If anything, the war initially boosted sales, since the American public had begun "scare buying"—making purchases of products they thought would soon be unavailable.

RED CHANNELS

In the early months of the Korean War, the CBS network televised sessions of the United Nations Security Council, meeting in New York, that dealt with Korea. The Soviet Union boycotted these sessions, and the People's Republic of China—the other major Communist nation—had been denied membership in the United Nations. The televised debate was thus one sided, in favor of U.S. involvement in Korea.

As to coverage of the war itself, the TV networks and stations used film footage—as had been the case with World War II. In one noteworthy incident, Edward R. Murrow, the most respected name in broadcast journalism, returned from a trip to Korea in August 1950 convinced that the war was becoming an American disaster. His news dispatch for CBS that criticized the U.S. military command was never aired: it was repressed by the company's president, Frank Stanton, and chairman, William Paley.[12]

The summer of 1950 was hardly a good time for Murrow, the heads of CBS, or anyone in the public eye to appear unsupportive of America's military and foreign policy. In June, Ed Sullivan, who was now in the good graces of the anti-Communists, leaked in his newspaper column that a "bombshell" was about to drop "into the offices of radio-TV networks, advertising agencies and sponsors."[13] The "bombshell" was a 200-page booklet titled *Red Channels,* and it was later described by writer Stephan Kanfer as "the most effective blacklist in the history of show business."[14]

Red Channels was a list of 151 broadcast performers, writers, guests, producers, etc., with the names of left-leaning organizations they were purported to have joined or supported. The information was compiled by a small group that included former FBI agents; on their list of Communist sympathizers were well-known performers— Orson Welles, Fredrick March, Leonard Bernstein, Arthur Miller, Dorothy Parker, Aaron Copeland, Gypsy Rose Lee, and others.

Listed as well in *Red Channels* were many noncelebrities, including Jean Muir, a radio and film actress. A popular NBC television series, *The Aldrich Family,* had recently hired Muir to play Mrs. Aldrich in its second season. It was the biggest part in her twenty-year career. When the casting announcement was made in late August 1950, letters and phone calls of protest quickly came into the offices of the program's sponsor, General Foods, its advertising agency, and NBC. Among the protesters were some of the same groups and individuals who had sparked the Paul Draper controversy.

The issue was bigger this time, however, since Jean Muir had been hired to appear every week on a network TV program watched in hundreds of thousands of American homes, with American soldiers now fighting troops from a Communist country. General Foods acted quickly. On August 28, the company dropped Jean Muir from the cast and delayed the program's new season of episodes to bring in a replacement. A spokesman for General Foods denied that the company was supporting the *Red Channels* group. Instead, the company wanted to avoid the "unfavorable criticism and even antagonism among sizable groups of consumers" that might result from televising "controversial personalities or the discussion of controversial subjects."[15]

Jean Muir immediately denied that she was ever a Communist and claimed to believe "that the Communists represent a vicious and destructive force, and I am opposed to them." In fact, her worst actions may have been that she supported a group of Spanish war refugees in the 1930s and sent a greeting to the Moscow Arts Theatre on their thirtieth anniversary. Moscow Arts was "a purely artistic organization," she told the press. "Since as an actress I did owe a lot to the acting techniques which they advanced, I did send them a congratulatory message."[16]

Jean Muir was just one of many performers who lost jobs because of the blacklist; some never knew they'd been blacklisted or that they'd even been considered for the jobs they had lost. Jean Muir, however, was dropped in public view by a leading food company, and the story was front-page news. A broadcasting "purge . . . appeared imminent," reported *The New York Times,* quoting an industry leader: "I think Miss Muir's case is just the beginning of what we're going to face. The 'Red Channels' book is now the Bible up and down Madison Avenue,"[17] where the nation's biggest advertising agencies resided.

When the *Times* ran a longer article on the Muir case in September 1950, readers wrote to express a range of opinions. "No General Foods products for me," proclaimed a reader who hoped that "the Jean Muir case will be the weapon to blow wide open the hysterical abrogation of fair trial before a guilty verdict." One reader told the *Times,* "Go back to Russia where you belong," and was seconded by another who thought the Muir article "belongs in The Daily Worker."[18] Soon, a new "Mrs. Aldrich" was hired, and Jean Muir remained off the air.

In December 1950, another blacklisting case emerged on TV when a local New York station canceled a series of Charlie Chaplin films after it had received a letter of complaint from a Catholic War Veterans commander. (Chaplin, too, had been branded a Communist supporter.) "It makes no difference if the pictures were made five, ten, twenty or more years ago," the letter read. "Entertainment for art's sake just does not exist when you talk about communism."[19]

Later that month, CBS ordered all of its 2,500 employees to take a loyalty oath, swearing that they weren't members of any Communist organization nor had they ever been. CBS was worried that some potential sponsors believed the network was too liberal politically; the oath would show that CBS was removing any Communist supporters from its employees. About twenty CBS employees did admit to some ties to Communist groups; upon further investigation by CBS, some of them were fired.[20] As for NBC, their management simply continued a practice they'd already begun of requiring loyalty oaths from new employees.

By removing from the airwaves some of the more liberal writers, journalists, producers, and performers, blacklisting helped make TV more politically conservative and less a source of diverse viewpoints. Those liberals who remained in broadcasting faced the threat of being blacklisted: it was a sword hanging over their heads should they become too controversial.

THE INVASION OF COMICS

On the screens of America's TV sets in the fall of 1950 came an invading force of comedians. Instantly, it seemed, comedy had replaced variety as the program of choice among the broadcasters. Actually, the stage had been set for comedy on television back in 1949, when CBS "raided" NBC's stock of popular radio comedians. NBC added a few more comedians to its stable of performers, and both networks planned the transfer of these well-paid talents from radio to TV, to help build their audience in the newer medium.

The comedians who invaded TV in late 1950 fell into several categories. Some were veterans of show business, with roots in vaudeville or in an even older form of entertainment, minstrel shows. Others had begun their careers in the 1930s and 1940s in radio, and a few were nightclub and resort performers.

One comic who added TV to his long career in show business was Jimmy Durante, who played piano and sang in the rowdy, illegal speakeasies of the 1920s' Prohibition years. On stage, Durante was a gravel-voiced, high-energy, mischievous lowbrow performer, with a thick Brooklyn accent and a prominent nose that earned him the nickname "Schnozzola." Durante was now one of four comics who alternated as the host of *Four Star Revue,* an NBC variety program televised on Wednesday nights.

On his first show, on November 2, 1950, Jimmy Durante began with what he did best: playing and singing one of his trademark numbers, "You Gotta Start Off Each Day With a Song." With Durante, however, no song was ever done straight through, as he'd jump up from the piano, yell "Stop the music!," tell a quick joke or two, then pick up the song where he had left off. To the audience, Durante's routine was fresh and spontaneous, but of course it was all scripted and well rehearsed. In that first program, for example, an actor was planted in the audience watching a TV set, so that Durante could run off the stage, yank away the set, and proclaim, "Nobody watches *The Goldbergs* when Durante's on!"

Jimmy Durante quickly became the most popular of the four comics who alternated on *Four Star Revue* (the others were Ed Wynn, Danny Thomas, and Jack Carson). Both *Variety* and *The New York Times* declared him "The most resounding success" of all the new TV comedians,[21] and Jack Gould ranked his TV shows among "the theatrical treats of the year."[22] With Durante's appearances on TV in 1950, the viewing audience was bestowed a special gift. For decades, Americans had listened to Durante and other great comedians on the radio. At times they'd seen the comics in films, although Hollywood movie scripts were not always written to highlight the funniest routines. Now the public could see their favorites performing live in their living rooms, doing the routines that had brought them fame.

Other "old-established vets" with popular TV shows in 1950 were Eddie Cantor and sixty-four-year-old Ed Wynn, who'd begun performing in vaudeville back in 1902. A common complaint among these veterans was how quickly their career's worth of material was used up in their TV shows. Eddie Cantor, for example, performed what he called the "Cavalcade of Cantor" on his first night as the star of the *Comedy Hour* (later known as the *Colgate Comedy Hour*), on September 25, 1950. These were the highlights of his long career in show business, including a song performed in blackface from his minstrel days decades earlier. Once done, however, Cantor could hardly repeat the numbers on his following programs. Unless, somehow, these troopers could perform new material that equaled their best from the past, their appeal on TV would inevitably drop.

Two former vaudeville performers who found greater success on TV were George Burns and Gracie Allen. This married couple had also been on network radio for nineteen years. During their first TV show—televised live from New York on October 12, 1950—Gracie Allen was petrified. During her many years on radio, she hadn't memorized a script; it wasn't necessary on radio, where the home audience couldn't see performers reading from the scripts they held. Live television, however, required her and other radio veterans to memorize their lines. Moreover, Gracie Allen had the most lines to learn in the script, and many of them were written to sound "daffy," and thus were convoluted and easy to confuse. "I haven't memorized anything for twenty years," she said afterward. "All I could think of was, 'What's the next line?' "23

In general, the transition of Burns and Allen from radio to TV had been carefully planned. George Burns first visited television studios in Hollywood to see how other programs were produced. Then he and his writers prepared the first few months of scripts in advance, using very little of the couple's vaudeville material. Instead, the scripts for the TV programs were similar to their radio shows, in which they played "Burns and Allen," a married show-business couple.

A new visual feature was added for this program on television. George Burns borrowed an idea from the theater, popularized just before the war by the Pulitzer prizewinning drama, *Our Town,* in which an actor walks in and out of the set, to serve as a narrator and interpreter for the audience. George Burns took that role on the show, used his cigar as a prop, and carried on a running conversation with his TV viewers: it was cleverly done and added to the show's pace, humor, and overall success. *The George Burns and Gracie Allen Show* aired from October 1950 until Gracie Allen's retirement in September 1958, making it the longest-running situation comedy of the 1950s.

JACK BENNY AND FRED ALLEN

The first words spoken by Jack Benny on his first TV program, in October 1950, were, "I'd give a million dollars to know what I look like on television!" His audience laughed because they thought they knew Jack Benny; they knew he was vain and sensitive about his looks, and they knew he was notoriously cheap. The comedian Jack Benny had been portraying this very familiar character for decades on radio; in late 1950, he made the switch to TV and succeeded. *The Jack Benny Show* was a popular half-hour program on TV for fifteen years, and Benny continued making TV comedy specials until his death in 1974.

As with *The George Burns and Gracie Allen Show,* Jack Benny's writers kept the essence of his character intact; they also transported from radio his cast of performers. They added a few visual effects for TV, such as a pay phone in his living room in the first show. Yet the best visual effect was Jack Benny himself: in particular, his facial expressions, such as his deadpan stare whenever his vanity and cheapness were being tested. In one of his most famous routines, for example, he was robbed at gunpoint by a thief who growled, "Your money or your life!" His answer, "I'm thinking!" drew a big laugh from the audience, but they'd already been laughing at the sight of Benny's deadpan stare, which seemed to last for minutes.

Also shifting his career to television in October 1950 was another comedy star from radio—Fred Allen. He was one of a group of four comedians alternating on NBC's new Sunday night program, *Comedy Hour,* airing opposite Ed Sullivan's *Toast of the Town* on CBS. Fred Allen's seventeen years on radio had established him as one of the country's sharpest wits, and he was expected to do well on TV. "Comedy has a real treat tonight," wrote Jack Gould in *The New York Times* on the day he premiered. "It's Fred Allen at 8 o'clock on N.B.C."[24] Fred Allen himself was less confident that he'd succeed on TV. In 1949, he said about himself and his fellow radio comics, "We have a great problem. We don't know how to duplicate our success in radio. . . . We don't know what will be funny or even whether our looks are acceptable."[25]

His fears proved to be true: both Allen himself and the contents of his TV program were disappointing. On his first program, for example, he was both antagonistic toward television and apologetic about his presence on it. Even "Allen's Alley," the most popular feature of his radio show, was less funny on TV. The assortment of quirky characters in the "Alley" had been transformed for TV from real people into puppets. "You can do better, Mr. Allen," *Life* wrote in its brief review of the program. Fred Allen was photographed with his back to the camera; the caption read, "Tired and dissatisfied during rehearsal, Allen slumps backstage." *Life* advised him to "simply relax, take TV for granted, and be Fred Allen."[26]

The ratings dropped for Fred Allen's second show; he was rated third among the four hosts of the *Comedy Hour* and lower than Ed Sullivan on CBS. After just two more programs, Fred Allen quit the *Comedy Hour.* He was taking "an extended vacation," he said, "for health reasons," following doctor's orders to rest because of high blood pressure. Allen later said that he quit "because of ill health. I make people sick."[27]

Fred Allen had replaced Mary Margaret McBride as the best-known radio performer to fail on TV. The press reported that Fred Allen was unhappy with the format of the *Comedy Hour* and might return to the airwaves with a different type of show, only half as long. Indeed, he did try TV again; first, as one of three alternating stars of a short-lived comedy series in 1951, and later—with success—as a panelist on *What's My Line* from 1954 until his death in 1956.

GROUCHO MARX AND MARTIN AND LEWIS

Fred Allen's discomfort regarding TV was part of a general displeasure he had toward the postwar culture, and that he often stated with wit and sarcasm. "Everything is for the eye these days," he said in 1949. "Nothing is for the mind. The next generation will have eyeballs as big as cantaloupes and no brain at all."[28] Conversely, another one of America's celebrated wits found TV to be an ideal medium for his humor.

Groucho Marx was part of America's most famous comic family in vaudeville and films, the Marx Brothers. Groucho had recently revived his career by becoming the host of a radio quiz show from Hollywood, *You Bet Your Life,* and he and his show made the shift to TV with ease. Each week, he performed a ninety-minute show in front of three pairs of 35 millimeter motion picture cameras, with one of each pair rolling at all times. He used the best thirty minutes of audio material for his radio show on Wednesday evening, while the best thirty minutes visually were edited into a TV program, then flown to stations for broadcast on Thursday night.

Groucho Marx used the format of *You Bet Your Life* as a springboard for his humor. His short conversations with the contestants were filled with his quips and barbs; many of the contestants were funny themselves. Many of them were also from America's minorities and ethnic groups. It was unusual for a TV program to feature members of these groups on the air, but the producers of *You Bet Your Life* had wanted the show to reflect the diversity of its audience.

The program itself was basically a quiz show. Its most memorable feature was a toy duck that dropped down into camera range whenever a contestant managed to "say the secret word" for the evening and win a bonus cash prize. An audience of 40 million Americans regularly watched Groucho Marx on *You Bet Your Life* during the early 1950s, when the show flirted with the top spot in ratings surveys. They watched one of the country's wittiest performers on TV until 1961, for 528 half-hours. *You Bet Your Life* with Groucho even outlasted its long-time sponsor, DeSoto automobiles, which ceased making cars in 1960.

The American public also saw on TV in 1950 a pair of young performers who were on a swift ride to the top of their ranks in show business: Dean Martin and Jerry Lewis. At their best, live and loosely scripted, Martin and Lewis were as wild an act as ever performed on television. Beginning on September 17, 1950, the American public could watch them monthly, as they alternated as stars of NBC's *Comedy Hour* on Sunday nights. By early 1951, Martin and Lewis had ratings above the other hosts of the *Comedy Hour* and above Ed Sullivan's show on CBS; their monthly appearances were among the most popular TV shows in the country.

Romantic singer Dean Martin and rubber-faced comic Jerry Lewis had formed a comedy act in Atlantic City in 1946. They found quick success in nightclubs and motion pictures, along with a mild setback on radio in 1949. Their act was better suited for TV than for radio. Although Dean Martin was a good singer, their popularity rested more on the physical humor and facial expressions of Jerry Lewis and on the slapstick interactions between the two.

For five years, Martin and Lewis sandwiched their monthly shows on TV in between their movies and personal appearances. They were the most popular comedy act in the country, but they split bitterly in 1955 in one of the most publicized show-business breakups. Dean Martin and Jerry Lewis then launched separate but equally successful careers, with Martin having a second popular TV series in the 1960s and 1970s.

JACKIE GLEASON
AND THE CAVALCADE OF STARS

Another comedian who launched a new TV program in 1950 became one of the medium's greatest stars. Although only thirty-four years old, Jackie Gleason was already a veteran of burlesque, vaudeville, nightclubs, movies, radio, and theater. He even had the lead role in one of the first TV comedy series filmed in Hollywood, *The Life of Riley,* that aired for six months in 1949.

In mid-1950, the Du Mont network needed a new host for their variety show, *Cavalcade of Stars,* after both Jack Carter and his replacement, Jerry Lester, left the network for NBC. Jackie Gleason was not their first choice; although some of his peers recognized his talents, the public hardly knew him. It was Jackie Gleason they hired nonetheless, and he debuted on *Cavalcade of Stars* on Saturday, July 8, 1950. In the words of his biographer, William Henry, it was "a date of transforming importance in his life and of considerable significance in the life of American culture."[29]

For his first show, Gleason performed old comedy sketches that had been purchased from their writers for the evening. On the second show, Jackie Gleason appeared as a new character in a sketch written just for him. He played a wealthy, rude, imbibing playboy, dressed in top hat, cape, and cane, who later was named Reggie Van Gleason III. The sketch also had a photographer, and for that role Gleason's writers, Coleman Jacoby and Arnie Rosen, suggested a comic who was working in another Du Mont show. After performing the sketch with him, Gleason told his writers, "Find something for him—he's great."[30] Thus began the comedy team of Jackie Gleason and Art Carney, who performed on TV together for twelve of the next twenty years.

Within a few months, Gleason and writers Jacoby and Rosen had created a wide range of characters for Gleason to portray in skits: the pathetic "Bachelor," performed in pantomime; the "loudmouths" Charlie Bratton and Rudy the Repairman; and Fenwick Babbitt, a meek soul turned violent by the frustrations of life. "I think a comedian has to develop characterizations to keep going on TV," Gleason told *The New York Times* in May 1951. "I don't care how strong a personality he might have, if he tries to be just himself for one hour every week his popularity is bound to fall off."[31]

Gleason's favorite character was his first one: Reggie Van Gleason III. "Reggie, one suspects, is the man Gleason would like to have been from his earliest childhood," writes William Henry. With enough money to be rude to anyone he chooses, Reggie wants "to be alone with his bottle, his hostility, his deep depression and anger toward the world."[32] Gleason's most popular character, the blustery and barely middle-class Ralph Kramden, first came to life on *Cavalcade of Stars* in 1951; he's survived all the others, including Gleason himself, through reruns of *The Honeymooners,* whose episodes aired originally in the 1950s.

With Gleason as host and star, *Cavalcade of Stars* became Du Mont's most popular program in 1950 and 1951, and the network moved it to Friday nights, away from NBC's *Your Show of Shows* on Saturday. The Du Mont network would soon lose Jackie Gleason, who was easily lured to CBS by a high salary offer in 1952. Using many of the same characters he'd developed on *Cavalcade of Stars,* Jackie Gleason became a true TV star himself, achieving fame and fortune in the 1950s and 1960s and even finding the success in Hollywood movies that had eluded him as a young man.

Jackie Gleason and all the other comics who began their TV careers in 1950 followed in the footsteps of Milton Berle and the cast of *Your Show of Shows.* Did they all share a common trait? It may well have been their experience performing live and being funny before audiences in nightclubs, vaudeville, or theater. George Burns explained it this way in December 1950: "If you're a good performer, know your business, and people like you, you're made. If they dislike you, if they detect a note of insincerity, you're a dead duck. Liking the show, they look forward to seeing it every chance they get."[33]

With the exception of Fred Allen, these comics had popular TV shows for five years (Martin and Lewis) to almost twenty-five years (Jack Benny). Their jokes, spoofs, funny faces, and pratfalls became something for a generation of Americans to talk about the day after watching them on TV. More immediately, they helped the TV boom continue in 1950 and early 1951, when the number of sets owned by Americans surpassed 10 million.

TRUMAN AND MACARTHUR

Television's comedy invasion in the fall of 1950 took place in the midst of a serious international crisis: the outbreak of fighting in Korea. At first, the news from Korea was good. Although American troops were again at war, and the daily newspapers again had casuality lists to print, at least this conflict seemed destined to end soon. Appearing on Eleanor Roosevelt's TV show on October 2, 1950, Secretary of State Dean Acheson assured the American public that the war in Korea was "close to an end."[34] Two weeks later, in Tokyo, General Douglas MacArthur promised to "have the boys home for Christmas."[35]

Then, with the North Korean army pushed back off the land it had taken in the summer, MacArthur sent his troops above the border in what he called his "End-the-War Offensive."[36] However, hundreds of thousands of Chinese troops had already crossed into North Korea from Manchuria, and, like the "bad guys" of a Western, they hid to await the U.S. offensive. Under a full moon on the night of November 24, 1950, the Chinese Red Army attacked the American troops—and a much bigger war had begun.

General MacArthur's command post in Tokyo at first misjudged the battle, describing it as North Korea's "one last dying gasp of effort before it was all over."[37] In a few days the U.S. Eighth army was in retreat, forty miles behind the line it had held on November 24, and the war had turned disastrous. In Washington, DC, Acheson gave the government's first public assessment in a speech on TV on November 29, 1950. "Now, this new act of aggression," he said, "has created a new crisis, a situation of unparalleled danger." He saved his harshest words not for China—the Truman administration was hoping to avoid an all-out war with China—but for the Soviet Union: the Chinese were simply their "dupes," Acheson told the public.[38]

Despite the importance of Secretary of State Acheson's speech, only the Du Mont network chose to televise it. Acheson may have been too controversial for CBS and NBC to broadcast, for fear of stirring up the anti-Communist *Red Channels* group and their supporters. He'd been accused by Republicans in Congress of acting "weak" toward China. In fact, the outspoken Senator Joseph McCarthy blamed Acheson for the Korean War's bad turn of events. Acheson was "tying MacArthur's hands," claimed Senator McCarthy, by not allowing him to bomb China directly, "where it hurts."39

General Douglas MacArthur did ask Truman to be allowed to bomb military and supply sites across the border in China. Mac-Arthur also wanted to send the non-Communist Chinese army, now stationed on the island of Formosa, to fight against the Communist Chinese on the mainland. Truman didn't want a wider war with China or the Soviet Union. When MacArthur went public with his requests, President Truman abruptly fired him, which ignited a storm of protest around the country. Stuffed dummies of Truman and Acheson were hung in effigy, while some Republicans called for their impeachment. The White House received 78,000 telegrams, with only one in twenty in favor of MacArthur's firing.

TV newscasts soon showed films of MacArthur's return to America, landing in California as crowds of his supporters broke through police lines. Hundreds of thousands of people lined his motorcade routes in California and in Washington, DC, when he came to address a joint session of Congress on April 20, 1951. In this case, all the TV networks televised MacArthur's speech live, shortly after noon, to an audience of over 30 million viewers.

The seventy-one-year-old MacArthur had never spoken on television before; in fact, he had never seen a TV set until he landed in California that week. Yet he gave one of the most dramatic speeches ever seen on TV by the American public. He spoke of Asia past and present, of Japan and its recovery, of Korea and China, and he repeated his call for stronger actions against China. "In war there is no substitute for victory," he said.40 MacArthur was interrupted thirty times by applause, mostly from Republicans who saw his message as politically damaging to President Truman and the Democrats.

MacArthur spoke to Congress on TV for thirty-four minutes, and he closed with a dramatic and eloquent farewell. "Old soldiers never die," he said with tears in his eyes, quoting from a West Point barracks song. "They just fade away. And like the old soldier of that ballad, I now close my military career and just fade away, an old soldier who tried to do his duty as God gave him the light to see that duty. Good-bye."41

In the west wing of the White House, President Truman and his staff were watching MacArthur as well on TV. "A hundred percent bullshit," said Truman as the speech ended.42 But the next afternoon, the President was booed throwing out the first ball on baseball's opening day; meanwhile, millions of cheering New Yorkers gave MacArthur a ticker-tape parade. MacArthur's televised speech had raised emotions among the public, favoring him and hurting Truman.

For the next few weeks, the general toured the nation's big cities, then its small cities, all triumphantly. This mood of national support lasted only into the early summer, when Congress held hearings on his dismissal and aired both sides of the controversy. Although Truman regained some respect for his handling of MacArthur, he never regained the public support he'd lost that afternoon in April 1951; facing likely defeat, he chose not to run for reelection the following year. By then, the Korean War had reached a stalemate, and General Douglas MacArthur was fulfilling his own televised prophecy, as the "old soldier" faded away from public attention.

EXPANDING THE DAILY SCHEDULE

MacArthur's memorable speech to Congress was televised during the daytime—when the viewing audience, in theory, was sparse. Most adults, after all, were too busy on the job or doing housework to watch TV, and most children were in school. Yet somehow tens of millions of Americans had watched those special programs; even accounting for those who'd taken the day off, it was still a surprisingly big audience. By the end of 1950, however, American television had expanded its viewing hours well into the daytime, as the networks and local stations alike saw the potential to attract viewers and sponsors.

In Detroit, for example, the TV day began at 7:00 a.m.; in Cincinnati, it began at 8:15 a.m. The daytime hours were now filled with programs that were targeted mainly at the American housewife, of which an estimated 7 million now had TV sets. Surveys showed that 5 million of those sets were on sometime during the afternoon, and that women were now watching TV an hour or two more per week than men. *Look* magazine profiled one of them, Eileen Turyn, mother of two infant baby boomers, in an April 1951 article titled, "Temptation." Turyn each day faced the new "housewife's dilemma," *Look* wrote, of choosing between her chores and television. "She knows that, once she turns her set on, her work schedule is doomed." Still, she "allows herself one afternoon program, but only if Kathy and Tommy are otherwise occupied and only if she has planned a simple dinner for her husband."[43]

For her one program a day, Eileen Turyn could choose among talk shows, cooking and fashion demonstrations, and even exercise shows that were aired on local stations around the country in 1950 and 1951. Such shows were inexpensive to produce but attractive to sponsors aiming for the family member who purchased household products. The networks, too, were now airing several hours of low-budget "housewife" shows, such as Du Mont's *Okay, Mother,* hosted by Dennis James, and CBS's *Homemaker's Exchange.*

Added to the daytime TV schedule were a few network programs that were produced on a bigger budget. *The First Hundred Years* and *Hawkins Falls—Population 6,200* were daytime serials; although neither lasted long, they helped make soap operas a permanent fixture for the networks. *Winner Take All* was a daytime quiz show, soon to be joined by *Strike It Rich* and later by a host of others. Both *The Garry Moore Show* and *The Kate Smith Show* were daytime network variety programs, with music, talk, and comedy. Kate Smith had been the leading female singer on network radio; now she was being watched in 2 million homes on weekday afternoons.

Also by the end of 1950, American television was filling in other hours of the week. The daytime hours of Saturday and Sunday now featured both local and network programs—Westerns, circus and children's shows, public issues programs—with audiences peaking late Saturday afternoon and from noontime through the afternoon on Sundays. On weeknights, TV had extended the viewing schedule beyond 11:00 p.m., thereby changing the sleeping patterns of the American public. In New York, for example, three out of four sets were on late at least one night per week; on any given night, half the sets were on after 11:00 p.m.

Two-thirds of the New Yorkers who reported watching late-night TV had previously been asleep at that time. Now they were watching, in particular, *Broadway Open House,* an NBC network program that aired weeknights in 1950 and 1951 from 11:00 p.m. to midnight. *Broadway Open House* created a new genre in American entertainment—the late-night talk show, featuring a comic as host, show business guests, a house band, sketches, "in-jokes," and risqué humor. Similar to *The Tonight Show* and the many others that succeeded it, *Broadway Open House* had Americans staying up later than they were supposed to, sharing an experience that was both trendy and informal—and a bit naughty.

Chapter 9

Linking Coast to Coast

COLOR TV BEGINS

In the fall of 1950 another decision by the FCC threw the TV industry off its stride. On the important matter of color TV, the FCC announced the result of eight months of testimony and 12,000 pages of reports and transcripts. The government agency would approve only one color system to sell to the public: surprisingly, it was the CBS spinning disk mechanism. The FCC claimed that the CBS system promised good pictures, unlike RCA's all-electronic technology thus far.

The switch to the CBS spinning disk technology would, however, make obsolete the 7 million TV sets in operation and the thousands still being sold each day. The FCC's answer was for the TV industry to begin making new sets with so-called "bracket standards," which meant they could receive both the current black-and-white signals and the new CBS color signals. RCA, Philco, Du Mont, and most other TV set manufacturers quickly announced they were unwilling to build new sets with bracket standards. RCA took their case to court, filing a suit with the United States Superior Court to overturn the FCC decision.

As for CBS, the apparent winners in the contest to bring color TV to the market, company president Frank Stanton advised the public not to buy new sets unless they could be adapted to receive color signals. His company announced plans to demonstrate the spinning disk color TV to the public and press in a series of special broadcasts. The color broadcasts began in New York on November 13, 1950, with five shows a day. To the press and public, the spinning disk was kept out of sight, hidden inside the TV consoles. Instead, CBS promoted an apparatus made by Teletone Radio to convert a black-and-white set to color. The converter had its own picture tube, with a 12-inch screen.

On screen again for the color broadcasts was model Patty Painter (who had displayed colors for CBS back in 1946), wearing a striped blouse and dropping red and yellow roses into a bowl. Other segments of the CBS show included a bowl of fresh fruit, packs of soap and cigarettes, a ballerina and puppets, a map of Europe and flags of nations, and Van Gogh reproductions. The colors were impressive, even if the technology was flawed.

On November 15, however, a federal court in Chicago put a temporary restraining order on CBS and the FCC, who were planning to begin commercial color broadcasts the following week. The judges declared it "unthinkable" to act hastily "in view of the importance and complications of this issue," and they set no date for their final decision.[1] Thus, TV would remain black-and-white for the near future.

By this time, RCA's David Sarnoff had his engineers working sixteen-hour shifts, including weekends, to prepare for a public demonstration of RCA's own color technology. In December 1950, the engineers showed the press and the public their latest work from their laboratories in Princeton. RCA's color demonstration matched CBS's almost point by point: they used Christmas toys, for example, instead of soap and cigarettes. The RCA demonstration had no effect on the U.S. District Court. The judges ruled in late December that the FCC and CBS could go ahead and launch commercial color TV using the spinning disk system.

In its decision, the Chicago federal court also questioned why the FCC would want to begin color television now, in view of the defense emergency that had recently been declared by President Truman. They noted that their ruling would no doubt be appealed before the U.S. Supreme Court.

THE CRIME COMMISSION HEARINGS

In New Orleans, St. Louis, and Detroit in February 1951, congressional hearings on organized crime were televised by local stations, and they caught on with the viewing public. In Detroit, for example, the two days of testimony on station WWJ-TV were watched on about 90 percent of the city's 435,000 TV sets.

The hearings were run by Senator Estes Kefauver of Tennessee, who was taking his Senate Crime Investigating Committee to fourteen big cities around the country. In each city, Kefauver and his committee heard testimony under oath from an assortment of lawmen, crooks, and politicians. The American public had a captivating "true life" TV drama to watch, filled with bad deeds and unsavory characters.

When the Senate Crime Investigating Committee moved to New York on March 12, 1951, daytime ratings for TV soared, as homemakers and workers alike stopped their chores to watch. Even the New York Stock Exchange slowed down its dealings. The biggest name testifying in New York was a leading crime figure, Frank Costello. In his first day of testimony, Costello objected to having his face on TV. Instead, the camera focused on his hands as they moved and gestured nervously. Costello refused to answer many of the questions he was asked, citing his rights under the Fifth Amendment.

By now, the hearings were being televised live to twenty cities in the East and Midwest, with an estimated 20 to 30 million people watching. "All along the TV cable," described *Life,* people "had suddenly gone indoors—into living rooms, taverns and clubrooms, auditoriums and back offices. There, in eerie half-light . . . people sat as if charmed." The hearings had become "almost the sole subject of national conversation."[2]

Once again, the audience for a TV program had become news in itself. To some, the news was good: TV had captured the interest of Americans in a public issue and in watching government proceedings. As one TV executive suggested, "Perhaps television is going to change the one great American habit which none of us thought too much about—apathy."[3] Yet the hearings did seem like entertainment. In St. Louis, TV stations rescheduled their programs so that the testimony of a local sports betting figure, James J. Carroll, could be aired. However, Carroll refused to testify in front of the TV cameras, saying he didn't want "to be made an object of ridicule."[4]

Senator Kefauver himself told Carroll that TV was now "a recognized medium of public information along with radio and newspapers."[5] The lines between news and entertainment, and between public officials and performers, were blurring. The Senate Crime Commission Investigation hearings had made Senator Kefauver a national celebrity, and he even appeared on the TV network quiz program, *What's My Line?* The first question posed to him by a blindfolded panel, who had to guess his occupation, was, "Are you in the entertainment business?" After the studio audience stopped laughing, he replied, "No, ma'am."

With roughly 12 million sets tuned to over 100 stations around the country, TV was supplanting radio as America's favorite home medium. The Crime Committee hearings in early 1951 would become the first of a number of public hearings on TV; through Watergate in the 1970s and beyond, the live televising of dramatic public debates in America would be a double-edged sword. Television added elements of mass entertainment to the controversies being aired. Video lights and cameras could transform a public hearing into a "three-ring circus," in which officials and testifiers played to the home audience.

AMOS 'N' ANDY

Another national controversy—racism—touched TV in the middle of 1951 when telecasts began of *Amos 'n' Andy,* one of the most successful entertainment shows of modern times. The creators of *Amos 'n' Andy,* Freeman Gosden and Charles Correll, had begun working together on radio in 1925. Their musical and comedy act was strongly influenced by American minstrel shows in which white performers wore blackface and spoke in heavy accents to portray clownish versions of African Americans.

Gosden and Correll soon developed their act into a comedy series for network radio, *Amos 'n' Andy,* which caught on with the public in the late 1920s, at the same time that radio itself became popular. In the 1930s *Amos 'n' Andy* had a remarkably large audience of 40 million listeners, and its popularity affected national daily life. Work stopped, stores and theaters closed, telephones were quiet and water usage dropped weeknights from 7:00 to 7:15 when the show aired. *Amos 'n' Andy* became less popular in the 1940s, and by 1947 Godsen and Correll were looking to TV as a new medium for their program.

Other radio shows that switched to TV, however, did not have to be recast with new performers before they could be televised as *Amos 'n' Andy* did. On the radio, many of the show's African-American characters were played by whites, including Godsen and Correll, who performed the leading roles themselves. On TV the black characters had to look realistic, so black performers were needed by the dozens. With much publicity, Godsen and Correll conducted a nationwide talent hunt for cast members, and even President Truman offered a tip on someone to hire for the show's major character, the "Kingfish."

By early 1951, Gosden and Correll had assembled a cast of veteran African-American performers and hired Charles Barton to direct them. Barton had directed Abbott and Costello movies and other comedies at Universal Studios. In February 1951, filming of the first episodes of *Amos 'n' Andy* began at Hal Roach Studios in Culver City, California, where the *Keystone Kops, Little Rascals,* and other classic comedy series were made in the 1920s and 1930s. By then, the TV series had secured a sponsor, Blatz Brewing Company, and a place in the CBS network schedule for the summer and fall seasons.

The show premiered on TV on June 28, 1951, with these words from the CBS announcer: "Out of the library of American folklore, those treasured stories of Huck Finn, Paul Bunyan, and Rip Van Winkle . . . come the warm and lovable tales of Amos and Andy." In that first episode the show's protagonist, the scheming Kingfish, plotted to marry off his mother-in-law at the expense of his friend, the gullible Andy Brown. Before the second episode could air the following week, however, *Amos 'n' Andy* had already set off a small social furor.

The problem was the way in which the series depicted African Americans. On the one hand, *Amos 'n' Andy* featured a middle-class community in New York's Harlem, peopled with successful black businessmen and professionals. Even to this day, only a handful of network TV series have been situated in black urban communities. *Amos 'n' Andy* provided work on network TV to scores of black performers—a group that the medium had mostly ignored up to this point. The actor who played the janitor Lightnin' in the series, Horace ("Nick") Stewart, used his earnings to fund a professional African-American theater company in Los Angeles.

On the other hand, the series focused on buffoonish characters who spoke with thick accents, misused the English language, acted irresponsibly, and avoided work. As *Variety* wrote in its review of the first episode, "Considering that this is the first major use of Negroes in commercial broadcasting," CBS and the show's producers and sponsor should not have "offend[ed] the sensibilities of a large segment of the U.S. population."[6]

Even before the first episode aired, America's leading civil rights group, the National Association for the Advancement of Colored People (NAACP), had filed for a court injunction to stop CBS. Once the series began, the NAACP called on Blatz Brewing to drop its sponsorship of the show, which they described as a "gross libel on the Negro and distortion of the truth."[7] They were later joined in protest by labor groups and church organizations.

But CBS and Blatz continued to televise new episodes of *Amos 'n' Andy* for two seasons, until June 1953 when Blatz withdrew as a sponsor. Even then, CBS continued to profit from *Amos 'n' Andy* for another dozen years. The network sold copies of the episodes on film to stations around the country, thus making *Amos 'n' Andy* the first network TV series to have a second life in syndication.

"We weren't kidding race. We were kidding people," said Correll years later of the series and controversy he and Godsen had created.[8] By the mid-1960s, American society had undergone a change in attitude toward racial stereotypes in the media. A program that portrayed African Americans so negatively, for whatever purpose, could no longer be televised without creating a storm of protest from a variety of people. *Amos 'n' Andy* has not been aired on TV since 1965, although videotapes of its episodes from 1951-1953 are regularly sold in stores and by mail order.

HOLLYWOOD AND THE COAST-TO-COAST LINK

Amos 'n' Andy had another distinction in the history of American television: it was the first big-budget comedy series to be filmed in Hollywood. In a sense, the roots of *Amos 'n' Andy* on TV were in *Hopalong Cassidy* as well as in minstrel shows. Back in 1949, the success of *Hopalong Cassidy* made it clear that TV could be a gold mine for filmed programs from Hollywood. *Hopalong* was followed quickly by *The Lone Ranger* in September 1949 and *The Gene Autry Show* in July 1950, both filmed in Hollywood.

These TV Westerns were joined in 1949-1951 by other programs filmed in Hollywood. *Your Show Time* was a series from Hollywood that adapted classic short stories into half-hour dramas for TV; it ran for six months in 1949 and won TV's first Emmy award for a filmed program. *The Life of Riley,* a domestic comedy, premiered in October 1949. It won the second Emmy and starred Jackie Gleason two years before he began hosting Du Mont's *Cavalcade of Stars.* The show was canceled after five months, only to resurface in 1953 with a new star, William Bendix, and higher ratings.

The Hank McCune Show, which ran on NBC from September to December 1950, was a comedy from Hollywood that carries the distinction of being the first TV series with a "laugh track" added to the show after it was filmed. Another domestic comedy, *The Stu Erwin Show,* starred film and radio actor Stu Erwin as a bumbling father and high school principal; it began its five-year run on network TV in October 1950.

Also premiering that month was *Beulah,* a comedy series about a black maid and the white middle-class family whose house she kept. Like *Amos 'n' Andy,* a white actor had played "Beulah" for years on the radio. On TV, Beulah was played first by Ethel Waters, a veteran of films, theater, and popular music, then by actress Louise Beavers. The series ran for three years despite protests from the NAACP and others because of its racial stereotyping.

Amos 'n' Andy followed in the footsteps of these pioneering TV series filmed in Hollywood, but with a generous weekly budget of $40,000 to spend on writers, sets, costumes, technicians, and talent. In fact, the debut of *Amos 'n' Andy* on TV in June 1951 signaled a new era for the industry in which Hollywood's money, resources, and talent would play much larger roles.

The motion picture industry had shunned TV throughout the 1940s, but now television was surpassing radio in its audience size and advertising dollars, and TV was making inroads in Hollywood's popularity as well. Movie box-office receipts had dropped as much as a third in markets with TV stations; the loss had led to cutbacks and layoffs among the Hollywood studios. In response, some of the studios (e.g., Warner Brothers, Republic, and Universal) had set up divisions or subsidiary companies to produce films for TV.

In mid-1951, TV was about to become a coast-to-coast live medium. AT&T was preparing to launch a $40 million relay system to link stations in the East and Midwest to stations on the West Coast. For the first time, live images would be transmitted in an instant from New York to Denver and over the Rocky Mountains to Salt Lake City, San Francisco, and Los Angeles. A million TV families in California would be able to see the popular network programs televised live from the East, while the rest of the country could now watch live TV shows from Hollywood.

The new AT&T link to the West Coast was pressed into an early opening on September 4, 1951, to televise a moment of history. Three thousand delegates from fifty-two nations had gathered in San Francisco's Opera House for the Japanese Peace Treaty Conference to officially end World War II. The first person to speak and be seen live on TV from the Atlantic to the Pacific was the Mayor of San Francisco, Elmer Robinson. All he did, however, was introduce Secretary of State Dean Acheson, who in turn introduced his boss, President Harry Truman. The President's striped tie and breast-pocket handkerchief were clearly seen by tens of millions of Americans, linked for the first time in a national TV network.

Truman spoke of America's war enemy, Japan, now starting to re-enter the world economy. "The new Japan will not find the world entirely friendly and trusting," Truman said. "It will have to keep on working to win the friendship and trust of other peoples over the years to come."[9] Coincidentally, Japan ordered its first TV set just a few weeks after Truman's speech. Little did Truman—or anyone else—realize that Japan would someday dominate the TV manufacturing industry with technology that Americans trusted, and that its Sony Corporation would come to own the RCA Building.

CBS used the new coast-to-coast link on Sunday, September 23, 1951, for a telethon to raise money for pro-democracy efforts in Europe. Television signals crossed the continent from New York in the morning and from Hollywood at night, sending live pictures of the *Amos 'n' Andy* cast and other performers and officials. On the following Sunday, September 30, 1951, the new age of regular coast-to-coast broadcasting began for real. "Hollywood TV Premiere!" trumpeted a newspaper advertisement in New York that day. "Now it's all yours—all the glitter and fun of Hollywood alive—and first-hand and this-very-instant."[10]

The CBS station in Los Angeles, KTSL, was the first to use the link, transmitting live programs from New York in the late afternoon and early evening. The first TV show from the West Coast was NBC's *Comedy Hour,* starring Eddie Cantor, televised live from the El Capitan Theater in Hollywood. Cantor recapped his long career in show business and marked the occasion by highlighting the cities he'd played that were now part of the vast TV network: St. Louis, Pittsburgh, Chicago, San Francisco, and others.

Later that night another show-business veteran, Red Skelton, premiered his NBC program from Hollywood. On stage almost the entire half hour by himself, Skelton played some of the comic characters he'd developed on radio: Clem Kadiddlehopper, the cowboy Dead Eye, the politician San Fernando Red, and the "mean little kid." Wrote Jack Gould the next day in *The New York Times,* Skelton is "a comedian who is something of an acquired taste," his humor "built around little hats and big grimaces," and he wondered what Red "[would] do five or six weeks from now."[11]

Instead, four months later Red Skelton had TV's top-rated show and an Emmy award for Best Comedian. Over the next few years, Skelton survived a series of personal and professional setbacks to become one of TV's most popular comedians. *The Red Skelton Show,* with its "little hats and big grimaces," was on the air from 1951-1971, ranking third on TV historians Brooks and Marsh's list of all-time top series.[12]

THE BIRTH OF I LOVE LUCY

The new coast-to-coast link allowed Red Skelton and other Hollywood stars to be seen live by tens of millions of people all at once. However, this immediacy carried a price. On live TV, an embarrassing mistake or poor performance might by seen by a big audience; Hollywood's film talent were accustomed to having such material reshot or edited before an audience could see it.

One Hollywood couple's first appearance on live TV, on *The Ed Wynn Show* in 1950, was marred by mistakes. When Desi Arnaz reached the finale of his one song on the show, "A Big Straw Hat," he tossed the straw hat into the air—and dropped it by mistake. He moved off camera to retrieve it—another mistake—and failed to sing the last line of the song. His wife, Lucille Ball, lost her wig at the climax of her big sketch, and the stage curtain closed on her by mistake during the final joke.

Thus, when Arnaz and Ball made plans in mid-1951 to begin their own TV series, *I Love Lucy,* from Hollywood, one of their first key decisions was to do their show on film. "We were doing situation comedy, which, to be funny and real, also has to be believable," Desi Arnaz wrote later. "I just knew we could do a better show on film."[13] The couple's network, CBS, and their sponsors, Phillip Morris, wanted *I Love Lucy* performed live on stage because they felt that Lucille Ball wasn't as funny without an audience.

They compromised, deciding to make *I Love Lucy* the first TV series of its kind to be filmed live before an audience. They chose a system for TV developed by Jerry Fairbanks, a former Hollywood cameraman, in which three movie cameras filmed the show simultaneously to get close-ups, medium shots, and long shots from different locations. Afterward, all the film footage was edited to create a half-hour show, with a quality that approximated a Hollywood movie.

Fairbanks was himself filming a TV situation comedy in Hollywood in 1951, *Jackson and Jill,* about a young husband and his scatterbrained wife. But *Jackson and Jill* was filmed on a sound stage, without an audience. Scenes could be reshot, or shot out of sequence, with lights and cameras moved and adjusted at will. This would not be the case for *I Love Lucy.* With an audience present, Ball and Arnaz wanted to perform each episode as if it were a short play, with a minimum of stops and distractions.

To design a system for filming with an audience in the studio, Arnaz and Ball hired Karl Freund, a legendary cameraman. Freund had won an Oscar for *The Good Earth* in 1937; he'd also filmed *Metropolis, Dracula,* and Greta Garbo in *Camille.* Freund and the show's production staff quickly refashioned a Hollywood film studio, General Service (where Shirley Temple had debuted in the 1930s) to film the first *I Love Lucy* on Saturday night, September 8, 1951.

That night 300 people took seats in the new bleachers built inside the General Service studio. They were welcomed by Desi Arnaz, a Cuban immigrant who had already built a career in Latin-American music, in films, in nightclubs, and on radio. Arnaz pointed out to the audience the three cameras, the dozens of lights, and the production and technical crew, including Karl Freund, situated between them and the set. He introduced Lucille Ball, who had been a Follies showgirl in the 1930s and a leading lady for RKO Pictures and CBS radio in the 1940s. She was followed on the set by William Frawley, a Hollywood character actor with nearly 100 screen credits, and by Vivian Vance, who had acted in only two movies. Vance later admitted she was "scared to death" that night.

The cast took their places, and the cameras began to roll. Playing Lucy Ricardo, Lucille Ball was engrossed in a mystery novel that would lead her to wonder if husband Ricky was plotting to murder her. It was basic "screwball comedy," using standard themes and plot lines from Hollywood and radio scripts, but the cast was talented, and the production was of top quality. For roughly an hour, the audience in the bleachers laughed at the funny lines, physical humor, and even a dog act that was part of the script. "When the laughs started coming," Lucille Ball later recalled, "I was very relieved. I remember saying, 'Whew! It's working.'"14

With their first show in the can, the cast and crew of *I Love Lucy* continued to film new episodes in front of studio audiences and edit the footage for their show's debut on TV. On October 15, 1951, two weeks after the coast-to-coast link had been launched, they gathered in the home of their director, Marc Daniels, after a long rehearsal to watch the first *I Love Lucy* telecast. According to Daniels, they all "just sat there motionless staring at the set."15 The only one laughing was Vivian Vance's husband, who was also the only one who hadn't seen the episode before.

Also laughing that night, however, were millions of other Americans from coast-to-coast: *I Love Lucy* was ranked among the week's top ten shows. In its review the following week, *Variety* called *I Love Lucy* a "slick blending of Hollywood and TV showmanship," with "all the Grade A qualities of major studio production [and] the desired intimacy for TV."16 *Variety* predicted the show would create a demand for similar filmed sitcoms on TV.

THE "HOLLYWOOD BOOM" BEGINS

Indeed, as *I Love Lucy* quickly climbed the ratings—seventh in December, fifth in January, second in March, and first in April—Hollywood's film studios began cranking out similar half-hour comedies to fill TV screens. *My Friend Irma* debuted in January 1952, followed by *My Little Margie* in June, *A Date with Judy* in July, *My Favorite Husband* and *Heaven for Betsy* in September, and in October 1952 *I Married Joan, Meet Millie,* and *Our Miss Brooks.* Focusing on the comic lives of their female stars, they were among 2,000 pilot TV shows filmed in Hollywood by late 1952. "The great Hollywood boom is underway," reported the *Saturday Evening Post.* "The word is out that fortunes are to be made in filming original programs for television.... Supermarkets, neighborhood theaters, and even private family garages had been converted to temporary or semipermanent sound stages."17

Within a year, the daily fare on TV screens was filling up with West Coast programming. From the networks came filmed situation comedies, family comedies, and live variety shows. The majority of these new programs were televised by CBS, which built a complex of TV studios and offices in Los Angeles in 1952 as a new West Coast production center. NBC opened its own West Coast production center in Burbank in late 1952 for its own Hollywood shows, which included *Dragnet, The Red Skelton Show,* and *This Is Your Life.*

From independent producers such as Jerry Fairbanks came syndicated TV shows on films, such as *Sky King, Annie Oakley,* and *Ramar of the Jungle*—all were low-budget Hollywood TV series in 1953, filmed in the style of Hollywood B movies. *Ramar of the Jungle,* for example, was filmed outside Los Angeles at the estate of an eccentric millionaire who had outdoor foliage resembling jungles and swamplands. Playing African natives were African-American college football players, and the series used film footage shot in Mexico of animals fighting each other. The Society for the Prevention of Cruelty to Animals (SPCA) wouldn't allow such footage to be filmed in the United States.

This Hollywood boom, however, brought fallout to another big city, Chicago, which for a few years had served as the second hub for network TV and live programs. Hollywood had become TV's new second hub, and the industry had no real need for a third. Chicago's programs soon dropped off the network schedules, and the Chicago School of Television shut down.

In one case a small storm resulted. Two months after the link to California opened, NBC cut its popular puppet show from Chicago, *Kukla, Fran and Ollie,* from thirty to fifteen minutes a day, just as Burr Tillstrom had predicted. Jack Gould of the *Times* had once described *Kukla* as "just about the only literate offering on the air." Now he called NBC's decision to cut it "cultural totalitarianism," and his paper ran a series of protest letters. "The main justification of TV's existence is 'Kukla, Fran and Ollie,' " wrote one viewer, while another described NBC executives as "myopic numskulls with more authority than brains."[18]

In one week, NBC received 3,000 letters on *Kukla, Fran and Ollie,* but six months later the network cut the show down to just once a week, on Sunday afternoons. "This treatment is a sad commentary," wrote Jack Gould,[19] but it symbolized the fate of TV shows from Chicago and cities other than New York and Los Angeles once the two coasts were linked.

Gould wondered "why in heaven's name" the networks didn't seek more programming outside of New York and Hollywood.[20] Jules Herbuveaux, who was in a position to know as NBC's chief of programming for Chicago, had a simple answer. "He who holds the gold," he would say, "makes the decisions."[21] And in the early days of network TV, the gold was in the hands of the sponsors and their advertising agencies. "With large sums at stake," wrote *Time* in 1951, the sponsors and agencies "prefer to have their programs produced and staged close at hand, where they can keep a firm finger in the pie."[22] "Close at hand" meant New York at first for the sponsors, then either New York or Hollywood and Los Angeles after 1951.

THE TODAY SHOW

As TV from Chicago faded from the network screen, a number of its performers and production figures headed where the "gold" was—to either coast. Among the Chicago School alumni who continued their careers in TV was Dave Garroway, who had been cast adrift by NBC when *Garroway at Large* was canceled in 1951. Garroway was not well regarded among NBC executives, despite his success in Chicago, but he managed to talk himself into a key role with a new network show, during an all-night conversation with one of its producers in a Chicago hotel room.

"The spot was made for me," Garroway claimed when he'd first heard of the show, called *Rise and Shine*.[23] It was the brainchild of Sylvester "Pat" Weaver, an NBC vice president who was one of the TV industry's visionaries. Pat Weaver had been partly responsible for the successful *Your Show of Shows,* and in 1949 he had lobbied for what he called "Operation Frontal Lobe," which was his notion to introduce high culture and educational material gradually into the regular network schedule. Operation Frontal Lobe failed quickly when it attracted little interest among sponsors.

Weaver's new idea was an early-morning network TV show that would compete with radio for the attention of the nation's families. Weaver envisioned an audience that would listen to the show from other rooms in the house, then come in to watch the set when something caught their interest. "We want America to shave, to eat, to dress, to get to work on time," Weaver explained in a memo. "But we also want America to be well informed, to be amused, to be lightened in spirit and in heart, and to be reinforced in inner resolution through knowledge."[24]

Weaver also envisioned a complex set for *Rise and Shine,* filled with all types of communications technology. The show's host would be "the Communicator," who would serve each morning as "the news center of the world." Instead, Weaver's show was televised from a storefront studio in the RCA Exhibit Hall, visible to New Yorkers and tourists walking by; its "Communicator" was a bemused, low-key Dave Garroway. The show premiered, on Monday, January 14, 1952, at 7 a.m., with a new name, *Today,* and with NBC advertisements proclaiming it "a television revolution" and "the most exciting thing that has happened in broadcasting in a decade."[25]

Today barely survived its first months on the air, however. The show had at first only one sponsor, *Changing Times* magazine, and half of NBC's affiliated TV stations around the country were refusing to air it. Uncooperative, too, was NBC's news division. They believed *Today* intruded on their domain, and they held back their best film footage for their own evening news program. In its first week on the air, *Today* received devastating reviews. "Do yourself a favor, NBC," wrote one TV critic. "Roll over and go to sleep."[26] The *Herald Tribune* called *Today* a "two-hour comedy of errors,"[27] and the *Times* described it as "excessively pretentious and ostentatious and unreasonably confusing and complex."[28] The critics ridiculed how Garroway phoned a reporter in Germany to hear about the weather and another in London to introduce a phonograph record. As for the series of clocks above Garroway's horseshoe-shaped desk, critic John Crosby asked, "Why would I want to know the time in Tokyo?"[29]

Midway through 1952, *Today* was losing money for NBC at a rate of $1.7 million a year. Yet many viewers were pleased with the show, especially those in parts of the country without a good source for national and foreign news. *Today* survived its shaky start and within a few years had become a big moneymaker for the network, with Dave Garroway as host until 1955.

Over the years, *Today* launched the careers of Hugh Downs, Barbara Walters, Tom Brokaw, Jane Pauley, Willard Scott, Frank McGee, Bryant Gumbel, John Chancellor, Katie Couric, and a chimp named J. Fred Muggs. Although one of its many imitators, *Good Morning America,* has surpassed it in ratings, *Today* now ranks with *Meet the Press* as the only programs from TV's early years that remain on the air.

NEW HAMPSHIRE AND "IKE"

Much of the news that *Today* reported in its early months was political, as the United States was beginning to undergo a great shift in leadership. The year 1952 would culminate in a presidential election, with the Republicans favored to oust the unpopular Harry Truman, should he choose to run again.

Television covered the first primary balloting of 1952, in New Hampshire, as it had no other previous election—in depth and in person. TV reporters and camera crews "swarmed over the state," noted Jack Gould in the *Times,* who suggested that "the vivid lesson of the New Hampshire primary is that campaigns in the TV age are going to be conducted in a goldfish bowl."[30] Notably absent from that goldfish bowl, however, was the Republican winner in New Hampshire, Dwight Eisenhower, who was stationed in Paris as the first supreme commander of the NATO armed forces.

As with Wendell Willkie in 1940, Eisenhower had never held or even run for a political office before; however, his World War II leadership had made him a popular national figure, with a short record of successful TV appearances. Eisenhower's return from Europe after V-E Day had been a highlight of American television in 1945; it was followed by his Lincoln Day wreath-laying ceremony in early 1946, in the first network broadcast from Washington, DC. His best-selling memoirs of the war, *Crusade in Europe,* had been turned into a TV series in 1949; it was television's first documentary series, and it featured much film footage of Eisenhower as well as passages from his book.

Eisenhower's biggest connection to TV, however, was in the company he kept, especially during his postwar years in New York, when he served as president of Columbia University before being called back into service to lead NATO. With the help of his brother, Milton Eisenhower, who had years of experience in managing government/ press relations, "Ike" became friends with RCA's David Sarnoff,

CBS's William Paley, with Henry Luce of *Time* and *Life*, and with the leaders of the top New York advertising agencies.

In the early months of 1952, these media moguls helped form and support a "Citizens for Eisenhower" movement that promoted him for president. In February 1952, the Citizens for Eisenhower and other groups of supporters staged a fund-raising rally in Madison Square Garden that was broadcast on television and radio. Hosted by TV's Jinx Falkenberg and Tex McCrary, the program featured Clark Gable, Mary Martin, Ethel Merman, Richard Rodgers, Fred Waring, and the legendary songwriter Irving Berlin, who sang his new composition, "I Like Ike," to the crowd.

By the middle of March, Ike had won the first two Republican primaries—in New Hampshire and a surprising write-in victory in Minnesota. Still stationed in Paris, he seemed propelled on a collision course with Republican conservatives, led by Robert Taft, and with his own boss, President Truman. As had Roosevelt in 1940, Truman refused to commit himself to another term and, in fact, kept his name off the ballot in New Hampshire. That primary was won instead by Senator Estes Kefauver, who had become a national figure through the televised crime hearings in 1950.

Then, on March 29, 1952, the race for the White House took a dramatic turn. In a speech to a dinner crowd of Democrats in Washington, DC, that was televised live on a third of the CBS network, President Truman departed from his text to say, "I shall not be a candidate for reelection. . . . I shall not accept a renomination."[31] Now, for the first time in two generations, since the 1920 election, the American public would truly have a fresh choice for President, with no incumbent running for reelection.

THE FREEZE IS LIFTED

Truman warned his audience at the dinner and on TV that night that his Republican opponents "have slick advertising experts" who would try to convince the public that "everything the Government has done for the country is socialism." With sarcasm, Truman said, "And here you are, with your new car, and your home, and better opportunities for the kids, and a television set—just surrounded by socialism." Vote Republican, he warned, "and you'll probably have a garage and no car, a crystal radio set and no television."[32]

In his speech, Truman conveniently ignored the fact that much of the country still had no TV because of the FCC's freeze on building stations, now in its fourth year. However, 1952 was a big national election year, and the freeze may have seemed too potent a campaign issue to continue much longer. Just two weeks after Truman's speech, on Easter Sunday in April 1952, the FCC lifted the freeze.

The agency announced that it would license up to 2,053 television stations in 1,291 communities around the nation, including the 108 currently on the air. Seventy percent of the licenses would be reserved for stations in the UHF (higher frequency) band of the spectrum, which the FCC was now subdividing into seventy channels to add to the twelve channels already on the lower VHF band. The licensing process would begin on July 1, 1952—eleven years to the day after the FCC had allowed commercial TV to begin.

The FCC's decree in April 1952 was sweeping; to a great extent, it shaped American television for the next thirty years. First, it thoroughly ended any chance that TV channels would be reserved for rural areas. In the early 1940s, the FCC had considered the idea of "community" channels, which would not be assigned to a city or town. Nothing along those lines could be found in the FCC's new allocations, and that led two of the agency's seven commissioners to vote against it.

A third FCC commissioner, Frieda Hennock, also voted against the allocations, claiming that they shortchanged the educational needs of the American public. In fact, the FCC was setting aside 242 of its licenses for educational stations, eighty in the VHF band. Hennock complained that New York City, for example, had only one such license available, despite the city's vast expanse of cultural and educational institutions. In allotting 242 potential licenses for education, the FCC seemed to have staked a middle ground between Frieda Hennock and others who wanted at least one-fourth of all stations for education and culture, and the TV industry—especially the networks—who wanted the broadcast spectrum to themselves.

The "middle ground" itself was on a slant toward the industry. The FCC rejected the request of some of the educational broadcasters that they be allowed to become part-commercial to help pay for their programs and facilities. In doing so, the FCC gave the networks the advantage of having less competition for the advertising dollars of sponsors. Instead, educational TV would have to seek its funding elsewhere—among governments, colleges, foundations, etc. This decision by the FCC put educational TV in a perpetual economic crunch.

The FCC's April 14 decree also began the endgame, finally, in the contest over color TV. With the freeze lifted, with new stations and new markets set to open, the public was again encouraged to buy TV sets, but these sets would be strictly black-and-white, since color sets and programming were not yet available.

For the future, RCA's color system became the likely winner in the contest against the spinning disks of CBS. RCA's electronic system was "compatible," which would allow the millions of Americans to someday watch color programs in black-and-white on the TV sets they already owned. That's exactly what happened when color TV entered the market later in the 1950s using the RCA system, and soon it became commonplace in the 1960s and 1970s.

In the end, the spinning color disks of the CBS system spun their way into oblivion. All the years of wrangling over color TV had merely slowed the pace of television's march into American culture. Did the money CBS spent on its color system go to waste? Not if the CBS corporate strategy was to thwart an RCA/NBC monopoly of American television. The color controversy and the FCC freeze had given CBS time to catch up to their rival NBC in building a network of TV stations and creating a schedule of popular shows.

LUCY *TAKES OVER*

By the spring of 1952, three of TV's four top-rated programs belonged to CBS, including *I Love Lucy,* the country's new number one show. *I Love Lucy* had quickly and steadily climbed over its competition. It had placed sixteenth in the ratings back in November 1951, but was second by March 1952. Then, on the night of April 7, 1952, *I Love Lucy* reached a milestone in TV history when 10 million homes tuned in to see its twenty-sixth episode, titled "The Marriage License." Thirty million Americans watched Lucy and Ricky Ricardo reexchange their marriage vows after discovering their original license was invalid. The audience was roughly one-fifth of the U.S. population, and it was just a sign of things to come.

Why was *I Love Lucy* so popular? Desi Arnaz gave some of the credit to their production system, which, he claimed, "proved to be the best way to do television comedies." Arnaz also cited the show's writers and the "chemistry . . . rapport and understanding" between the four performers, which had "somehow naturally transfered to the characters" they portrayed.[33]

Another reason for the show's popularity may have been its realism. Within its framework of farce and visual comedy, *I Love Lucy* portrayed two middle-class married couples—friends and neighbors—fighting the eternal battle of the sexes, armed with passion, jealousy, humor, anger, and love. In this case, the show's two main stars were married in real life as well. The Ricardos seemed a genuine couple, sharing a single bed; often the show's themes, plots, and details were rooted in Lucy and Desi's real life together. "The Marriage License," for example, was based in part on the fact that Ball and Arnaz had renewed their vows in 1949, after nine years of marriage.

When Desi Arnaz was asked to assign the credit for the show's success, he said, "I would give Lucy ninety percent and then divide the other ten percent among the rest of us."[34] Lucille Ball was another one of the show business veterans who became TV's first comedy stars. Like Berle, Durante, Gleason, Burns and Allen, and Benny, she brought a wide array of talent and comic skills to the TV screen. She had learned how to handle comic props, for example, from master film comedian Buster Keaton.

In *Lucy,* the hyperactive, overdramatic, but ultimately loveable center of attention, Lucille Ball had found an ideal part to play. The character of Lucy Ricardo may have been easy to identify with among many postwar women, in love with their husbands and homes but feeling constrained and rebellious. Lucy Ricardo is "the embodiment of female energy with no valid outlet," writes Gerard Jones in a study of TV families; she's "a comic demon called forth from the boredom and frustration of an entire generation of housewives."[35]

THE 1952 CONVENTIONS

As the 1952 political conventions approached, Dwight Eisenhower returned to the United States from his post in Europe as the chief of NATO forces to officially join the race for the White House.

Back in 1945, when Ike returned from World War II to a ticker-tape homecoming in New York, it was televised live as a major news event. So, too, was his second homecoming. His home this time, however, was his childhood home in Abilene, Kansas. It was roughly America's geographic center and a telegenic place for him to enter the race—even if he hadn't lived there since 1911.

Abilene had no TV station, but CBS rushed in their cameras and transmitters for live, free coverage of Eisenhower's visit, which brought demands for equal time from Eisenhower's opponent in the primaries, Senator Robert Taft. CBS answered the charge of favoritism by claiming that the Abilene speech was a news event, not a political rally. CBS had good reason to "like Ike" in 1952. In general, the TV industry was counting on a freer hand from the FCC in an Eisenhower administration—indeed, Ike promised in his Abilene speech to curtail the power of federal agencies to regulate industry. In particular, CBS's founder and CEO William Paley had worked for the general in England during the war, socialized with him in New York in the late 1940s, and belonged to the "Citizens for Eisenhower" group that brought him into the race—all of which was true for David Sarnoff, as well. Paley even hoped to become ambassador to England if Eisenhower was nominated and elected.[36]

In the weeks before the Republican convention, more TV stations in the South and Southwest were added to the national network. Viewers in Texas, Louisiana, and elsewhere had been promised "ringside seats for politics," in advertisements run by the TV industry during the weeks prior to the convention.[37] "Ringside seats" they had indeed, as the conservative and moderate wings of the Republican party swatted and slugged each other. (At one point, in fact, a fistfight actually did erupt among the delegates.)

As for television, it finally found in Chicago, where both conventions were held in 1952, the respect it deserved for having become the nation's biggest medium. Television was the reason why Chicago's International Amphitheater was selected as the site: it had the most space—not for the delegates, but for all the TV people. Given the best vantage points inside the hall were TV's cameras, news anchors, and reporters, and its walls were painted blue and gray to look better on TV. The GOP's agenda was squeezed into the prime TV viewing hours, and almost every speaker used a new piece of TV technology, the TelePrompTer, so their eyes kept in contact with the voters in America's living rooms.

TV even affected the convention's outcome. Going into Chicago, conservative Senator Robert Taft needed the votes of just seventy-five more delegates to win the nomination. Eisenhower's supporters made a last-ditch stand at a committee meeting in which delegates from several contested states were to be chosen. CBS and NBC had planned to televise the meeting, but Taft's supporters wouldn't allow TV cameras inside. At one point, the cameras panned an empty meeting room instead. Taft appeared to have something to hide, striking a blow to his image, and the political tide shifted to Eisenhower.

The most dramatic moment on TV at the 1952 convention came during a speech by one of Taft's supporters. At the rostrum and with a big TV audience watching, Senator Everett Dirkson of Illinois pointed a finger right at New York's Governor Tom Dewey, the party's nominee—and loser—in 1944 and 1948. "To all our good friends from the Eastern seacoast," Dirkson said. "We followed you before and you took us down the road to defeat. Don't do it to us again."[38]

The convention hall erupted in howls and boos and even fistfights, all in front of the network TV cameras. But Tom Dewey was an "Ike" supporter, along with most of the Eastern wing of the party, and they held sway. By the time the balloting began, Eisenhower had picked up enough delegates to win the nomination. It would be another dozen years before Republican conservatives finally won the nomination, behind Barry Goldwater, and almost thirty years before they won the Presidency with Ronald Reagan.

The Republican convention also made a national celebrity out of an unknown young actress, Betty Furness. On the set of a kitchen that was built inside the Amphitheater, Furness opened refrigerator doors and pointed to shelves and freezer space. She was the spokesperson/model for Westinghouse appliances in the thirty-four hours of commercials the company televised during the conventions and campaign that summer. Westinghouse paid an estimated $3.6 million for the airtime—a far cry from the few dollars paid by TV's first sponsors back in 1941. The money spent by Westinghouse and other sponsors in 1952 was another indication of TV's new status as the country's most popular medium.

CONGRESS AND THE CODE

Back in 1940, television was caught up briefly in election-year politics when Republicans in Congress held a hearing on the FCC and its red light on TV's growth. In June 1952—another election year—Congress again held hearings on television. This time, the rhetoric focused on the contents of TV programs and whether television caused "juvenile delinquency, loose morals, and crime."39

Congressman Ezekiel Gathings of Arkansas had called for the hearings. Because television "comes right into the living room," Gathings told the House Commerce Committee as the hearings began, TV's content should be of concern to the American public. He noted that a week of early-evening TV in Los Angeles showed ninety-one murders, ten thefts, seven robberies, three kidnappings, as well as "drunkenness and brawls."40 The solution was simply to "turn the damn thing off," Gathings was told by a New York congressman.41

Throw "the damned thing out of the window," the same congressman told members of the Women's Christian Temperence Union (WCTU) and other antiliquor groups at the next session.42 These groups claimed that TV showed "the attractive side of the barrooms and their brothels." Maybe Congress couldn't legislate morality, said the WCTU's director, but "by not legislating you can definitely legislate immorality."43 Next, Chicago radio commentator Paul Harvey told Congress that New York's "bawdy night life" comedians were imposing "their distorted views on the rest of the forty-seven states."44

Violence on TV, liquor commercials, and New York comedians were safe and handy topics for campaign rhetoric. Simply by airing in public these concerns, Congressman Gathings and others hoping to be reelected in the Bible Belt and elsewhere could win favor with blocs of voters. By mid-1952, however, TV had officially surpassed radio as the biggest source of income for the broadcast industry. Television had generated over $12 million in profits the previous year, with nine out of ten TV stations now making money. Any politician who introduced or supported legislation against the TV industry would have to contend with its new status and power as America's most popular medium.

Not surprisingly, Congressman Gathings and the House committee took no action against TV and its contents, despite several weeks of well-publicized hearings. Instead, Congress let the broadcasters continue to police themselves with an industry "code of ethics" written the previous year. It called on the networks and local stations to voluntarily exclude programs in poor taste or with excessive violence. Programs that followed the code could display a seal of approval on air. The broadcast code was revised and reissued that November, but it still remained voluntary.

Thus, a resolution of sorts was reached in Washington in 1952 between Congress, the American public, and the TV broadcasters. Congress would allow the public to voice complaints about programs, and the broadcasters would assure Congress that they responded to the public's complaints. This public display of concern and assurance would occur every few years—especially in a big election year, but Congress would rarely intrude any farther.

Instead, social and economic forces held sway. At times, when public concern was especially strong, the TV industry was threatened with the loss of advertising dollars or with new regulations from the FCC. The TV networks and stations responded on their own, implementing a "family hour" of primetime shows appropriate for children in the 1970s, for example, and a rating code in the 1990s.

THE FCC AND BLACKLISTING

On another controversial issue in 1952, a second branch of the government backed off from confronting the newly powerful TV industry. In April, the FCC was petitioned by the American Civil Liberties Union (ACLU) to investigate blacklisting in the TV and radio industries. Specifically, the ACLU accused the four TV networks (NBC, CBS, ABC, and Du Mont), along with two stations in New York and Los Angeles, of blacklisting performers and others.

The ACLU's petition called on the FCC to investigate and put an end to blacklisting, and to deny licenses to those stations that continued the practice. The petition was filed with a copy of Merle Miller's *The Judge and the Judged,* a report on blacklisting in TV and radio commissioned by the ACLU. Miller's book documented such cases as the editing out of Paul Draper on Ed Sullivan's *The Toast of the Town* and the firing of Jean Muir from the cast of *The Aldrich Family.*

A dozen years earlier, the FCC under President Roosevelt and with Larry Fly as chairman might have investigated the blacklisting issue. The agency might well have backed the rights of the blacklisted employees to be treated fairly by the TV industry. In 1952, though, anti-Communism was at its peak in the United States, and few people in the public arena dared speak against it. Early in the year, for example, actor Philip Loeb was dropped from the role of Jake Goldberg, the husband and father in *The Goldbergs.* No sponsor would support the program with Loeb in the cast after his name appeared on an anti-Communist blacklist.

Six weeks later, the FCC voted behind closed doors to renew TV licenses belonging to CBS, NBC, and ABC that would have expired on June 1. The next day, however, the FCC reversed itself (in response to a motion by Commissioner Frieda Hennock) and announced publicly that the licenses for the three networks were only temporary. Sounding as if it were taking the first step toward hearings, the FCC asked for legal briefs from the ACLU and explanations about blacklisting practices from the networks.

The following night, however, the popular radio commentator Fulton Lewis spoke against Frieda Hennock and the ACLU on his network news program. Lewis claimed that they opposed the efforts of the broadcasters to "weed out Communists, Communist sympathizers and subversives."[45] The June 6 issue of *Counterattack,* a newsletter from the *Red Channels* publishers, ran an item headlined "Are Broadcasting Networks Required by Law to Hire Subversives?" The writer urged readers to write to Congress to protest "this amazing move to foist Communist agents on [the] U S broadcasting industry."[46]

Criticism of the FCC also came from the TV industry, whose trade publication, *Broadcasting,* wrote that blacklisting was "none of the FCC's business." The fact that the government agency had voted to make the license renewals temporary, claimed *Broadcasting,* showed that "the FCC is made up of a gang of left wing (or worse) sympathizers."[47]

The FCC quickly voted to drop the "temporary" from all the license renewals in question, before the briefs on the case were even submitted. Blacklisting would not be an issue in renewing licenses, said the FCC. Writing an immediate, angry response was one of the ACLU's directors, former FCC Chairman Larry Fly from the Roosevelt administration. "As one who has something more than a passing acquaintance with this Commission's practices," wrote Fly, "I know that a license is generally never renewed when an unresolved complaint is pending before it."[48]

DRAGNET

Amidst the controversies over TV contents and purported Communists in the industry, one phrase became popular as a symbol of law, justice, and retribution: "Dum da dum dum. Dum da dum dum daaah." A new TV program emerged in 1952 that made the singing of those nine tones, in a deep voice, an instant national fad. The program, *Dragnet,* which aired Thursday nights on NBC, also made popular a brisk and official attitude toward police work and the solving of crimes: as the show's hero, Sergeant Joe Friday, put it, "Just the facts, ma'am." Portraying Joe Friday was the show's creator, producer, director, and frequent writer, Jack Webb, a former radio news announcer and Hollywood bit player who had transferred *Dragnet* from radio to TV in early 1952. Webb's concept for *Dragnet* was rooted in part in the film-noir genre of Hollywood crime movies in the 1940s and early 1950s. The dialogue was terse; the settings were realistic and grim; and the crimes involved the shady dealings of California's urban underworld. Webb added more reality by shooting *Dragnet* on location in Los Angeles and using real stories and jargon from the city's police precincts. He emphasized the faces of his characters with frequent close-up camera shots, but he kept the use of makeup to a minimum. Webb used radio actors who were chosen for their vocal inflections, not their looks. "Movies have stereotypes for policemen and bank clerks," he explained. "What does a policeman look like? People look like people."[49]

Webb's formula of realistic stories, settings, characters, and dialogue worked perfectly on television, in part because it matched TV's own ability to present realistic and intimate images. *Dragnet* quickly became one of TV's top-rated programs in 1952, then surpassed Milton Berle and Arthur Godfrey in 1953 to challenge *I Love Lucy* as America's most popular show. Jack Webb made the cover of *Time*; inside, the magazine exclaimed, "Sherlock Holmes himself never captured the instantaneous interest of so many millions of people." *Time* also suggested that Webb and *Dragnet* were creating a new apprecia-tion in America, "a nation of incipient cop haters," for the "under-paid, long-suffering ordinary policeman" and its "first rudimentary understanding of real-life law enforcement."[50]

Webb did indeed use real police officers as technical advisors, and he took pains to create sets that resembled actual precincts, down to the doorknobs and calendars. Each episode of *Dragnet* began with the narrated words, "The story you are about to see is true. Only the names have been changed to protect the innocent." As such, *Dragnet* was the forerunner of *Naked City, The FBI, Hill Street Blues, NYPD Blue, Law and Order, Cops,* and other TV police shows that have car-ried the aura of reality.

Dragnet was televised fiction, however, not reality. The deeper issues involving crime and justice were shortchanged as Webb wrapped up his plotlines in a half hour, with justice meted out to the perpetrators in the narrator's terse closing words. Webb's police officers carefully followed correct procedures, even as real Los Angeles cops were being indicted and disciplined in the early 1950s in brutality cases involving minorities. Although *Dragnet* may have given many Ameri-cans their "first rudimentary understanding of real-life law enforce-ment,"[51] the popular program's reality was selective and limited. *Dragnet* was really "Just *some* of the facts, ma'am."

LIVE DRAMA FROM NEW YORK

Dragnet was also a forerunner of countless dramatic programs on TV to be filmed in and around Hollywood studios in the decades to come. In the meantime, however, most TV drama shows were tele-vised live from New York City. Live drama had been a regular feature on TV since the *Kraft Television Theater* began televising plays from NBC's New York studios in 1947. In the early 1950s, the TV sched-ule had live drama every night—mostly adaptations of Broadway plays, short stories, and other works written for other venues. By 1952, however, these sources of TV plays were becoming depleted. According to Fred Coe, NBC's leading drama producer, "I started to look for writers who could not only adapt other people's work, but who maybe might come in with some original ideas for plays of their own."[52]

One of these scriptwriters was Paddy Chayevsky, whose first original TV play, *Holiday Song,* aired on NBC's *Philco Playhouse* in 1952. In it, Chayevsky portrayed a world-weary Jewish cantor who is reborn spiritually when he reunites two European refugees—a husband and wife—he meets mysteriously on separate Manhattan subway trains. Chayevsky's third TV play, a year later, was *Marty,* one of TV's most famous single programs. By then, Chayevsky was writing dialogue that sounded, in his own words, "as if it had been wiretapped. I tried to envision the scenes as if a camera had been focused upon the unsuspecting characters and had caught them in an untouched moment of life."[53]

The story of *Marty* was simple: a lower-middle class butcher meets a schoolteacher who's the mate for his lonely soul at a local dance hall. Chayevsky's dialogue and the live performances of Rod Steiger and Nancy Marchand rang true. The play became a motion picture two years later, winning Oscars for Best Picture and Best Screenplay. "With 'Marty,' " write TV historians Irving Settel and William Laas, "the television tail began to wag the motion picture dog."[54]

With *Marty,* too, American TV entered the peak of a so-called "Golden Age" for TV drama, with New York productions that were sophisticated, well-performed, and relevant. These were exciting, memorable times for TV's growing group of playwrights. "There was something of the theater" in live TV, explained writer Rod Serling,[55] whose career began with the broadcast of his play, *The Sergeant,* on April 29, 1952, and continued with nine more scripts by the end of the year. One of his colleagues, Tad Mosel, described the thrill of each performance: "this rush of music" came first, "and you'd hear this voice say, 'LIVE FROM NEW YORK,' and you knew that your little play was going out to forty million people."[56] The next morning, "you would walk down the street," said Gore Vidal, who also wrote TV plays during this period, "and you would hear people talking about it."[57]

"We'd go on at nine and off at ten, and it was a complete living experience," described film director Arthur Penn, who began his career as a floor manager on NBC's *Comedy Hour,* then became a director of TV live dramas. Penn recalled, "What we had was this wonderful confluence of superb acting talent, superb writing talent, and really emerging directorial talent."[58] Among other directors were Sidney Lumet, John Frankenheimer, and Fred Zinnemann, all of whom became leading Hollywood filmmakers after practicing their craft on live TV.

Many hungry young actors performed in live TV dramas during this period, including twenty-year-old James Dean. The Indiana farm boy had moved to New York in late 1951 to pursue an acting career. He supported himself in part with TV acting jobs that came in spurts: three roles in May and June 1952, then seven months idle, followed by six roles in the first half of 1953. His performances in live TV plays in 1952 and 1953 showcased the great profile, hair, and physique; the twitches, slouches, and smirks; the mumbles and shouts; and the intensity and charisma that was pure James Dean.

In an episode of *You Are There,* televised live on his twenty-second birthday and directed by Sidney Lumet, James Dean played Robert Ford, the man who shot Jesse James. A year later, film director George Stevens watched a kinescope of Dean's performance and decided to cast Dean as the Western character Jett Rink in the movie *Giant.* Another TV role in August 1953, as a delinquent street kid, earned him a rave review in *Variety,* calling him "magnetic" with "quite a future ahead of him."[59]

From then on, James Dean worked steadily and appeared on nine live TV dramas in three months, including a starring role as another delinquent in a teleplay written by Rod Serling. After a successful screen test for film director Elia Kazan, who was casting for *East of Eden,* James Dean flew off to Hollywood. He had been in New York for two and a half years and had appeared in twenty-two live TV dramas. In Hollywood, he acted in only three motion pictures before his death in an auto accident in September 1955.

James Dean's career shift from live TV dramas in New York to major motion pictures in Hollywood was followed in the 1950s by Paul Newman, Joanne Woodward, Jason Robards, Grace Kelly, Anne Bancroft, and Rod Steiger, among others. In more recent decades, the same path from TV to film stardom has been taken by Clint Eastwood, Warren Beatty, Goldie Hawn, Robin Williams, Sally Field, Tom Hanks, Eddie Murphy, Denzel Washington, Meg Ryan, Bruce Willis, and many others.

Thus, TV may have lured a big portion of the audience away from the film industry, but it eventually fed the movies what they needed to survive: talented and popular performers. To the performers themselves, the career shifts meant a change in the craft they practiced. As explained by one TV actress, Bethel Leslie, who moved from New York to Hollywood along with the industry in the early 1950s: "When I went out to Hollywood, the first thing they did was fit me with falsies that went out to here. The whole atmosphere was different. In New York, there was always a sense that what was important was the work and the performance. Out there, the hair and the lighting was most important."[60] The serious, intellectual world of New York theater versus the artificial, glamorous Hollywood scene: it's a contrast in American cultural values that remains just as potent today.

Chapter 10

Liking Ike and Loving Lucy

THE CHECKERS SPEECH

A change was in the air in 1952, as the American public seemed likely to vote for an end to the Roosevelt and Truman administrations that had led the country for twenty years, through the Great Depression, World War II, and the postwar period. This change would be televised coast to coast, in a society where over half the population now had TV sets in their homes.

The 1952 presidential election was the first to be covered from start to finish on national TV, beginning with the New Hampshire primary and continuing through Eisenhower's Abilene homecoming in June. The live telecast from Abilene, however, was a disaster for Ike—"history's first demonstration of bad political television," wrote Craig Allen in *Eisenhower and the Mass Media.* He spoke outdoors during a rainstorm and "stumbled through an ill-prepared speech with water dripping from his glasses."[1] In the words of David Halberstam, Eisenhower looked "like a tired, somewhat dispirited old man doing something he did not want to do."[2]

After the disaster in Abilene, Eisenhower had his image remade for TV by advertising men from BBD&O, a leading New York ad agency. They switched his eyeglass frames from metal to horn-rimmed and applied makeup to his face and his bald head. His campaign team spent $1.5 million on TV advertisements after the Chicago convention, employing the same writer who was selling aspirin tablets with commercials that featured pounding hammers and bubbling stomach acid. The scripts he wrote for Eisenhower were just as basic, often using a simple question and a noncommittal answer, e.g., "Mr. Eisenhower, what about the high cost of living?" "My wife, Mamie, worries about the same thing. I tell her it's our job to change that on November fourth."[3]

The best use of TV that election year—a historic broadcast, in fact—was the "Checkers speech" made by Eisenhower's young running mate, Senator Richard Nixon. On Saturday, September 17, 1952, on live network TV, Nixon's train pulled out of the station in Pomona, California, on an old-fashioned whistle-stop campaign. At his first stop he learned that newspapers back East were charging that he had a secret stash of money donated from political supporters—a "Nixon fund." He didn't deny it; the fund was legitimate, he said, to be used for mailings and for trips back home.

Suddenly, however, Nixon's place on the ticket and his future in politics were dependent on whether he could clear at once his name and reputation. "I had . . . to tell my story to millions," Nixon later wrote, "[and] there was only one way to do this—through a national television broadcast."[4] The Republicans purchased a half hour of airtime on CBS on Tuesday night, September 20, 1952, and Nixon flew to Los Angeles for the live broadcast at 6:30 p.m. Pacific time.

Nixon spoke live that night from the same stage of the El Capitan Theater where a year earlier Eddie Cantor on the *Comedy Hour* had launched coast-to-coast TV. Just as Cantor had recapped on TV his show-biz career, Nixon now highlighted his life in politics and every dollar he claimed to have earned and spent and borrowed. With his wife Pat sitting on stage, Nixon quoted in his defense a homily from Abraham Lincoln and an audit from Price Waterhouse.

Nixon borrowed his most famous reference from Franklin Roosevelt, who in the 1944 election had cleverly turned a charge against his own honesty into a personal attack against the family dog, Fala. "I decided to mention my own dog Checkers," Nixon wrote in *Six Crises*. "Using the same ploy as FDR would irritate my opponents and delight my friends, I thought."[5] The family puppy, Nixon told the nation on TV, was indeed a gift from a political supporter—but his two little girls loved it, and "regardless of what they say about it, we are going to keep it."[6]

Nixon also revealed later that he'd purposely delayed going on TV for a few days and kept his intentions secret to build the size of his audience. It worked. Roughly 30 million Americans watched him that night, and up to a million of them wrote or phoned or wired their support afterward. Eisenhower had no choice now but to keep Nixon on the ticket, although Ike was furious, breaking his pencil on a notepad as he watched Nixon say on TV that opponent Adlai Stevenson should release his financial records. If Stevenson did, Eisenhower figured, he too would have to—against his will.

LUCY IS PREGNANT

As big as Nixon's TV audience was that night in September 1952, even more people watched Lucy Ricardo the night before, as she auditioned for Ricky's band by playing "Glow Worm" on the sax. It was the second episode of *I Love Lucy*'s second season and was filmed back in June, just before Hollywood columnist Louella Parsons broke the news that Lucille Ball was pregnant. During that summer of 1952, while the politicians squabbled in Chicago, the Arnazes, CBS, and Philip Morris held their own closed-door meetings, debating how best to handle the condition of the top star of the top show on TV.

Lucille Ball was not the first pregnant woman on a TV series. Back in the late 1940s, Mary Kay of a little-watched and long-forgotten TV series on Du Mont stations, *Mary Kay and Johnny,* had made her pregnancy part of the plot line. With that one exception, however, pregnant women were whisked off the TV screen back then just as they were dispatched from the offices, schools, stores, or wherever they worked in public view. In 1952 the Arnazes had clout, and they used it that fall to film seven new episodes of *I Love Lucy* that chronicled for America the full pregnancy of Lucy Ricardo.

Some concessions were made. Lucy quit smoking on the air, and they ran each script by a reverend, a priest, and a rabbi, to ensure that nothing would be considered religiously offensive. The word "pregnant" was replaced by the more polite "expecting"—or "'specting," as Desi said, who noted wryly in his 1976 autobiography that now on TV "they not only use the word but also show you how to get in that condition."[7] As the *I Love Lucy* team filmed the seven shows in the fall of 1952, they secretly planned a big publicity campaign to begin when the first one aired in early December. They had an ace up their sleeve, too. When Lucille Ball had given birth in 1951 to her first child, Lucie Arnaz, she'd had a C-section, which meant she would this time as well. The birth of the real baby could be scheduled in advance; thus, the Arnazes could secretly plan for both the real and the TV baby to arrive on the very same day.

Halfway between the filming and the broadcast of the first pregnancy episode, America elected the President who served for the rest of the 1950s, Dwight Eisenhower. On Election Night, the TV networks hardly needed computers to pick the winner—Ike swept all but the South—yet they used them anyhow, for the first time. CBS's big Univac computer was panned by *Variety*—it didn't project "the warmth and the spirit of America at the polls."[8] *Variety* instead praised the new CBS anchorman, Walter Cronkite, who would occupy that position for decades. So, in a few short weeks, America had picked its new leader, found its new anchor, and discovered it was "'specting" another baby boomer.

OZZIE AND HARRIET

The fall of 1952 also introduced on TV a family whose first names have since come to symbolize a rosy 1950s' America: Ozzie, Harriet, David, and Ricky—the Nelsons. As with *I Love Lucy,* this family featured a couple who were married in real life and who'd been moderate successes elsewhere in show business. Ozzie Nelson grew up in a small town in New Jersey where Mom baked cookies, Dad worked at the bank, and Ozzie himself played sports, read Horatio Alger novels, and was an Eagle Scout.

Harriet Hilliard, on the other hand, grew up in a vaudeville family, living on the road or in boarding schools, and maybe dreaming of the home that her future husband had all along. Together, they found success first as a Big Band leader and vocalist, then as radio performers—with Harriet also in films—in New York and Hollywood. And they found houses for themselves and their two boys on both coasts that harkened back to Ozzie's idyllic childhood.

In 1944, Ozzie and Harriet Nelson created their own radio show, a domestic comedy with child actors playing their sons and with plots that dealt with the little incidents of family life—what their writers called "homey shit."[9] In October 1952, *The Adventures of Ozzie and Harriet* moved to TV on the ABC network, with their real sons, David and Ricky, playing themselves. By now, the Nelsons lived in a two-story white Cape Cod colonial, with Early American furniture and a knotty-pine kitchen that overlooked the dining room table. Was that the TV Nelsons or the real Nelsons? Actually, it was both: the set they'd built at General Service Studios (where *I Love Lucy* was filmed) was a perfect clone of their real home in Hollywood.

After all, if Dwight Eisenhower could stage his homecoming in Abilene, if the Arnazes and Ricardos could both have their babies on the same day, if Richard Nixon could rally support with his children and their puppy, then surely the Nelsons could live in the same house on TV and in reality. Those images on the screen and in real life were starting to merge coast to coast, in the culture forming in and around the 20 million homes that now had TV.

In particular, the image of the American family that *The Adventures of Ozzie and Harriet* presented weekly was a nostalgic recreation of a simpler world, before the Depression, World War II, and the Cold War had complicated modern life. The outside world rarely intruded into the life of the Nelsons; in fact, Ozzie Nelson had no occupation to interfere with the "homey" plotlines of the series. Instead, the good-natured father remained totally focused on the daily doings of himself and his family—and on David and Ricky, in particular, who grew up on the TV screen as role models for America's millions of baby boomers.

Ironically, the real Ozzie Nelson not only had a job as the show's producer, he was a workaholic who devoted much of his life off-camera to it. As a father, he imposed strict rules on his sons to ensure their good public image, and he micromanaged the recording career of young Ricky, who became a popular rock 'n' roll performer. But the intense off-screen Ozzie somehow combined with the easygoing on-screen Ozzie to produce a lighthearted and likeable show. *The Adventures of Ozzie and Harriet* remained on the air for fifteen years, from 1952 to 1966. It outlasted all other family comedies on TV and set the tone for many of them with its "sponsor-pleasing concept," as described by Gerard Jones in *Honey I'm Home! Sitcoms: Selling the American Dream,* "that TV comedy should present ideal situations that make us feel good about the world."[10]

SEE IT NOW

On the opposite end of the spectrum from *Ozzie and Harriet* was *See It Now,* a CBS news program that prided itself on the true images of the world it transmitted to the American public. On the show's premiere, for example, in the fall of 1951, TV cameras stationed at both San Francisco's Golden Gate Bridge and New York's Statue of Liberty gave viewers live pictures of the two coasts at the same time. It was a historic moment—the first instance of Americans seeing coast-to-coast images simultaneously—but another segment later on that first *See It Now* may have proven more significant. CBS reporter Robert Pierpoint was televised as he followed a company of U.S. troops stationed in Korea, and instantly TV journalism entered a new era.

Up until that first *See It Now*, television had relied on the films of newsreel companies for footage of the Korean War, as the early TV industry had done during World War II. In fact, the news clips that had aired on TV from Korea had the format and content of World War II film coverage, with an emphasis on military hardware, troop movements, and combat. Pierpoint's report, on the other hand, was personal and intimate, focusing on the daily lives of the young men on the front. The feature ended, for example, with each soldier in a platoon filing in front of the CBS camera and stating his name and hometown. The platoon had recently suffered casualties, viewers were told by Edward R. Murrow, staring into the camera in the CBS studio in New York. "They may need some blood. Could you spare a pint?"

"Mr. Murrow's sparing comments cut to the viewer's heart," wrote Jack Gould in the *Times* the next day.[11] Murrow's comments that night also echoed his reports on network radio during the Nazi bombings of London in 1940, when his descriptions and interviews of Londoners under siege won the compassion of listeners in America. *See It Now* was coproduced by Murrow and Fred Friendly, a young and experienced radio news producer, and the two men filled the series with interviews and fresh, on-location footage. "We try to handle stories differently from the way they were presented earlier," Murrow explained in mid-1952. "There is nothing less satisfying than tired newsreel clips [and] a man reading the news."[12]

Murrow had reported from Korea shortly after the war broke out in 1950, but his broadcast never aired, nor had he returned to Korea as the war became stalemated. In December 1952, with the war now in its third year, he brought a fifteen-member *See It Now* production team to South Korea. They split into five groups and filmed, in the *See It Now* style, troops at the front, nurses in a MASH medical unit,

Korean children, soldiers at mail call and in downtown Seoul, and wounded and bandaged young men. Coaxed by the *See It Now* reporters, the troops stated their names and hometowns, wished their loved ones a merry Christmas, sang Christmas carols and an Army blues song, and commented wryly on their situation. "Tell me, how do you guys feel about this war situation?" a soldier was asked as mortar fire boomed in the background. "Well, I don't know. It is pretty hard to figure out. I tried to think of it in different ways, but I come up with the same answer—that I think it's a bunch of nonsense."

That soldier's comment was the most direct criticism of the Korean War made on the program, which was televised on December 28, 1952, as "Christmas in Korea." In general, the program showed the futility of the war, symbolized by a memorable opening scene of a soldier trying to dig a foxhole in frozen dirt. "Christmas in Korea" gave Americans a view of both a landscape and a war that was cold, hard, and bleak. "Most of these hills look alike, and they stretch all the way from Pusan up to the front," Murrow described, looking down from an airplane. "And each one of the hills . . . has been paid for in blood." He closed the broadcast by saying, "There is no conclusion to this report from Korea because there is no end to the war."

The reaction to "Christmas in Korea" was swift and supportive. "Compelling, heart-tugging, throat-catching," for example, wrote *Variety*. "The impact was socko. . . . This is an historic chapter in the new American journalism." *Variety* also predicted, "This Murrow show will have historic significance and influence in the future thinking of America in relation to Korea."[13] Actually, the incumbent president, Dwight Eisenhower, had visited Korea earlier that month and had concluded too that the war seemed futile. In the spring of 1953, ceasefire talks resumed, prisoners of war were exchanged, and an armistice was signed in July. The war had taken the lives of over 30,000 Americans and 4 million people altogether; it was settled by creating a 150-mile long Demilitarized Zone between North and South Korea that's patrolled by troops to this day.

As for the "new American journalism" that Murrow, Friendly, and the *See It Now* team had created, it resurfaced in late 1953 and 1954 with a new target: Senator Joseph McCarthy and his Communist witch-hunt. Using TV's power to transmit realistic images close up, *See It Now* conveyed the bullying style of Senator McCarthy and the sympathetic plight of the people he attacked; he fell quickly from power in late 1954 and died less than three years later. By then, *See It Now* was off the CBS weekly schedule. The program had won every major award in TV and journalism, but it had also triggered controversy, lost sponsors, and strained the CBS news budget. Then, in the 1960s, the *See It Now* approach to covering the Korean War resurfaced when American troops returned to Asia to fight in Vietnam. Once again, teams of TV journalists filed reports from front lines, hospitals, hillsides, and villages, transmitting the personal side of the conflict. As the war continued, the images that Americans viewed on their living-room TV screens were strong enough to weaken their support of U.S. involvement.

THE BIRTH AND THE INAUGURATION

Finally came a climactic two days in January 1953 in which the extent of TV's growth since 1939 became dramatically clear. At 8:15 a.m. on Monday, January 19, Lucille Ball gave birth in Hollywood to a boy, Desi Arnaz Jr., right on schedule. All the publicity that had built during the airing of her pregnancy episodes had made this birth a national—even worldwide—media event. As was Richard Nixon after the Checkers speech, the Arnazes were deluged with letters, telegrams, and phone calls. Ten hours later, the birth episode, "Lucy Goes to the Hospital," was broadcast, and around 45 million people watched it—easily a record audience and an impressive portion of the American public.

Fourteen hours after the televised birth of Lucy's baby, a somewhat smaller but still huge audience of about 40 million watched the nation's reins of power pass from Harry Truman and the Democrats to Dwight Eisenhower and the Republicans. It was the first presidential inauguration viewed from coast to coast, and those who watched the parade afterward also saw some new technology put to use: portable TV cameras down along the parade route.

On that Inauguration Day in 1953, Harry Truman became the first President to relinquish the office on live TV. At 11:00 a.m., NBC televised Truman and Eisenhower shaking hands beside the limousine parked outside the White House. It may have looked like a friendly gesture, but it wasn't. In a breach of protocol, Eisenhower had forced President Truman to walk outside the White House to meet him; it symbolized the chill that had settled in between the two. Later, during

Eisenhower's inaugural address, Truman had his moment of impoliteness when TV cameras caught him slumped over and seeming inattentive.

This inauguration also began a new era for the Presidency and TV, symbolized perhaps in a moment during his Inaugural Parade when a cowboy actor on horseback stopped in front of the new President and actually lassoed him. News anchor Walter Cronkite, reporting on TV, gasped and said, "Oh, no." Afterward, it was revealed that the lassoing of President Eisenhower on TV had been set up with his consent beforehand: just the latest event staged for TV in his postwar career. Indeed, the lassoing of Eisenhower on TV that afternoon was symbolic of a new relationship between the TV industry and the White House that would continue throughout the decade.

With the ascent of Dwight Eisenhower to the White House, David Sarnoff and Bill Paley and other key figures in broadcasting and advertising now had a President they had helped get elected. An immediate effect was a change in the makeup of the FCC, which had been controlled by Democratic appointees since its creation back in 1934. After the Republicans took over the Presidency in 1953, two of the FCC's Democrat commissioners left their positions and were replaced by Republicans appointed by Eisenhower. On April 18, 1953, Rosel Hyde became the first Republican appointee to head the commission, and the days of the "amber light," the "freeze," and other serious conflicts between the FCC and the TV industry were over. The FCC was now firmly in the hands of a pro-business administration, and it would remain so for the rest of the decade.

THE ABC-PARAMOUNT MERGER

The FCC's first important decision after Eisenhower's inauguration was to resolve an issue that had been left hanging for almost two years: a proposed merger between a budding TV network and an established motion picture company. Back in May 1951, ABC announced plans to merge with United Paramount Theatres. It was the biggest deal in broadcast history at the time, and it would bring $30 million in fresh capital to ABC in its effort to create a TV network to compete with NBC, CBS, and Du Mont. The FCC held up the merger until early February 1953, and even then its approval came with a strong dissension from Frieda Hennock, the FCC commissioner who had earlier pushed for more educational TV stations.

Hennock warned, "The amalgamation of motion pictures and television that appears fairly certain to come about cannot help but hamper the maximum development of television as a most powerful medium in its own right."[14] In hindsight, Frieda Hennock was only half right. The ABC/Paramount merger, despite her warning, helped the development of ABC into a national TV network. In fact, ABC survived and grew in the 1950s because of its Hollywood connections to Paramount, Walt Disney Studios, and Warner Brothers—with the latter two motion picture companies supplying the ABC network with some of its most popular shows of the decade, including *Disneyland, Cheyenne, Maverick,* and *77 Sunset Strip.*

This "amalgamation of motion pictures and television," in retrospect, seems inevitable. Throughout the 1940s, television was viewed as an upstart and an enemy in Hollywood. The idea that millions of Americans might watch entertainment on their home screens for free every day was mortifying to the film industry. The big studios generally wanted to have little to do with TV, even as it grew in popularity, hoping it would just go away. Warner Brothers, for example, wouldn't show TV sets or refer to television in their movies.

However, TV was a strong magnet, pulling in Hopalong Cassidy in 1949, Lucille Ball and Desi Arnaz, the radio comics, in 1951 and 1952, and finally the movie studios in 1954 and 1955. Walt Disney Studios went in first, in October 1954, with the premiere on the ABC network of the long-running Walt Disney TV series, named at first *Disneyland.* The series was an immediate success—especially when the "Davy Crockett" episodes began airing in December 1954—and it was the inspiration for two less-successful Hollywood-studio shows in 1955, *The 20th Century-Fox Hour* on CBS and *MGM Parade,* also on ABC.

Hollywood was a magnet, too, pulling the TV industry all the way from New York in the 1950s to make use of Hollywood's talent, its sets and stages, and its money. In the end, Hollywood became so basic to television that even shows that take place in New York have been filmed in California: *I Love Lucy,* of course, but also *All in the Family, Taxi, Barney Miller,* and more recently, *Seinfeld* and *NYPD Blue.*

THE END OF THE DU MONT NETWORK

On the other hand, Frieda Hennock's warning about the "amalgamation" of Hollywood and TV proved correct in the case of Du Mont. The FCC's approval of the ABC/Paramount merger marked the beginning of the end for the pioneering TV network.

When the FCC announced its approval, the agency also settled a long-running dispute with Du Mont. Back in 1937, Allen Du Mont had turned to Paramount Pictures during a financial pinch and had received $36,000 from them in exchange for 30 percent of Du Mont's stock. But because Paramount already owned TV stations in Chicago and Los Angeles, the FCC refused to let Du Mont acquire any more stations than the three it had in New York, Washington, and Pittsburgh. No single company could own more than five TV stations: that was an FCC regulation, and to no avail Du Mont argued that it should be considered a separate entity from Paramount.

As NBC and CBS built their TV networks after 1946, Du Mont was held back by not having those two additional stations; they would have increased Du Mont's revenues and guaranteed to sponsors two more cities in Du Mont's budding network. Even when Paramount Theatres split in half in 1949, and the half that now retained the Du Mont stock kept only one TV station, the FCC still refused to let Du Mont acquire any others.

With the lifting of the freeze in 1952, the financial gap only widened between Du Mont and NBC and CBS. The FCC was still restricting the number of channels on the VHF band of the spectrum in most cities, and Du Mont still had no affiliated stations in much of the country. Du Mont's losses in TV rose to $2.5 million in 1952.

Finally, when the ABC/Paramount merger was approved in 1953, the FCC resolved the Du Mont/Paramount issue by allowing Du Mont to acquire two more TV stations. Du Mont quickly applied for a license to build a station in Boston, but the network didn't survive long enough to use it. The company lost another $3.8 million in its TV operations in 1953, and finally $5 million in 1954. As a Du Mont executive later recalled, "The dike was crumbling and we didn't have enough thumbs to put in it. Finally, the dike broke and we were out of the network business."[15]

The end came in 1955 when, having already sold its Pittsburgh station, Du Mont Laboratories sold WABD in New York, WTTG in

Washington, and its TV production studios; *Business Week* labeled it an "amputation."[16] Under new management, the stations and studios renamed themselves Metropolitan Broadcasting, then Metromedia— "to change our aura," as one executive explained, "so as not to be identified with the failure that was associated with Du Mont."[17]

Failure though it might have seemed in the mid-1950s, Du Mont was a true pioneer in American TV. Du Mont had the first commercial network, the first top-rated show, the first soap opera, the first day-time programming, and the first Saturday night variety show. Most important, Du Mont was the first third network, and it challenged the monopoly over America's airwaves of NBC and CBS. In that sense, Du Mont paved the way for the other TV networks and cable channels that comprise today's diverse broadcasting schedule.

Du Mont's final accomplishment was perhaps its most improbable: knocking the mighty Milton Berle from the top ranks of the ratings—and with a religious program, no less. In early 1952, Du Mont began televising *Life Is Worth Living,* basically a half-hour Catholic sermon, opposite Berle's variety show on Tuesday nights. Delivering the weekly lesson was Bishop Fulton J. Sheen, who stood on a simple set and, without notes, spoke earnestly to the American public on issues of morality, spirituality, and a heavy dose of anti-Communism. "I went on television to help my sponsor, the good Lord," Bishop Sheen told the *Times,*[18] but *Life Is Worth Living* attracted other sponsors, too, as it climbed up in the ratings—and Berle's show fell. In the middle of 1956, these two pioneers of American TV—the Du Mont network and "Mr. Television"—suffered the same fate: Du Mont aired its final program, a boxing match, and NBC dropped Milton Berle off its schedule.

THE END OF THE BEGINNING

In February 1953, a month after the birth of their real and TV sons, Lucille Ball and Desi Arnaz reaped the rewards of *I Love Lucy.* They signed an $8 million contract with sponsor Philip Morris, by far the largest TV deal to date. Of that $8 million, CBS received $3 million from Philip Morris to reserve the Monday night 9:00-9:30 time slot for the next two and a half years. It was a huge leap from the $4 paid by Bulova Watches to RCA a dozen years earlier for television's first commercial, but just the beginning of decades of big TV advertising deals. (In June 2001, for example, Procter and Gamble agreed to pay a hundred times as much—$300 million—for just a year's worth of commercial airtime on cable channels owned by a single media conglomerate, Viacom.)

The remaining $5 million went to Arnaz and Ball to fill the Monday night time slot with roughly a hundred new *I Love Lucy* episodes. In addition, the new contract granted them ownership of all the *I Love Lucy* episodes. The couple's earlier decision to film the show instead of televising it live would pay off royally in 1957, when they sold the rights to rebroadcast the filmed episodes to CBS for another $4.5 million in cash.

"Lucy's $50,000,000 Baby" was the headline on the front cover of the first issue of *TV Guide,* which went to press a few weeks after the big contract was signed. Their estimate of $50 million was based on the total revenues for Ball and Arnaz, including sales from items bearing their names and images: magazines, books, comic books, a daily cartoon strip, coloring books, dolls, paper dolls, toys, diaper bags, aprons, sheet music and records, cigarette lighters, baby furniture, bedroom and living room furniture—even kitchen linoleum. Arnaz and Ball had followed the trail from film to TV blazed by William Boyd *(Hopalong Cassidy),* and it brought them the riches that Boyd had found—and that other TV stars would find in the future. By the late 1990s, the highest-paid TV performers were making from $250,000 to over $1 million *per episode.*

The $8 million contract from Philip Morris, the $5 million payment to Arnaz and Ball, the $50 million estimate by *TV Guide,* and the 40 million Americans watching *I Love Lucy* on Monday nights— all these numbers in the millions swirled around TV in the spring of 1953. The lofty numbers signaled the end of the beginning of television's history in American society. TV had become one of the nation's most popular activities and possessions. TV sets were in over half of American homes in 1953, and every day the medium was capturing a mass audience to watch people, programs, and events.

Also, by 1953, the overall structure that characterized American TV for the next thirty years was now in place. The two rival networks in radio, NBC and CBS, had become the two rival networks in TV. Both NBC and CBS were supplying scores of local affiliated stations coast to coast with programs very similar to what they had aired on radio in the 1930s and 1940s. A third network, ABC, was using its

Hollywood connections to build its own national base of stations and programming.

Although the structure had reserved space for educational TV and non-network stations, the odds were stacked against them. Many of these stations were assigned frequencies in the UHF portion of the broadcast spectrum, which few TV sets built to that point could receive. They were often shortchanged as well in acquiring commercial sponsors, because national brands and advertising agencies targeted their support to the network programs of NBC, CBS, and ABC.

Fourteen years earlier, David Sarnoff had proudly announced "the birth in this country of a new art so important in its implications that it is bound to affect all society. It is an art which shines like a torch of hope in a troubled world. It is a creative force which we must learn to utilize for the benefit of all mankind."[19] Of course, Sarnoff hadn't promised a television industry based on equality and open access, yet it's disappointing how the medium so quickly became so restrictive.

The structure in place by early 1953 allowed the radio industry—and NBC and CBS, in particular—to continue its hold on the broadcast band of the spectrum. American TV might have taken a different shape had that not happened. The Du Mont network, for example, proved that popular TV shows could emerge from a company that wasn't part of the radio industry. The Chicago School of Television proved that good and enjoyable shows could be produced somewhere other than New York or Los Angeles, the two hubs of radio. Eventually, the growth of cable and satellite technology in the 1980s would break down TV's structure and allow more stations and channels to operate successfully.

In the spring of 1953, however, Du Mont and the Chicago School were falling to the wayside of American TV. Maybe neither was fit enough to survive in the capitalistic system that governs American industry—or maybe they were victims of national politics. A federal agency of appointed government officials, after all, regulates the airwaves in the United States, and the FCC played an active role in the growth of TV after 1939. Only two FCC commissioners, Larry Fly and Frieda Hennock, were strong and vocal supporters of an open structure for American TV—Hennock more so than Fly.

All too often, the FCC and the politicians who debated TV wanted to restrict the medium, from the number of stations to the contents of programs. Given the nature of the times, it's not surprising that Congress and the FCC supported the blacklisting on TV of Americans with strongly dissenting views, such as Paul Robeson, or with rumored links to communism. But blacklisting was a restriction on the use of the public airwaves in a democracy, and so too were government policies and regulations that allowed TV to be dominated for decades by a handful of corporations, acting in their own best interests. As a result, Americans lost a rare chance to widen dramatically the range of people, viewpoints, and experiences they shared.

On the other hand, TV's rise in popularity was rooted in shows and performers that the American public eagerly shared, from the Louis-Conn fight in 1946, through Howdy Doody and Milton Berle in 1948, to the birth of Lucy's baby in 1953. Maybe it's the comedians and writers, the athletes and announcers, the producers and directors, the camera operators and the rest of the talent and technical people from TV's early years who merit the most consideration. Without their skills, creativity, and hard work, television may have taken on a smaller role in American society—as a recreational activity, for example, instead of a dominant daily medium.

From this viewpoint, the economic and political structure that nurtured American TV was a blessing: it brought into the new medium of TV enough "old money" from radio and advertising to support a high level of professional talent. In the early 1940s, for example, when TV was a novelty and sets and stations were few and far between, a local puppet troupe could attract a small audience to watch Schenectady's WRGB. However, only master puppeteers, such as Burr Tillstrom or Howdy Doody's Frank Paris, working with writers and songwriters and gifted performers with a high level of professional talent, could make watching TV a basic part of our daily lives.

Yet right from the day the 1939 New York World's Fair opened, Americans showed an interest in anything, it seemed, that was televised. Even today, many Americans keep their TV set on almost constantly, watching dramas that are hardly riveting, comedy shows that aren't always funny, and sports events that are blowouts. Why is it that people watch TV when the quality of the telecasts is clearly below the standards set by the best programs? It may well be that TV's most basic attraction is television itself: the "window" that expands our sight to other places, and the "magic" that brings performers, programs, and events into our daily lives. In other words, television adds to our individual worlds; it satisfies a basic desire for seeing and experiencing life outside our inner selves.

Maybe the final conclusion to be drawn from the early history of TV in the United States is that a uniquely American—and fortuitous—combination of factors brought success and popularity to this new medium. The economic and political structure, despite its shortcomings, nurtured a TV industry that produced sets, stations, networks, and daily programming on a professional level. The gifted talent, whether on screen or behind the scenes, worked hard to create TV programs that attracted big audiences and often kept them glued to their sets. Finally, the technology of TV itself blessed Americans with the ability to laugh, wonder, be thrilled, caught up, and amazed, and even learn, just by looking at images moving on a small screen.

Notes

Chapter 1

1. "Thousands See Pageantry by Television." *The New York Herald Tribune,* May 1, 1939, p. 4.
2. Ibid.
3. Ibid.
4. Jenkins, C.F. "Radio Movies." *Transactions of the Society of Motion Picture Engineers.* New York, 1925, p. 7.
5. Kisseloff, Jeff. *The Box: An Oral History of Television, 1920-1961.* New York, Penguin, 1995, p. 22.
6. "Dedication of RCA Seen on Television." *The New York Times,* April 21, 1939, p. 16.
7. Barnouw, Erik. *Tube of Plenty: The Evolution of American Television.* New York: Oxford, 1990, p. 78.
8. Dunlap, Orrin E. "Act I Reviewed." *The New York Times,* May 7, 1939, Section 10, p. 12.
9. Ibid.
10. Ibid.
11. "Television Attracts Throngs to Stores." *The New York Times,* May 2, 1939, p. 19.
12. "Television Reviews." *Billboard,* May 13, 1939.
13. Dunlap, Orrin E. "Televiews of Pictures." *The New York Times,* September 3, 1939, Section 9, p. 8.
14. Dunlap, Orrin E. "First Television of Baseball Seen." *The New York Times,* May 18, 1939, Section 9, p. 29.
15. Dunlap, Orrin E. "Batter Up!" *The New York Times,* May 21, 1939, Section 9, p. 10.
16. Advertisement. *The Evening News* (Newburgh, NY), October 26, 1939, p. 9.
17. Ibid.
18. "FCC Hangs Up Amber Light." *The New York Times,* November 19, 1939, Section 10, p. 12.
19. "FCC Cautions on Speedy Prospect of Commercializing Television." *The New York Times,* November 15, 1939, p. 25.
20. "Mr. Fly Is Interviewed on Television Outlook." *The New York Times,* December 10, 1939, Section 10, p. 12.
21. "FCC Moves to Widen Use of Television." *The New York Times,* March 1, 1940, p. 13.
22. "A Go-Ahead Signal." *The New York Times,* March 10, 1940, Section 10, p. 12.
23. Ibid.

24. Advertisement. RCA Television. *The New York Times,* March 20, 1940, p. 21.

25. Advertisement. Davega City Radio. *The New York Times,* March 20, 1940, p. 22.

26. Advertisement. Bloomingdale's Department Store. *The New York Times,* March 20, 1940, p. 20.

27. "A Statement by the Radio Corporation of America." *The New York Times,* March 20, 1940, p. 21.

28. "A Go-Ahead Signal." *The New York Times,* March 10, 1940, Section 10, p. 12.

29. "FCC Stays Start in Television, Rebukes R.C.A. for Sales Drive." *The New York Times,* March 24, 1940, p. 1.

30. Ibid.

31. "FCC Member Hits Television Delay." *The New York Times,* April 3, 1940, p. 1.

32. "FCC Head Explains Television Delay." *The New York Times,* April 7, 1940, p. 25.

33. "Fly Challenges Television Plea." *The New York Times,* April 10, 1940, p. 20.

34. "Senate Unit Urges Television Peace." *The New York Times,* April 11, 1940, p. 31.

35. "Early Television Is Hope of Fly." *The New York Times,* April 12, 1940, p. 14.

36. Dunlap, Orrin E. "Looking in on a Hearing." *The New York Times,* April 14, 1940, Section 10, p. 12.

37. Ibid.

38. "FCC Television Aim Set by President." *The New York Times,* April 13, 1940, p. 9.

Chapter 2

1. Johnston, Alva. "Trouble in Television." *The Saturday Evening Post,* September 28, 1940, p. 24.

2. Ibid., p. 25

3. Ibid., p. 25.

4. Dunlap, Orrin E. "Seeing Democracy at Work." *The New York Times,* June 30, 1940, Section 10, p. 10.

5. Ibid.

6. "Candidates Put Before Delegates." *The New York Times,* June 27, 1940, p. 4.

7. "Sidelights on the Big Show." *The New York Times,* June 27, 1940, Section 10, p. 10.

8. Parmet, Herman S. and Marie B. Hecht. *Never Again: A President Runs for a Third Term,* New York: Macmillan, 1968, p. 83.

9. Ibid.

10. Kennedy, T.R. "Televiews on the Air." *The New York Times,* October 13, 1940, Section 10, p. 12.

11. "Text of Roosevelt's Speech at the Garden and During His City Tour." *The New York Times,* October 29, 1940, p. 17.

12. "Pictured Election Returns Win Acclaim for Television." *The New York Times,* November 10, 1940, Section 10, p. 12.

13. Schaffner, Franklin J. *Worthington Miner.* Lanham, MD: Scarecrow Press, 1985, p. 166.

14. "President's Call for Full Response on Defense." *The New York Times,* December 30, 1940, p. 6.

15. "Roosevelt Calls for 'All Out' Drive." *The New York Times,* March 16, 1941, p. 1.

Chapter 3

1. Wheen, Francis. *Television: A History.* London: Century, 1985, p. 38.

2. "Urge FCC to Permit Television Start." *The New York Times,* March 22, 1941, p. 31.

3. Ibid.

4. "Television Ready To Go, FCC Is Told." *The New York Times,* March 25, 1941, p. 25.

5. Kennedy, T.R. "Engineers Send Theatre-Size Images." *The New York Times,* April 6, 1941, Section 10, p. 12.

6. Ibid.

7. "Television Show Given in Theatre." *The New York Times,* May 10, 1941, p. 17.

8. Ibid.

9. Ibid.

10. "RCA Studies Future of Video But Sees Rather Dim Future." *Broadcasting,* May 12, 1941, pp. 92-93.

11. "Text of the President's Address Depicting Emergency Confronting Nation." *The New York Times,* May 28, 1941, p. 2.

12. *Broadcasting,* August 15, 1941, p. 80.

13. "Television's Pioneer Sponsors." *Variety,* July 9, 1941.

14. Ibid.

15. Stewart, R.W. "Television's Commercials Steal the Show." *The New York Times,* Section 10, p. 10.

16. Ibid.

17. "Television's Pioneer Sponsors." *Variety,* July 9, 1941.

18. Ibid.

19. "Television Reviews: Dancing Lessons." *Variety,* July 23, 1941.

20. Ibid.

21. "RCA Beats the Promises." *Broadcasting,* August 8, 1941, p. 48.

22. "Television Develops New Presentation of War News As Events Occur Swiftly." *Broadcasting,* December 15, 1941, p. 16.

23. "Air Chief Warns of Possible Raids." *The New York Times,* March 26, 1942, p. 15.

24. Lescarboura, Austin. "Television, the Wartime Instructor." *Radio News,* May 1942, p. 77.

25. Ibid., p. 42.

26. "Radio Priority Freeze Order Not Strict Enough, Says Fly." *Broadcasting,* March 16, 1942, p. 22.

27. "Television." *The GE* [General Electric] *Monogram,* May 1944, pp. 17-19.

28. "What Will Postwar Television Be Like?" *Newsweek*, December 20, 1943, p. 69.

29. "Living Newspaper Is Televised in Schenectady Laboratory Test." *The New York Times*, November 6, 1943, p. 15.

30. "The Promise of Television." *Fortune*, August 1943, p. 140.

31. "Joyce Predicts 60% in Video Range 5 Years After War Ends." *Broadcasting*, November 15, 1943, p. 16.

32. "New Products Planned by Radio Industry Seen as Field for Post-War Employment." *The New York Times*, December 27, 1943, p. 11.

33. Sobel, Robert. *RCA*. New York: Stein and Day, 1986, p. 139.

34. Sarnoff, David. "Introduction to Technical Papers on Airborne Television." *RCA Review*, September 1946.

35. Advertisement for Du Mont. *Broadcasting 1943 Yearbook*, p. 303.

36. "Television Review: Romeo and Juliet." *Variety*, April 26, 1944.

37. "Television Broadcasting Not Limited to Wealthy." *Science News Letter*, February 8, 1941, p. 84.

38. "NBC Affiliate Policy to Apply to Television." *Broadcasting*, March 6, 1944, p. 9.

39. Ibid.

40. Joyce, Thomas F. "Television—A Post-War Maker of Jobs." *Broadcasting*, March 20, 1944, p. 28.

41. Ibid., p. 11.

42. Ibid., p. 28.

43. Ibid., p. 28.

44. Advertisement for RCA. *The New York Times*, May 2, 1944, p. 35.

45. "Cantor Censored in Televised Act." *The New York Times*, May 27, 1944, p. 17.

46. Ibid.

47. DeSilva, B.G. and Joseph Meyer. "If You Knew Susie." 1925.

48. "Cantor Censored in Televised Act." *The New York Times*, May 27, 1944, p. 17.

49. "Tele Followup." *Variety*, May 17, 1944.

Chapter 4

1. "Television Industry Opposes CBS Stand." *The New York Times*, April 30, 1944, p. 17.

2. "Television When?" *Business Week*, May 20, 1944, p. 88.

3. Robertson, Bruce. "No Stopping Television, Fly Tells REC." *Broadcasting*, May 22, 1944, p. 10.

4. Advertisement for RCA. *The New York Times*, May 2, 1944, p. 35.

5. Advertisement for RCA. *Broadcasting*, May 26, 1944, back cover.

6. "Clare Luce Says Republicans Will Build Better America for Returning 'G.I. Joes.'" *The New York Herald Tribune*, June 28, 1944, p. 5.

7. Ibid.

8. Kennedy, T.R. "What Television Learned at Chicago." *The New York Times*, July 2, 1944, Section II, p. 5.

9. Shadegg, Stephen C. *Clare Boothe Luce: A Biography*. New York: Simon & Schuster, 1970, p. 197.

10. Martin, Ralph G. *Henry and Clare, An Intimate Portrait of the Luces*. New York: Putnam's, 1991, p. 239.

11. "Second Place Race Sets Session Afire." *The New York Times,* July 22, 1944, p. 8.

12. "Radio Issue Stand Stated by Dewey." *The New York Times,* September 11, 1944, p. 9.

13. "Text of President's Radio Campaign Speech." *The New York Times,* November 3, 1944, p. 14.

14. Miner, Worthington. "Was It All So Golden?" *Television Quarterly,* Fall 1972, p. 15.

15. "Chi Tele Scene Lags Behind N.Y." *Variety,* November 8, 1944.

16. "Chairman Fly Resigns As Member of FCC As Hearings on Post-War Allocations End." *The New York Times,* November 3, 1944, p. 12.

17. "New Band for FM Proposed by FCC." *The New York Times*, January 16, 1945, p. 36.

18. Robertson, Bruce. "TBA Urges United Television Effort." *Broadcasting,* December 18, 1944, p. 14.

19. Anderson, Lansdell. "The 'Eye's' Have It." *Electrical Merchandising,* October 1944, p. 19.

20. Ibid., p. 21.

21. "President's Address." *The New York Times,* January 21, 1945, p. 26.

22. Kennedy, T.R. "Television in Action." *The New York Times,* June 24, 1945, Section 2, p. 5.

23. Groves, Leslie R. *Now It Can Be Told: The Story of the Manhattan Project*. New York: Harper, 1962, p. 296.

24. Ibid, p. 298.

25. Gannon, Mary. "Programming." *Television,* September 1945, p. 30.

Chapter 5

1. "A Television Camera 'With the Eyes of a Cat.'" Advertisement. Radio Corporation of America. *Radio News*, January 1946, p. 22.

2. "Television 'Eye' Vastly Improved." *The New York Times,* October 26, 1945, p. 21.

3. Stahl, Bob. "Long-Range Video Passes Mark in NBC's Coaxial Football Transmish." *Variety,* December 5, 1945.

4. Advertisement. WNBT. *Television,* February 1946: p. 45.

5. "TV Hearing." *Broadcasting,* October 15, 1945, p. 15.

6. Ibid., p. 10.

7. Gannon, Mary. "Public Service . . . Entertainment." *Television,* February 1946, p. 10.

8. Ibid.

9. "At the Knife & Fork." *The New Yorker,* June 29, 1946, p. 16.

10. Advertisement. NBC Television. *Television,* June 1946, front cover.

11. "Dignitaries Liked the Title Fight." *Broadcasting,* June 24, 1946, p. 16.

12. Brooks, Tim, and Earle Marsh. *The Complete Directory to Prime Time Network TV Shows, 1946-Present.* New York: Ballantine, 1995, pp. 482-483.

13. Gannon, Mary. "How to Buy a Television Set." *Television,* December 1946, p. 16.

14. Ibid.

15. "Army Checks Late Navy Rally to Win Thriller, 21-18." *The New York Times,* December 1, 1946, Section 5, p. 1.

16. "Television Review: Army-Navy Game." *Variety,* December 4, 1946.

17. "Army Checks Late Navy Rally to Win Thriller, 21-18." *The New York Times,* December 1, 1946, Section 5, p. 1.

18. Schoor, Gene. *One Hundred Years of Army-Navy Football.* New York: Henry Holt, 1989, p. 127.

19. Laurence, William L. "Fiery 'Super Volcano' Awes Observer of 3 Atom Tests." *The New York Times,* July 2, 1946, p. 1.

20. Baldwin, Hanson W. "The Press and Bikini." *The New York Times,* August 3, 1946, p. 6.

21. "They Like Video." *Broadcasting,* October 7, 1946, p. 82.

22. Borland, Hal. "The Town That Tested Television, Newburgh, N.Y." *Better Homes & Gardens,* October 1946, p. 28.

23. Ibid, p. 26.

24. "Programming." *Television,* March 1947, p. 27.

25. Donovan, Robert. *Conflict and Crisis: The Presidency of Harry S Truman, 1945-1948.* New York: Norton, 1977.

26. "Television Is Used at House Opening." *The New York Times,* January 4, 1947, p. 2.

27. "Rayburn Presents Martin." *The New York Times,* January 4, 1947, p. 2.

28. White, William S. "Congress Sparing with Its Applause." *The New York Times,* January 7, 1947, p. 18.

29. Bailey, Bill. "Reporting by Television Wins Convert." *Broadcasting,* January 13, 1947, pp. 20, 66.

30. "The Text of President Truman's Call on Congress to Meet the Country's Grave Problems." *The New York Times,* January 7, 1947, p. 18.

31. "Spot Radio News." *Radio News,* May 1947, p. 18.

32. Mallon, Winifred. "FCC Decision Bars Color Television." *The New York Times,* March 19, 1947, p. 27.

33. Bilbey, Kenneth W. *The General: David Sarnoff and the Rise of the Communications Industry.* New York: Harper and Row, 1986, p. 183.

34. Ibid.

35. Schaffner, Franklin J. *Worthington Miner.* Lanham, MD: Scarecrow Press, 1985, pp. 179-180.

36. "CBS Not to Abandon Video Activities." *Broadcasting,* May 12, 1947, p. 17.

37. "Negro Dancing with White Gal Brings Tele Rap." *Variety,* October 22, 1947.

38. "Only 6% of New Yorkers Ready to Buy Television Sets Now, 25% Within Year." *Broadcasting,* February 17, 1947, p. 83.

39. "Television's Audience Problem." *Business Week,* September 13, 1947, p. 70.

40. Schumach, Murray. "Television Attracts the Bar Trade." *The New York Times,* June 22, 1947, Section 2, p. 9.

41. Ibid.

42. Rice, Robert. "Onward and Upward with the Arts: Diary of a Viewer." *The New Yorker,* August 30, 1947, p. 47.

43. Ibid., p. 48.

44. Ibid., pp. 53-55.

45. "Television Reviews." *Variety,* May 14, 1947.

46. "American Woman's Dilemma." *Life,* June 16, 1947, p. 111.

47. Ibid., pp. 106-107.

48. Ibid., p. 109.

49. "Television Reviews." *Variety,* July 16, 1947.

50. Rubin, Joan Shelley. *The Making of Middlebrow Culture.* Chapel Hill: University of North Carolina Press, 1992, p. 322.

51. Ibid., p. 323.

52. Miner, Margaret and Hugh Rawson. *American Heritage Dictionary of American Quotations.* New York: Penguin, 1997, p. 303.

Chapter 6

1. "Short Stops on Video." *Variety,* October 8, 1947.

2. Ibid.

3. McGowen, Roscoe. "Wild Celebration in Dressing Room." *The New York Times,* October 4, 1947, p. 1.

4. Golenbock, Peter. *Bums: An Oral History of the Brooklyn Dodgers.* New York: Putnam, 1984, p. 191.

5. "Short Stops on Video." *Variety,* October 8, 1947.

6. Davis, Stephen. *Say Kids! What Time Is It?* Boston: Little, Brown, 1987, p. 30.

7. "Child Listeners Recall Product Names." *Broadcasting,* June 10, 1947, p. 26.

8. "How Many Strings to a Puppet?" *Television,* May 1948, front cover.

9. Gould, Jack. "The News of Radio." *The New York Times,* November 8, 1947, p. 28.

10. "Networks." *Television,* January 1948, p. 14.

11. Ibid., p. 16.

12. Advertisement. WPIX. *Television,* June 1948.

13. "Television Boom." *Fortune,* May 1948, p. 79.

14. "The Infant Grows Up." *Time,* May 24, 1948, p. 73.

15. Gould, Jack. "A Pretty Girl." *The New York Times,* May 2, 1948, Section 2, p. 9.

16. "Television Reviews: For Your Pleasure." *Variety,* May 19, 1948.

17. "Television Reviews: Alan Dale Show." *Variety,* June 9, 1948.

18. Gould, Jack. "A Pretty Girl." *The New York Times,* May 2, 1948, Section 2, p. 9.

19. Ibid.

20. Gould, Jack. "Television Review." *The New York Times,* July 4, 1948, Section 2, p. 7.

21. Rosen, George. "'Vaudeo' Comes of Age in Texaco Show." *Variety,* June 16, 1948.

22. "Television at Philadelphia." *The New York Times,* June 27, 1948, Section 4, p. 8.

23. Ibid.

24. Lowe, Herman A. "Television Steals Spotlight from Delegates at GOP Philly Convention." *Variety,* June 23, 1948.

25. Ross, Irwin. *The Loneliest Campaign.* New York: Greenwood, 1977, p. 109.

26. Lowe, Herman A. "Dems Study Radio-Tele 'Bugs' of GOP to Give Facelift to Own Convention." *Variety,* June 30, 1948.

27. Ross, p. 125.

28. Ibid., p. 127.

29. "Truman Predicts Defeat of Rivals." *The New York Times,* July 15, 1948, p. 3.

30. Ibid.

31. Gould, Jack. "Television and Politics." *The New York Times,* July 18, 1948, Section 2, p. 7.

32. "Text of Wallace's Acceptance Speech." *The New York Times,* July 24, 1948, p. 28.

33. "Text of President Truman's Talk at Princeton." *The New York Times,* June 18, 1947, p. 20.

34. "Tele Follow-up Comment." *Variety,* December 15, 1948.

35. Gould, Jack. "Television Review." *The New York Times,* July 4, 1948, Section 2, p. 7.

36. Schaffner, Franklin J. *Worthington Miner.* Lanham, MD: Scarecrow Press, 1985, p. 185.

37. Harris, Michael David. *Always on Sunday: Ed Sullivan, An Insider's View.* New York: Meredith Press, 1968, p. 90.

38. MacDonald, J. Fred. *Blacks and White TV: African Americans in Television Since 1948.* Chicago: Nelson-Hall, 1992, p. 14.

39. Beach, James C. "Shake Hands with Schaefer." *Television,* September 1949, p. 28.

40. Owens, Jim. "TV Structure in Agencies." *Television,* April 1949, p. 18.

41. Loewi, Mortimer W. "New York TV Will Pass AM by Fall." *Television,* July 1949, p. 7.

42. Burns, George. *Gracie: A Love Story.* New York: Putnam, 1988, p. 241.

43. "Television Reviews: Mary Margaret McBride." *Variety,* September 29, 1948.

44. Ibid.

45. "Garnered from the Studios." *The New York Times,* November 28, 1948, Section 2, p. 11.

Chapter 7

1. Advertisement for *Kukla, Fran and Ollie. The New York Times,* January 12, 1949, p. 54.

2. Wilk, Max. *The Golden Age of Television.* New York: Delta, 1976, p. 230.

3. Gould, Jack. "Television in Review." *The New York Times,* January 23, 1949, Section 2, p. 9.

4. Gould, Jack. "Kukla and Ollie." *The New York Times,* March 27, 1949, Section 2, p. 9.

5. Gould, Jack. "Video Standards." *The New York Times,* January 30, 1949, Section 2, p. 9.

6. "In the Mailbag." *The New York Times,* February 6, 1949, Section 2, p. 11.

7. "Television Feared As Foe to Culture." *The New York Times,* January 3, 1949, p. 25.

8. Greenberg, Doris. "'Sit-Down' America Seen in Television." *The New York Times,* January 30, 1949, p. 49.

9. "In the Mailbag." *The New York Times,* January 9, 1949, Section 2, p. 9.

10. "Niebuhr Assails 'Vulgarization' of U.S. by Video." *The New York Herald Tribune,* January 29, 1949.

11. Gould, Jack. "Video Standards." *The New York Times,* January 30, 1949, Section 2, p. 11.

12. Ibid.

13. James, Edwin H. "NBC Code Relaxed." *Broadcasting,* February 14, 1949, p. 25.

14. Ibid.

15. Seldes, Gilbert. "Television, The Golden Hope." *Atlantic,* March 1949, p. 36.

16. Ibid.

17. Horn, John. "About Molly Goldberg and/or Gertrude Berg." *The New York Times,* March 27, 1949, Section 2, p. 9.

18. "Follow-Up Comment on 'The Goldbergs.'" *Television,* April 1949, p. 39.

19. Ibid.

20. Kisseloff, Jeff. *The Box: An Oral History of Television, 1920-1961.* New York: Penguin, 1995, p. 119.

21. Sennett, Ted. *Your Show of Shows.* New York, Da Capo, 1985, p. 7.

22. Sennett, p. 18.

23. Sennett, p. 18.

24. "Child Wonder." *Time,* May 16, 1949, p. 70.

25. Schaffner, Franklin J. *Worthington Miner.* Lanham, MD: Scarecrow Press, 1985, p. 138.

26. "Child Wonder." *Time,* May 16, 1949, p. 71.

27. Ibid.

28. "From the Studios: Television and Radio News." *The New York Times,* March 27, 1949, Section 2, p. 9.

29. *Television,* November 1949.

30. "On the Washington Screen—WMAL." Advertisement. *Broadcasting,* February 28, 1949, p. 10.

31. "It Pays to Sponsor Television Corn: Wrestling on Television." *Business Week,* October 7, 1950, p. 26.

32. "Dog Bones and Flying Mares." *The New Yorker,* September 18, 1948, p. 23-44.

33. "Roller Derby: Industry Made by Television." *Business Week,* June 4, 1949, p. 23.

34. Gould, Jack. "Is It Television, Sport or Narcotic?" *The New York Times,* June 5, 1949, Section 2, p. 9.

35. Halberstam, David. *Summer of '49.* New York: W. Morrow, 1989, p. 252.

36. "Beer Nursers Jam Bars Having Video." *The New York Times,* October 6, 1949, p. 43.

37. Ibid.

38. Ibid.

39. Van Horne, Harriet. "Entertainment: Television Is a Big Boy Now." *Holiday,* January 50, p. 7.

40. Wilk, Max. *The Golden Age of Television.* New York: Delta, 1976, p. 233.

41. Metz, Robert. *The Today Show.* Chicago: Playboy Press, 1977, p. 131.

42. Mills, Ted. "Garroway and 'Chinese Opera' Technique." *Television,* September 1949, p. 18.

43. Ibid., p. 19.

44. Gould, Jack. "Television in Review." *The New York Times,* September 7, 1950, Section 2, p. 11.

45. "School's Out: Chicago Style." *Time,* May 10, 1951, p. 82.

46. Ibid., p. 83.

47. Ibid., p. 82.

48. Lohman, Sidney. "New of TV and Radio." *The New York Times,* January 8, 1950, Section 2, p. 15.

49. *The New York Times,* October 9, 1949, Section 2, p. 3.

50. MacDonald, J. Fred. *Who Shot the Sheriff?: The Rise and Fall of the Television Western.* New York: Praeger, 1987, p. 22-23.

51. "Hopalong Hits the Jackpot." *Life,* June 12, 1950, p. 65.

52. Kisseloff, Jeff. *The Box: An Oral History of Television, 1920-1961.* New York: Penguin, 1995, p. 276.

53. MacDonald, p. 24.

54. "Dr. Einstein's Address on Peace in the Atomic Era." *The New York Times,* February 30, 1950, p. 3.

55. "Einstein Sees Bid to 'Annihilation.'" *The New York Times,* February 30, 1950, p. 1.

56. Kanfer, Stephan. *A Journal of the Plague Years.* New York: Atheneum, 1973, p. 103; Duberman, Martin. *Paul Robeson.* New York: Knopf, 1988, p. 384.

57. "Mrs. Roosevelt Sees a 'Misunderstanding.'" *The New York Times,* March 16, 1950, p. 33.

58. "Radio and Television." *The New York Times,* April 3, 1950, p. 38.

59. Barson, Michael. *Better Dead Than Red.* New York: Hyperion, 1992.

60. "Coy Warns Radio on Crime and Smut." *The New York Times,* March 15, 1950, p. 54.

61. Ibid.

62. Wilson, Earl. "That Happy, Happy Accident." *The New York Post,* April 15, 1951, p. M5.

63. Crosby, John. "Radio and Television." *The New York Herald Tribune,* January 23, 1950.

64. "Radio & TV." *Time,* April 24, 1950, p. 57.

65. Crosby, John. "Radio and Television." *The New York Herald Tribune,* March 12, 1951.

66. "Plunging Neckline Poses TV Problem." *The New York Herald Tribune,* April 20, 1951.

67. "Television Backs a Code of Ethics." *The New York Times,* October 20, 1951, p. 21.

68. "Late Video Ruining Marks, School Principal Asserts." *The New York Times,* December 10, 1949, p. 10.

69. "Youngsters 5 to 6 Give 4 Hours to TV." *The New York Times,* April 11, 1950, p. 54.

70. "I Believe in Television." *The Catholic World,* March 1950, p. 404.

71. Gould, Jack. "Video and Children." *The New York Times,* January 8, 1950, Section 2, p. 15.

72. "Picked from the Radio Mailbag." *The New York Times,* May 23, 1950, Section 2, p. 10.

73. Gould, Jack. "Stamford Survey." *The New York Times,* May 12, 1950, Section 2, p. 11.

74. Lamb, Edward. "Anarchy on TV?" *The New York Times,* April 2, 1950, Section 2, p. 9.

75. Cerf, Bennett. "Trade Winds." *Saturday Review of Literature,* February 26, 1949.

76. "What Shall We Do About Television?" *Parents,* December 1950, pp. 98-99.

Chapter 8

1. Davidson, Bill. "Hail Sid Caesar!" *Collier's,* November 11, 1950, p. 25.

2. Sennett, Ted. *Your Show of Shows.* New York: Da Capo, 1985, pp. 42-43.

3. Wilk, Max. *The Golden Age of Television.* New York: Delta, 1976, pp. 167-168.

4. Sennett, T., p. 85.

5. "U.S. 'Not at War,' President Asserts. *The New York Times,* June 30, 1950, p. 7.

6. Ibid.

7. "Text of President's Broadcast on the Korean Crisis." *The New York Times,* July 20, 1950, p. 15.

8. Ibid.

9. "Televising Democracy." *The New York Times,* July 21, 1950, p. 18.

10. Gould, Jack. "Radio and TV in Review." *The New York Times,* July 20, 1950, p. 50.

11. "Text of the President's Address on Economic Controls." *The New York Times,* September 10, 1950, p. 26.

12. Smith, Sally Bedell. *In All His Glory: The Life of William S. Paley, the Legendary Tycoon and His Brilliant Circle.* New York: Simon and Schuster, 1990, pp. 322-323.

13. Kanfer, Stephan. *A Journal of the Plague Years,* New York: Atheneum, 1973, p. 107.

14. Ibid.

15. Gould, Jack. "Aldrich's Show Drops Jean Muir, TV Actress Denies Communist Ties." *The New York Times,* August 29, 1950, p. 1.

16. Ibid.

17. Gould, Jack. "'Red Purge' Seen for Radio, Television in Wake of Jean Muir Ouster." *The New York Times,* August 30, 1950, p. 33.

18. "Jean Muir: Pro and Con." *The New York Times,* September 10, 1950, Section 2, p. 9.

19. "TV Station Drops Old Chaplin Films." *The New York Times*, December 7, 1950, p. 52.

20. Smith, p. 304.

21. Gould, Jack. "Television Treats." *The New York Times*, December 12, 1950, Section 2, p. 13.

22. Ibid.

23. Adams, Val. "Just a Couple of Performers." *The New York Times*, October 22, 1950, Section II, p. 13.

24. Gould, Jack. "Television Comedy." *The New York Times*, September 24, 1950, Section II, p. 11.

25. Crosby, John. "Fred Allen." *The New York Herald Tribune*, December 5, 1949.

26. "You Can Do Better, Mr. Allen." *Life*, October 23, 1950, p. 86.

27. Burns, George. *All My Best Friends*. New York: G. P. Putnam's, 1989, p. 283.

28. Crosby, John. "Fred Allen." *The New York Herald Tribune*, December 5, 1949.

29. Henry, William A. *The Great One: The Life and Legend of Jackie Gleason*. New York: Doubleday, 1992, p. 92.

30. Henry, p. 98.

31. Adams, Val. "Not Tough At All." *The New York Times*, May 20, 1951, Section 2, p. 11.

32. Henry, pp. 99-100.

33. Gannon, Mary. "George Burns Votes for Studio Audience." *Television*, December 1950, p. 13.

34. "Acheson Asks Pooling of Technical Skills By U.S. to Aid in Reconstruction of Korea." *The New York Times*, October 2, 1950, p. 3.

35. Parrott, Lindesay, "U.N. Forces Launch a General Assault in West Korea to Close Vise on Reds; M'Arthur at Front, Aims to End War." *The New York Times*, November 24, 1950, p. 1.

36. Ibid.

37. Hoyt, Edwin P. *The Day the Chinese Attacked: Korea, 1950*. New York: McGraw-Hill, 1990, 140.

38. "Acheson's Address on New Communist Threat to Peace of World." *The New York Times*, November 30, 1950, p. 14.

39. "3 Republican Senators Accuse Acheson of Trying to Oust MacArthur in Korea." *The New York Times*, October 2, 1950, p. 3.

40. "Text of General MacArthur's Address to Joint Meeting of Congress." *The New York Times*, April 20, 1951, p. 4.

41. Ibid.

42. Manchester, William. *American Caesar*, Boston: Little, Brown, 1978.

43. Welch, Mary Scott. "Temptation!" *Look*, April 24, 1951, p. 73.

Chapter 9

1. "Color TV Delayed Until Court Rules on R.C.A. Complaint." *The New York Times*, November 16, 1950, p. 1.

2. Gorman, Joseph Bruce. *Kefauver: A Political Biography*. New York: Oxford, 1971, p. 92.

3. Gould, Jack. "Major Issues Seen in Television Now." *The New York Times,* March 23, 1951, p. 12.

4. Blair, William M. "'Outraged' Over Video at Hearing, Carroll, Bet Expert, Defies Senators." *The New York Times,* February 25, 1951, p. 1.

5. Ibid., p. 62.

6. "Television Review: Amos 'n' Andy." *Variety,* July, 1951.

7. "Video Show Deplored." *The New York Times,* September 21, 1951, p. 36.

8. Andrews, Bart and Ahrgus Juilliard. *Holy Mackerel!: The Amos 'n' Andy Story.* New York: E.P. Dutton, 1986, p. 103.

9. Reston, James. "Conference Opens." *The New York Times,* September 5, 1951, p. 1.

10. "Hollywood TV Premiere!" *The New York Times,* September 30, 1951, Section 2, p. 12.

11. Gould, Jack. "Radio and Television." *The New York Times,* October 3, 1951, p. 47.

12. Brooks, Tim, and Earle Marsh. *The Complete Directory to Prime Time Network TV Shows: 1946-Present.* New York: Ballantine, 1995, p. 1277.

13. Arnaz, Desi. *A Book.* New York: William Morrow, 1976, p. 203.

14. Andrews, Bart. *The 'I Love Lucy' Book.* New York: Doubleday, 1985, p. 62.

15. Ibid., p. 67.

16. "Television Review: I Love Lucy." *Variety.* October 17, 1951.

17. Hawley, Lowell S. "Look What TV's Doing to Hollywood." *Saturday Evening Post,* February 7, 1953, p. 34.

18. "The Fate of 'Kukla': A Growing Controversy." *The New York Times,* December 19, 1951, Section 2, p. 15.

19. Adams, Val. "Radio and Television." *The New York Times,* October 27, 1952, p. 36.

20. Gould, Jack. "'Ding Dong School.'" *The New York Times,* January 18, 1953, Section 2, p. 13.

21. Heinemann, George. "Chicago, Chicago, That Television Town." *Television Quarterly,* 22(3): (1986), p. 43.

22. "School's Out." *Time,* September 10, 1951, p. 82.

23. Metz, Robert. *The Today Show.* Chicago: Playboy Press, 1977, p. 18.

24. Ibid., p. 25.

25. Advertisement for *Today. The New York Times,* January 3, 1952, Section 2, p. 13.

26. Metz, p. 39.

27. Weaver, Pat. *The Best Seat in the House: The Golden Years of Radio and Television.* New York: Alfred A. Knopf, 1994, p. 236.

28. Gould, Jack. "Comment on 'Today.'" *The New York Times,* January 20, 1950, Section 2, p. 11.

29. Metz, p. 38.

30. Gould, Jack. "Video and Politics." *The New York Times,* March 16, 1952, Section 2, p. 11.

31. "Text of Truman's Speech at Jefferson-Jackson Dinner." *The New York Times,* March 30, 1952, p. 64.

32. Ibid.

33. Arnaz, pp. 257-258.

34. Ibid., p. 269.

35. Jones, Gerard. *Honey, I'm Home! Sitcoms: Selling the American Dream.* New York: St. Martin's, 1992, p. 68.

36. Smith, Sally Bedell. *In All His Glory: The Life of William S. Paley, the Legendary Tycoon and His Brilliant Circle.* New York: Simon and Schuster, 1990, pp. 363, 367.

37. "Nine Markets Go Live." *Television,* June 1952, p. 37.

38. "Dirksen Induces Booing for Dewey." *The New York Times,* July 10, 1952, p. 18.

39. "House Votes Inquiries on Elections, Crime on Radio-TV, Immoral Books." *The New York Times,* May 13, 1952, p. 1.

40. Ibid.

41. "Inquiry Casts Eye on TV Necklines." *The New York Times,* June 4, 1952, p. 38.

42. "Drys Ask Congress to Ban Beer Ads on TV." *The New York Times,* June 5, 1952, p. 33.

43. Ibid.

44. "Night Club Comics Scored on TV Jokes." *The New York Times,* June 6, 1952, p. 18.

45. Foley, Karen Sue. *The Political Blacklist in the Broadcast Industry.* New York: Arno Press, 1979, p. 344.

46. Ibid., pp. 346-347.

47. Ibid., p. 344.

48. Ibid., p. 345.

49. "Detective Story." *Newsweek,* January 14, 1952, p. 74.

50. "Life of Crime: Dragnet." *Time,* September 22, 1952, p. 75.

51. Ibid.

52. Wilk, Max. *The Golden Age of Television.* New York: Delta, 1976, p. 127.

53. Sturcken, Frank. *Live Television, The Golden Age of 1946-1958 in New York.* Jefferson, NC: McFarland, p. 49.

54. Settel, Irving and William Laas. *A Pictorial History of Television.* New York, Grossett & Dunlap, 1969, p. 99.

55. Sander, Gordon F. *Serling: The Rise and Twilight of Television's Last Angry Man.* New York: Dutton, 1992, p. 88.

56. Ibid., p. 87.

57. Winship, Michael. *Television,* New York: Random House, 1988, p. 26.

58. Sander, p. 82.

59. Bluttman, Susan. "Rediscovering James Dean: The TV Legacy." *Emmy Magazine,* October 1990, p. 53.

60. Kisseloff, Jeff. *The Box: An Oral History of Television, 1920-1961.* New York: Penguin, 1995, p. 268.

Chapter 10

1. Allen, Craig. *Eisenhower and the Mass Media: Peace, Prosperity, & Primetime TV.* Chapel Hill: University of North Carolina, 1993, p. 24.

2. Halberstam, David. *The Fifties.* New York, Villard Books, 1993, p. 211.

3. Chester, Edward W. *Radio, Television and American Politics.* New York: Sheed and Ward, 1969, p. 83.

4. Nixon, Richard. *Six Crises.* Garden City: Doubleday, 1962, p. 95.

5. Ibid., p. 103.

6. "Text of Senator Nixon's Broadcast Explaining Supplementary Expense Fund." *The New York Times,* September 24, 1952, p. 22.

7. Arnaz, Desi. *A Book.* New York: William Morrow, 1976, p. 236.

8. "Machine vs. Man." *Variety,* November 12, 1952.

9. Bashe, Philip. *Teenage Idol, Travelin' Man: The Complete Biography of Rick Nelson.* New York: Hyperion, 1992, p. 22.

10. Jones, Gerard. *Honey, I'm Home! Sitcoms, Selling the American Dream.* New York: St. Martin's, 1992, p. 121.

11. Gould, Jack. "Radio and Television." *The New York Times,* November 19, 1951, p. 32.

12. Adams, Val. "Ed Murrow Offers Case for TV News." *The New York Times,* May 4, 1952, Section 2, p. 11.

13. "Murrow's Korea: The 'New Journalism.'" *Variety,* December 31, 1952.

14. Loftus, Joseph A. "Paramount, A.B.C. Cleared to Merge." *The New York Times.* February 10, 1953, p. 43.

15. Hess, Gary Newton. *An Historical Study of the Du Mont Television Network.* Dissertation. Northwestern University, 1960, p. 86.

16. "Du Mont Will Spin Off a Long-Time Loser." *Business Week,* August 20, 1955, p. 114.

17. Hess, p. 88.

18. Adams, Val. "The Bishop Looks at Television." *The New York Times,* April 6, 1952, Section 2, p. 13.

19. "Dedication of RCA Seen on Television." *The New York Times,* April 21, 1939, p. 16.

Index